THREE ESSAYS ON THE
THEORY OF SEXUALITY

SIGMUND FREUD

THREE ESSAYS ON THE
THEORY OF SEXUALITY

With a Foreword by

NANCY J. CHODOROW

With an Introductory Essay by

STEVEN MARCUS

Translated and Edited by

JAMES STRACHEY

BASIC
BOOKS

A Member of the Perseus Books Group

Library of Congress Catalog Card Number: 62-11202
ISBN-10: 0-465-08607-1 (cloth)
ISBN-13: 978-0-465-08607-8 (cloth)
ISBN-10: 0-465-09708-1 (paper)
ISBN-13: 978-0-465-09708-1 (paper)

Printed in the United States of America
EBC   07 08 09   20 19 18 17 16 15

CONTENTS

Foreword by Nancy J. Chodorow   vii
Editorial Note   xix
Editor's Note   xxi
Preface to the Second Edition   xxvi
Preface to the Third Edition   xxvi
Preface to the Fourth Edition   xxix
Introductory Essay by Steven Marcus   xxxi

I

THE SEXUAL ABERRATIONS   1

1   Deviations in Respect of the Sexual Object   2
    (A) Inversion   2
    (B) Sexually Immature Persons and Animals as Sexual Objects   14
2   Deviations in Respect of the Sexual Aim   15
    (A) Anatomical Extensions   16
    (B) Fixations of Preliminary Sexual Aims   21
3   The Perversions in General   26
4   The Sexual Instinct in Neurotics   29
5   Component Instincts and Erotogenic Zones   33
6   Reasons for the Apparent Preponderance of Perverse Sexuality in the Psychoneuroses   36
7   Intimation of the Infantile Character of Sexuality   37

II

INFANTILE SEXUALITY   39

1   The Period of Sexual Latency in Childhood and its Interruptions   42
2   The Manifestations of Infantile Sexuality   45

3 The Sexual Aim of Infantile Sexuality   49
4 Masturbatory Sexual Manifestations   51
5 The Sexual Researches of Childhood   60
6 The Phases of Development of
   the Sexual Organization   63
7 The Sources of Infantile Sexuality   66

III

THE TRANSFORMATION OF PUBERTY   73

1 The Primacy of the Genital Zones and Fore-Pleasure   74
2 The Problem of Sexual Excitation   78
3 The Libido Theory   83
4 The Differentiation Between Men and Women   85
5 The Finding of an Object   88

SUMMARY   97

Appendix: List of Writings by Freud Dealing
              Predominantly or Largely with Sexuality   110
Addenda   112
List of Abbreviations   113
Bibliography   114
General Index   123

FOREWORD

BY NANCY J. CHODOROW

Sexuality is one of the oldest clinical and theoretical problems in psychoanalysis, and one of the most perplexing. We know that sexuality in all its forms—as identity, behavior, fantasy, drive, passion, physical sensation, way of relating—is unique among human experiences and central to life. Yet this same sexuality in all its forms remains for psychoanalysts, as for everyone else, basically mysterious as we try to define it and describe its contours and significance. Psychoanalytic thinking on the subject begins with Freud's original and threatening *Three Essays on the Theory of Sexuality*—uneven, internally contradictory, puzzling . . . and extraordinary.

I cannot begin before affirming that, for me, it is always a pleasure to see Freud's mind at work, to admire the style of his rhetoric and the elegance of his prose, regardless of what he is writing about. Here, characteristically, he starts from what "we" have traditionally believed—i.e., from "popular opinion" that the sexual instinct is "generally understood to be absent in childhood" and to awaken only at puberty, and that it is "revealed in the manifestations of an irresistible attraction exercised by one sex upon the other" and from our "habit of regarding the connection between the sexual instinct and the sexual object as more intimate than it in fact is." Then, also characteristically, Freud marshals every argument and all the evidence in his power to puncture the conventional assumptions: prepubertal childhood sexuality does, indisputably, exist; men are, demonstrably, attracted to men and women to women; and both empirical observation and clinical investigation reveal that "the sexual instinct and the sexual object are merely soldered together." On almost the last page of the *Three Essays*, Freud, typically forthright about the limits of his knowledge, says, "we are not in a position to give so much as a hint as to the causes of [such] temporal disturbances of the process of development [as precocity and other variations among individuals in the timing and duration of the different elements of childhood sexuality]. A prospect opens before us at this point upon a whole phalanx of biological and perhaps, too, of historical problems of which we have not even come within striking distance."

Among the most salient elements substantively and rhetorically in this work, and surely among the most challenging to convention and hardest (both consciously and unconsciously) to embrace, are Freud's arguments first for continuity among all forms of adult sexuality and then for infantile sexuality as part of the same continuum. The first essay addresses the "Sexual Aberrations," and Freud opens by questioning assumptions widely taken for granted about sexual object choice, specifically about the radical difference between homosexuality and heterosexuality. He claims that there is continuity rather than discontinuity between homo- and heterosexual object choice, in that everyone has both homosexual and heterosexual libidinal attachments in his or her unconscious, and that heterosexual object is just as restricted in choice and aim as homosexual: both, Freud points out, involve a "tyranny" of one object and aim. He expands on this observation in the 1915 addendum to the original:[1] "The exclusive sexual interest felt by men for women is also a problem that needs elucidating and is not a self-evident fact based upon an attraction that is ultimately of a chemical nature."

Nor is there, in Freud's view, a single homosexuality that can be contrasted with a single heterosexuality. There is, rather, great variability among homosexualities. (Freud, ironically, has less to say about the heterosexualities, as a consequence of his focus on the sexual aberrations.) While he does not say, as some contemporary commentators would wish he did, that all sexual orientations are equally normal or healthy—indeed, he makes clear in the third essay, "The Transformations of Puberty," that the desirable developmental path leads to heterosexual object choice with coitus as final aim—he does not think that heterosexuality and homosexuality are different in kind or in their developmental process in the individual. Moreover, in keeping with his goal of making all sexual outcomes developmentally contingent, Freud suggests that heterosexual object choice is generally helped along by family process as well as by laws against homosexuality instead of being innately determined.

Freud makes a different kind of argument for the "normality" of the perversions, which are defined mainly by aim rather than by the sex of the object in relation to the self—in particular, the use of organs other than the genitals in the final sexual act and

---

[1] Freud continued to add to the *Three Essays* into the 1920s. Indeed, even some sections that we now think of as central were among those added after the original 1905 publication.

the sexualization of non-human objects, as, for example, in fetishism. In this section he also identifies what he calls the "component instincts"—the pairs, sadism and masochism and scopophilia (the desire to look) and exhibitionism, which can also be criterial in defining perversion. Here as in homosexuality, perversions exist on the same continuum as normality for Freud, and he in two ways folds in an assumption that defines perversion in relation to a normative heterosexual coital aim. First, on a behavioral level, many activities that count as perversions are quite normal when part of the process leading to heterosexual coitus ("most of these extensions . . . are rarely absent from the sexual life of healthy people"), and any organ, on the level of arousal and fantasy, can come to function as an erotogenic zone. It is "exclusiveness and fixation" that distinguish a perversion. The same applies to the component instincts: the extent of their psychological and behavioral exclusivity is the determinant, so whereas looking and showing, say, are often integrated into sexuality, voyeurism and public exhibitionism are perversions.

Second, on a psychological level, perversion and neurosis are two sides of the same psychic formation: "neuroses are, so to say, the negative of perversions." Freud concludes, radically, that those who are conflicted about or condemn sexual desires they define consciously or unconsciously as perverse or abnormal may repress them and constitute neurotic symptoms in their place. Symptoms originate from the repression and transformation not only of normal sexuality, but also of perverse aims and component instincts, so that the unconscious fantasies underlying the symptoms, as well as the symptoms themselves, reproduce or mimic perverse forms—as when masochism is transmuted into something moral and the person constantly engages in self-punishment and verbal self-flagellation, or when sadistic anal desires are expressed in attacking and attempting to destroy the creations of others through ridicule or mental demolition, or transformed into compulsive withholding and orderliness.

Even more radically and astonishingly, Freud connects neurosis and civilization—a connection he develops further, especially in his later works on group psychology, religion, civilization, and artists and their art. All that is highest and best in human civilization—creativity, religion, art, order, and progress—depends on reaction formations and sublimations that result from psychic transformations and displacements of sexual aims and interests. There is continuity rather than discontinuity, then, among all forms of adult sexuality—heterosexual and homosexual object choice, perverse and non-perverse sexual aims—and among all the transformations of sexuality—perversion and neurosis, sexuality and all forms of creativity, and social and cultural practices that make up civilized life.

In the second essay, "Infantile Sexuality," Freud advances beyond the argument he and Breuer make in the *Studies on Hysteria* (1893/95) for the centrality of sexuality in the etiology of the neuroses, and beyond his subsequent affirmation in *The Interpretation of Dreams* (1900/01) that he is talking about infantile sexuality. This essay specifies exactly whence sexual wishes come—from innate psychobiological propensities beginning from birth that combine with family experience. Indeed, Freud describes both childhood and family as seething arenas of sexuality and sexual curiosity, and he investigates at some length the various forms of infantile sexual behavior, including thumb-sucking, sensual sucking, and anal and genital masturbation. He names the polymorphous perversity of childhood, in which different parts of the body can bring erotic gratification through different modes—sucking, skin contact, touching and being touched, masturbating—none of which has primacy. He points out that in spite of the fluidity and lack of synthesis of aim in childhood sexuality, object choice is singular and relatively fixed, especially during the oedipal phase. And he shows how the latency period is crucial in instituting the "civilized" reaction to sexuality (which any reader can recognize) of disgust, shame, and moral condemnation, all of which figure centrally in the genesis of neurosis as well as in the reaction formations and sublimations of culture and high culture.

So, here was Freud, in 1905, describing childhood masturbation and childhood sexual curiosity and insisting that, just as there are continuities between perverse and normal, heterosexual and homosexual, genital and non-genital sexuality, there are also continuities between child and adult sexuality.[2] Here was Freud,

---

[2] I was surprised on rereading the *Three Essays* to discover that, although Freud writes about orality and anality in the perversions and in infantile masturbation thoroughout, the section on the development of the pregenital phases of the sexual organization, in which he names the oral and anal-sadistic phases and points to the diphasic nature of sexual development, was not added until 1915, and that his naming of the phallic phase, in which children recognize the male genital only, does not appear until after his 1923 paper on "The Infantile Genital Organization."

moreover, claiming that mothers—as pure, almost, as children in mid-nineteenth- and early-twentieth-century iconography and ideology—are themselves complicit in fostering this childhood sexual development. But mothers should not be horrified by their complicity, he says, because it is the very sexuality they foster in their children that will enable these children, in adulthood, to love and work. Children are sexual, the mother-child relation is sexual, and childhood sexuality is different from but continuous with adult sexuality. The relations between perverse and normal, heterosexual and homosexual, perverse and neurotic or sublimated, all can be found in the expression and development of sexuality from childhood. All sexuality is like in kind, originates in childhood, and is related in manifold ways: "not only the deviations from normal sexual life but its normal form as well are determined by the infantile manifestations of sexuality."

The cultural and personal threat of this essay on "Infantile Sexuality," perhaps even greater than that of "Sexual Aberrations," continues to the present, notwithstanding the complacent presumption that now, at the end of the Freudian century, its postulates are widely embraced. People are still skeptical about the unconscious, and their skepticism seems to center today, as one hundred years ago, on the existence and residues of childhood sexuality. People still believe that if they have no conscious memory of particular experiences of childhood sexuality, then the experiences did not occur. Turning to conscious memory or family mythology, they wonder how a girl could want a penis if she never saw one, or how a boy could fear castration if he never saw the female genitals. They are sure that the difference between the sexes, or the role of sex in reproduction, was never known to them. They do not remember wanting one parent and finding the other in the way. Clinical experience may also elicit the opposite observation: the active approach of a person in therapy to childhood sexual memories, images, and feelings may be rooted in knowledge about the centrality of sexuality to psychoanalytic theory, and this conscious focus may actually mask less conscious (or equally conscious) disbelief or skepticism. Sexuality in general makes people uneasy and anxious and Freud's proposal of infantile sexuality makes people especially uneasy and anxious—close to a century after its unveiling.

In addition to the general argument of the *Three Essays*, connecting all forms of sexuality, connecting sexuality to the non-sexual realms of individual and social life, and documenting the existence and development of childhood sexuality, Freud shares other importantly generative insights—not, however, without leaving contradictions in their wake, as we shall see.

First among Freud's specific insights in evocative power as well as in accuracy is, to my mind, his account of the genesis of adult object choice—the beautifully and originally put claim that "the finding of an object is in fact the refinding of it." (Or, as put more fully if less evocatively in 1915, "the innumerable peculiarities of the erotic life of human beings as well as the compulsive character of the process of falling in love itself are quite unintelligible except by reference back to childhood as being residual effects of childhood.") This insight illuminates an entire literary corpus and the sociology and anthropology of love, family, and kinship, as well as our clinical and personal experience. And Freud makes a profound contribution to social theory, by indirect extension, as he explains why the social prohibition on incest is so intensely invested psychologically; everyone's original object choice is incestuous and parental. Thus, an evolutionarily developed latency period conspires with reinforcing moral precepts and social rules to turn the child after puberty toward non-incestuous love objects. As Freud notes, and as literature, sociology, anthropology, and clinical and personal experience attest, the incest taboo does not succeed in wiping out all incestuous fantasy and desire, even if it modulates behavior in most cases.

Second among generative insights is the simple but persuasive theory Freud lays out of the relations of the organic and the psychological, in his pivotal developmental and clinical conception of the "complemental series." Throughout the *Three Essays* he wrestles with the question of constitution and experience. How is it that the same constitution can result in different sexualities, or the same experiences have different effects? How do we explain developmental outcomes, or, in current parlance, how do we choose between or reconcile essentialism and constructionism? Freud claims that, although the organic or physiological givens vary by individual, everyone is born with some innate disposition or "constitution." Everyone also has "accidental" experiences arising in his or her family, sometimes involving trauma. Constitution and accident interact: "the relation between the two is a co-operative and not a mutually exclusive one. The constitutional factor must await experiences before it can make itself felt; the accidental factor must have a constitutional basis in order to come into operation." Any particular sexual outcome will be the result of both, so that neither constitution nor experience alone can predict outcome. While accidental experiences in early childhood will have more determinative effect than later experience, Freud hypothesizes that constitution and experience play off against each other. A strong constitutional propensity needs less experience to have its effect, and, by complement, intense experiences can offset the near absence of constitutional propensity and produce the same impact.

Third among Freud's most generative insights is his documentation of the inextricable but complicated relationship between sexuality and gender. Indeed, his writings have spawned a veritable gender and sexuality industry, beginning early in the history of psychoanalysis and continuing into contemporary psychoanalysis, feminist psychoanalysis, psychoanalytic feminism, and gay and lesbian theory. Freud makes explicit what "everyone" supposedly knows: that gender and sexuality are not the same thing but cannot be separated one from the other, that body image and sexual experience relate in complex ways to sense of gender, that there is no one-to-one correspondence between sexual (or gendered) anatomy and sexual (or gendered) object choice. At the same time, of course, he also says that there is an inescapable connection between anatomy and sense of gender; the castration complex comes with having a penis in boys, and penis envy comes with not having one in girls.

As someone who has written both appreciatively and critically about Freud's account (developed mainly in his later writings) of femininity, I am struck by the discovery of a particular asymmetry that prevails throughout the *Three Essays* whenever women and men or boys and girls are noticed. On the one hand, Freud definitely begins from a male norm: girls' sexuality before puberty is "of a wholly masculine character," and libido is masculine; possession of the penis is central to boys and girls. On the other hand, Freud in these essays pays little attention to males. In the section "The Differentiation between Men and Women," for example, he is entirely preoccupied, in spite of the tacit comparison to men, with how it is with girls and women, both in their development and in their adult sexuality. Freud is fascinated and absorbed with understanding women and femininity more than men and masculinity, and this fascination grows out of and presages his whole oeuvre, from the *Studies on Hysteria* to *Analysis Terminable and Interminable*.

Three Essays on the Theory of Sexuality is in no way a seamless whole. The contradictions that surface, contributing to its curious or baffling spots and its unevenness, explain, I believe, some of the crucial developments and remaining difficulties in post-Freudian thought. More surprising than several minor puzzles, which serve to remind us of the patchwork texture of these essays, is the relative absence of psychological underpinnings to the work, especially when compared to Freud's intense interest in body and behavior.[3]

What is going on when Freud, supposedly the psychoanalyst passionate about the mind, spends pages as a sexologist in long, puzzled ruminations on the exact physiology of stimulation, sexual arousal, excitation, and discharge? Or when he reminds us that the external and internal genitals take final physiological form at puberty, or that the stimulation of the erotogenic zones from without both provides pleasure and generates further sexual tension? In the pages on "The Primacy of the Genital Zones and Fore-pleasure" and "The Problem of Sexual Excitation," over and over we find stunningly and bizarrely mundane statements of the obvious, filtered through the quirky and original mind of Freud. Nevertheless, we are fascinated even here when he takes us step-by-step through the solutions to straw-man problems—for instance, the curious claim that sexual excitation is so bewildering because of our "complete ignorance."

Of course, Freud's understanding of repression, neurosis, character, and sublimation is what links the biological-physiological aspect of sexuality to psychic life, but you would barely know that from a reading of the *Three Essays* alone. Freud here is, I think, both somewhat unaware of and determinedly disingenuous about his intentions—to use his study of physiological sexuality to underpin a psychological pleasure principle theory of tension release as the central goal of human functioning, and to draw our attention to the role of internal, mental forces (fantasy and wish) in generating sexual excitation or tension. In fact, the key section on "The Libido Theory" that makes such unrecognized intentions manifest, was not added until the 1915 version of the *Three Essays*. Thus, it is not until then that Freud blended his physiological discussion into libido theory—claiming that his earlier

---

[3] Among the several minor puzzles: Freud's scant attention to "normal" sexuality in comparison to his attention to the sexual aberrations; also his beginning an essay on infantile sexuality with latency rather than with infancy.

"hypotheses" about the chemical basisof sexual excitation could now be understood in terms of libido—that special energy that is qualitatively different from other forms of energy underlying mental processes.

Similarly, Freud is interested in infantile sexuality because its various forms (through regression and fixation, condensation, displacement, reaction-formation and symbolization) generate varieties of neurosis and character—especially hysterical, phobic, and obsessional—as well as feeding into adult sexualities of all sorts, but here again he displays the fascination with body and behavior that characterizes his investigation of sexuality in general. Even in the section on fixation that concludes the *Three Essays*, where we find Freud returning to the account of childhood sexuality and its significance that is for him the chief contribution of this work, we discover regrets about our lamentable lack of biological knowledge. Throughout these essays, then, Freud's interest in how, exactly, physiological sex works and how the sexual body develops seems a passion in itself, not to be subsumed under his interest in the mind. Indeed, I believe that Freud's obsession with the actual body (or body parts and their function) and with actual sexual behavior and excitement rather than with mind, desire, wish, and fantasy may also contribute to and rationalize popular resistance to and disbelief about childhood sexuality.

Like Steven Marcus in his Introduction, I myself have remarked on another contradiction as consequential as, but more explicit than, Freud's obsession with biology and physiology in an ostensibly psychoanalytic work. I refer to Freud's mutually exclusive claims for the primacy of the breast and the primacy of autoerotism—sources of competing psychoanalytic theories. Freud contends that the breast is the first sexual object, and that autoerotism follows after, providing "a second erotogenic zone, though one of an inferior kind." But he makes the equally strong assertion that infantile sexuality is *originally* autoerotic. Then, in *On Narcissism*, when he is interested not only in sexual pleasure in the self or the mother but also in the primary ego state of being narcissistic or object-related, he asserts that the child has originally two objects, himself and the mother who feeds him. The two mutually exclusive claims (and later the third) are left to stand, unresolved. Freud says, "a child sucking at his mother's breast has become the prototype of every relation of love. The finding of an object is in fact a refinding of it."

Now, whether the infant is originally libidinally attached to an object or not, and whether he or she gets erotic satisfaction from another or herself—indeed, whether humans are initially connected to others, so that forms of connection need explaining but not connection itself—is a pivotal question. Its extensions have separated drive theorists from object relations theorists for many years concerning whether libido is originally pleasure-seeking or object-seeking, and what are the kinds of unconscious fantasies that constitute psychic reality. Furthermore, it has implications for conceptions of human possibility, politics, and society as well and has divided psychoanalytic social theorists accordingly.

Psychoanalysts continue to write clinically about sexuality, and many elements in the *Three Essays* have been elaborated, challenged, or revised: female development has been studied and rethought creatively and with great depth; the claim for the universality of penis envy has been countered by arguments for a primary genitally-based femininity located in the female body; analysts have argued that the first genital phase takes place in the second year of life rather than the third or fourth year; and perversions and homosexualities have been extensively studied. French psychoanalysts in particular, like Chasseguet-Smirgel, McDougall, Laplanche and Green, have continued to make sexuality central, defining its nature, exploring further the perversions, and describing the forms of perverse thinking in the rejection of gender and generational difference that deny and distort reality and undermine genuine creativity.

At the same time, psychoanalytic commentators note these days that the place of sexuality in psychoanalysis has been inappropriately diminished and remains hard to determine. None of the elaborations, critiques, or revisions is comparable in scope or depth to the theoretical and clinical developments that have extended and transformed all other aspects of the Freudian corpus, and none of these latter developments itself offers us a theory of sexuality or indeed even makes sexuality a central point of interest. Neither the ego psychologies of Anna Freud, Hartmann, Arlow, or Brenner, the interpersonal and relational theories, Kleinian theory, the British object-relations tradition, or self-psychology has generated a serious challenge to the *Three Essays* or any kind of revisionist analogue.

(Indeed, it was probably Freud himself who came up with the major revision of his work when, in *Beyond the Pleasure Principle,* he introduced the death drive and argued that it limited the role of libido and sexuality in the psyche.)

Psychoanalysts also continue to be interested in development from infancy throughout the life cycle, and have directed attention to attachment, affective development, self and emotional development, cognitive development, the interaction of developmental lines, the extension of developmental stages past puberty, the move from paranoid-schizoid to depressive position, the idea of the transitional object and transitional space. But with the exceptions noted above, the 1905–1923 developmental theory of sexual phases and infantile sexuality has either been tacitly relegated to a place of secondary importance in the overall schema of development, or it has been left fundamentally unchanged.

While Steven Marcus is certainly right that no other theory has come along to replace Freud's, and is probably right that no theory "resembles it in explanatory power," he is surely wrong about the "coherence and integrity" of the ideas put forth in the *Three Essays*, which, though fertile, are completely fragmentary, as he also notes. And burdened as they are by the riveted attention to physiological experience, behavior, and development as well as by that fragmentation, the *Essays* themselves are at least partially responsible for the curious lack of cohesion in psychoanalytic thinking about sexuality and the diminution of its role.

Still, the topic of sexuality pervades psychoanalytic thinking, just as it pervades contemporary culture. Psychoanalysts, like other therapists, are interested clinically in actual sexual behavior, in sexual orientation, in desire, passion, and lust, that is, in sex as sex. We are interested in body image and sexual identity. We are interested in childhood sexual development, in order to understand both children and adults. All these issues are intertwined with gender identity and the sense of gender. This is the ground covered in the *Three Essays* by the sections on the sexual aberrations, libido theory, the component instincts and erotogenic zones, the differences between men and women, and childhood sexuality and its transformations and outcome in puberty.

But psychoanalytic thinkers in all fields are interested in sexuality in the mind as well as the body—sexual fantasy both conscious and unconscious, erotic transference and countertransference, perverse thinking in addition to perverse behavior. We are interested, as was Freud, in sexuality as a foundation of human life—in drives, libido theory, neurosis, character, and in the idea of libido/eros, in all its transformations and substitutions, as a basic motivating force. And psychoanalysts, like Freud, pay attention to cultural definitions and redefinitions of sexuality, sexual orientation, and gender, because these so centrally affect practitioners and their patients, in relation to both their behavior and their conscious and unconscious fantasies; psychoanalysis itself has led ordinary people to have different ways of thinking about their sexuality. And of course, no practitioner can work without being continually aware of the anxiety sexuality can evoke, in him or herself as well as in the patient—anxiety deriving from thinking and fantasizing about sexuality, acting sexual, or addressing childhood sexuality; about erotic transference and countertransference; or about one's own body integrity and sexuality.

Freud's thinking about these sexual matters of mind, being, and body is foundational to and shapes our thinking about all of them today, but it is ironic that so many of the roots can barely be uncovered in the one work most exclusively focused on sex. Yet even as other parts of Freud's oeuvre devote more attention to a number of these matters, none of them , nor our contemporary culture either, can be understood without reference to the *Three Essays*. The *Three Essays on Sexuality* require persistence, imagination, and openness to the unfamiliar on the part of the reader, but—with unevenness and remarkable flashes of brilliance at once—they tell us what sex is all about.

NANCY J. CHODOROW

BERKELEY, CALIFORNIA
November 1999

Nancy J. Chodorow, Ph.D. is a faculty member at the San Francisco Psychoanalytic Institute, Professor of Sociology and Clinical Professor of Psychology at the University of California, Berkeley, and a psychoanalyst in private practice. She is the author of *The Power of Feelings, Femininities, Masculinities, Sexualities, Feminism and Psychoanalytic Theory,* and *The Reproduction of Mothering.*

EDITORIAL NOTE

The present translation of Freud's *Three Essays on the Theory of Sexuality* forms an important addition to the International Psycho-Analytical Library. Since the original publication of the English translations of Freud's works there has been appearing the new authoritative text of *The Standard Edition of the Complete Psychological Works of Sigmund Freud*, translated from the German under the general editorship of James Strachey, in collaboration with Anna Freud, assisted by Alix Strachey and Alan Tyson. The Institute of Psycho-Analysis therefore thought it would be desirable to use this new text when reprinting the International Psycho-Analytical Library edition as the stocks of these began to get low or when, as in the present case, a work is published for the first time in the Library. With the generous co-operation of Mr. Strachey and his collaborators and of the Hogarth Press this aim has been achieved, and in future as it becomes necessary to reprint any of Freud's works they will appear in a new edition in the International Psycho-Analytical Library with the text of *The Standard Edition*.

The present edition of Freud's *Three Essays on the Theory of Sexuality* contains the completely revised and fully annotated text of The Standard Edition with a few extra editorial footnotes. A bibliography and index have been provided and the volume has been prepared for publication by Angela Richards.

It is the hope of the Publications Committee that these revised texts with their annotations will be useful to the growing number of students of psycho-analysis.

J. D. SUTHERLAND
General Editor of
The International Psycho-Analytical Library

EDITOR'S NOTE

DREI ABHANDLUNGEN ZUR SEXUALTHEORIE

(a) GERMAN EDITIONS:

1905   Leipzig and Vienna: Deuticke. Pp. ii + 83.

1910   2nd ed. Leipzig and Vienna: Deuticke. Pp. iii + 87. (With additions.)

1915   3rd ed. Leipzig and Vienna: Deuticke. Pp. vi + 101. (With additions.)

1920   4th ed. Leipzig and Vienna: Deuticke. Pp. viii + 104. (With additions.)

1922   5th ed. Leipzig and Vienna: Deuticke. Pp. viii + 104. (Unchanged.)

1924   *G.S.*, **5**, 3–119. (With additions.)

1925   6th ed. Leipzig and Vienna: Deuticke. Pp. 120. (= *G.S.* **5**.)

1942   *G.W.*, **5**, 29–145. (Unchanged.)

(b) ENGLISH TRANSLATIONS:

Three Contributions to the Sexual Theory

1910   New York: Journal of Nerv. and Ment. Dis. Publ. Co. (Monograph Series No. 7). Pp. x + 91. (Tr. A. A. Brill; Introd. J. J. Putnam.)

Three Contributions to the Theory of Sex

1916   2nd ed. of above. Pp. xi + 117. (With additions.)

1918   3rd ed. Pp. xii + 117.

1930   4th ed. Pp. xiv + 104. (Revised.)

1938   *Basic Writings*, 553–629. (Reprint of above.)

Three Essays on the Theory of Sexuality

1949   London: Imago Publishing Co. Pp. 133. (Tr. James Strachey.)

1953   *S.E.*, **7**, 125–245. (Revised and expanded version of above.)

The present translation is a corrected reprint of the Standard Edition version, with a few editorial additions.

Freud's *Three Essays on the Theory of Sexuality* stand, there can be no doubt, beside his *Interpretation of Dreams* as his most momentous and original contributions to human knowledge. Nevertheless, in the form in which we usually read these essays, it is difficult to estimate the precise nature of their impact when they were first published. For they were submitted by their author, in the course of a succession of editions over a period of twenty years, to more modifications and additions than any other of his writings, with the exception of, perhaps, *The Interpretation of Dreams* itself.[1] The present edition differs in an important respect from all previous editions, whether in German or English. Though it is based on the German sixth edition of 1925, the last published in Freud's lifetime, it indicates, with dates, every alteration of substance that has been introduced into the work since its first issue. Wherever material has been dropped or greatly modified in later editions, the cancelled passage or earlier version is given in a footnote. This will enable the reader to arrive at a clearer notion of what these essays were like in their original shape.

It will probably come as a surprise to learn, for instance, that the entire sections on the sexual theories of children and on the pregenital organizations of the libido (both in the second essay) were only added in 1915, ten years after the book was first published. The same year, too, brought the addition of the section on the libido theory to the third essay. Less surprisingly, the advances of biochemistry made it necessary (in 1920) to rewrite the paragraph on the chemical basis of sexuality. Here, indeed, the surprise works the other way. For the original version of this paragraph, here printed in a footnote, shows Freud's remarkable foresight in this connection and how little modification was required in his views (p. 82).

But in spite of the considerable additions made to the book after its first appearance, its essence was already there in 1905 and can, indeed, be traced back to still earlier dates. The whole history of Freud's concern with the subject can now, thanks to the publication of the Fliess correspondence (1950*a*), be followed in detail; but here it will be enough to indicate its outlines. Clinical observations of the importance of sexual factors in the

---

[1] Freud himself commented at some length on this circumstance, and the possible inconsistencies it might have introduced into the text, in the second paragraph of his paper on the 'phallic phase' (1923*e*).

causation, first, of anxiety neurosis and neurasthenia, and later, of the psychoneuroses, were what first led Freud into a general investigation of the subject of sexuality. His first approaches, during the early nineties, were from the physiological and chemical standpoints. A hypothesis on neuro-physiological lines, for instance, of the processes of sexual excitation and discharge will be found in Section III of his first paper on anxiety neurosis (1895*b*); and a remarkable diagram illustrating this hypothesis occurs in Draft G in the Fliess letters at about the same date but had been mentioned a year earlier (in Draft D). Freud's insistence on the chemical basis of sexuality goes back at least as far as this. (It, too, is alluded to in Draft D, probably dating to the spring of 1894.) In this case Freud believed that he owed much to suggestions from Fliess, as is shown in, among other places, his associations to the famous dream of Irma's injection in the summer of 1895 (*The Interpretation of Dreams*, Chapter II). He was also indebted to Fliess for hints on the kindred subject of bisexuality (p. 9, footnote), which he mentioned in a letter of December 6, 1896 (Letter 52) and later came to regard as a 'decisive factor' (p. 86), though his ultimate opinion on the operation of that factor brought him into disagreement with Fliess. It was in this same letter at the end of 1896 (Freud, 1950*a*, Letter 52) that we find the first mention of erotogenic zones (liable to stimulation in childhood but later suppressed) and their connections with perversions. And, again, at the beginning of the same year (Draft K, of January 1, 1896)—and here we can see indications of a more psychological approach—a discussion appears of the repressive forces, disgust, shame and morality.

But though so many elements of Freud's theory of sexuality were already present in his mind by 1896, its keystone was still to be discovered. There had from the very first been a suspicion that the causative factors of hysteria went back to childhood; the fact is alluded to in the opening paragraphs of the Breuer and Freud 'Preliminary Communication' of 1893. By 1895 (see, for instance, Part II of the 'Project', printed as an appendix to the Fliess letters) Freud had a complete explanation of hysteria based on the traumatic effects of sexual seduction in early childhood. But during all these years before 1897 infantile sexuality was regarded as no more than a dormant factor, only liable to be brought into the open, with disastrous results, by the intervention of an adult. An apparent exception to this might, it is

true, be supposed to follow from the contrast drawn by Freud
between the causation of hysteria and obsessional neurosis: the
former, he maintained, could be traced to *passive* sexual experiences in childhood, but the latter to *active* ones. But Freud makes
it quite plain in his second paper on the 'Neuro-Psychoses of
Defence' (1896*b*), in which this distinction is drawn, that the
active experiences at the bottom of obsessional neurosis are
invariably *preceded* by passive ones—so that once again the
stirring-up of infantile sexuality was ultimately due to external
interference. It was not until the summer of 1897 that Freud
found himself obliged to abandon his seduction theory. He
announced the event in a letter to Fliess of September 21
(Letter 69),[1] and his almost simultaneous discovery of the
Oedipus complex in his self-analysis (Letters 70 and 71 of
October 3 and 15) led inevitably to the realization that sexual
impulses operated normally in the youngest children without
any need for outside stimulation. With this realization Freud's
sexual theory was in fact completed.

It took some years, however, for him to become entirely
reconciled to his own discovery. In a passage, for instance, in
his paper on 'Sexuality in the Aetiology of the Neuroses' (1898*a*)
he blows hot and cold on it. On the one hand he says that
children are 'capable of every psychical sexual function and of
many somatic ones' and that it is wrong to suppose that their
sexual life begins only at puberty. But on the other hand he
declares that 'the organization and evolution of the human
species seek to avoid any considerable sexual activity in childhood', that the sexual motive forces in human beings should be
stored up and only released at puberty and that this explains
why sexual experiences in childhood are bound to be pathogenic. It is, he goes on, the *after-effects* produced by such experiences in maturity that are important, owing to the development
of the somatic and psychical sexual apparatus that has taken
place in the meantime. Even in the first edition of *The Interpretation of Dreams* (1900*a*), there is a curious passage towards the end

[1] His abandonment of the seduction theory was first publicly announced in a brief passage and footnote in the present work (p. 56)
and soon afterwards at greater length in his second paper on 'The Part
Played by Sexuality in the Aetiology of the Neuroses' (1906*a*; *S.E.*,
7, p. 274 ff.). He later described his own reactions to the event in
his 'History of the Psycho-Analytic Movement' (1914*d*) and in his
Autobiographical Study (1925*d*).

of Chapter III (*Standard Ed.*, **4**, 130), in which Freud remarks that 'we think highly of the happiness of childhood because it is still innocent of sexual desires'. (A correction was added to this in 1911: cf. p. 112.) This was no doubt a relic from an early draft of the book, for elsewhere (e.g. in his discussion of the Oedipus complex in Chapter V) he writes quite unambiguously of the existence of sexual wishes even in normal children. And it is evident that by the time he drew up his case history of 'Dora' (at the beginning of 1901) the main lines of his theory of sexuality were firmly laid down. (1905*e*, *S.E.*, **7**, 5.)

Even so, however, he was in no hurry to publish his results. When *The Interpretation of Dreams* was finished and on the point of appearing, on October 11, 1899 (Letter 121), he wrote to Fliess: 'A theory of sexuality might well be the dream book's immediate successor'; and three months later, on January 26, 1900 (Letter 128): 'I am putting together material for the theory of sexuality and waiting till some spark can set what I have collected ablaze.' But the spark was a long time in coming. Apart from the little essay *On Dreams* and *The Psychopathology of Everyday Life*, both of which appeared before the autumn of 1901, Freud published nothing of importance for another five years.

Then, suddenly, in 1905 he brought out three major works: his book on *Jokes*, his *Three Essays* and his case history of 'Dora'. It is certain that the last-named of these had for the most part been written four years earlier, in 1901: see the Editor's Note to this case history (1905*e*), *Standard Ed.*, **7**, 3 ff. It was published in October and November, 1905. The other two were published, almost simultaneously, some months earlier, though the exact dates are not known: see a longer discussion of this in the Editor's Preface to the book on *Jokes* (1905*c*), *Standard Ed.*, **8**, 5.

In the German editions the sections are numbered only in the first essay; and indeed before 1924 they were numbered only half-way through the first essay. For convenience of reference, the numbering of the sections has here been extended to the second and third essays.

Editorial additions, whether to the text or the footnotes, are printed in square brackets.

PREFACE TO THE SECOND EDITION [1]

THE author is under no illusion as to the deficiencies and obscurities of this little work. Nevertheless he has resisted the temptation of introducing into it the results of the researches of the last five years, since this would have destroyed its unity and documentary character. He is, therefore, reprinting the original text with only slight alterations, and has contented himself with adding a few footnotes which are distinguished from the older ones by an asterisk. [2] It is, moreover, his earnest wish that the book may age rapidly—that what was once new in it may become generally accepted, and that what is imperfect in it may be replaced by something better.

VIENNA, *December* 1909

PREFACE TO THE THIRD EDITION

I HAVE now been watching for more than ten years the effects produced by this work and the reception accorded to it; and I take the opportunity offered by the publication of its third edition to preface it with a few remarks intended to prevent misunderstandings and expectations that cannot be fulfilled. It must above all be emphasized that the exposition to be found in the following pages is based entirely upon everyday medical observation, to which the findings of psycho-analytic research should lend additional depth and scientific significance. It is impossible that these *Three Essays on the Theory of Sexuality* should contain anything but what psycho-analysis makes it necessary to assume or possible to establish. It is, therefore, out of the question that they could ever be extended into a complete 'theory of sexuality', and it is natural that there should be a number of important problems of sexual life with which they do not deal at all. But the reader should not conclude from this that the branches of this large subject which have been thus passed over are unknown to the author or have been neglected by him as of small importance.

[1] [This preface was omitted from 1920 onwards.]
[2] [The distinction was dropped in all subsequent editions.]

The fact that this book is based upon the psycho-analytic observations which led to its composition is shown, however, not only in the choice of the topics dealt with, but also in their arrangement. Throughout the entire work the various factors are placed in a particular order of precedence: preference is given to the accidental factors, while disposition is left in the background, and more weight is attached to ontogenesis than to phylogenesis. For it is the accidental factors that play the principal part in analysis: they are almost entirely subject to its influence. The dispositional ones only come to light after them, as something stirred into activity by experience: adequate consideration of them would lead far beyond the sphere of psycho-analysis.

The relation between ontogenesis and phylogenesis is a similar one. Ontogenesis may be regarded as a recapitulation of phylogenesis, in so far as the latter has not been modified by more recent experience. The phylogenetic disposition can be seen at work behind the ontogenetic process. But disposition is ultimately the precipitate of earlier experience of the species to which the more recent experience of the individual, as the sum of the accidental factors, is super-added.

I must, however, emphasize that the present work is characterized not only by being completely based upon psycho-analytic research, but also by being deliberately independent of the findings of biology. I have carefully avoided introducing any preconceptions, whether derived from general sexual biology or from that of particular animal species, into this study—a study which is concerned with the sexual functions of human beings and which is made possible through the technique of psycho-analysis. Indeed, my aim has rather been to discover how far psychological investigation can throw light upon the biology of the sexual life of man. It was legitimate for me to indicate points of contact and agreement which came to light during my investigation, but there was no need for me to be diverted from my course if the psycho-analytic method led in a number of important respects to opinions and findings which differed largely from those based on biological considerations.

In this third edition I have introduced a considerable amount of fresh matter, but have not indicated it in any special way, as I did in the previous edition. Progress in our field of scientific work is at present less rapid; nevertheless it was essential to make a certain number of additions to this volume if it was to be kept in touch with recent psycho-analytic literature.[1]

VIENNA, *October* 1914

[1] [The following footnote appeared at this point in 1915 only:] In 1910, after the publication of the second edition, an English translation by A. A. Brill was published in New York; and in 1911 a Russian one by N. Ossipow in Moscow. [Translations also appeared during Freud's lifetime in Hungarian (1915), Italian (1921), Spanish (1922), French (1923), Polish (1924), Czech (1926) and Japanese (1931).]

PREFACE TO THE FOURTH EDITION

Now that the flood-waters of war have subsided, it is satisfactory to be able to record the fact that interest in psycho-analytic research remains unimpaired in the world at large. But the different parts of the theory have not all had the same history. The purely psychological theses and findings of psycho-analysis on the unconscious, repression, conflict as a cause of illness, the advantage accruing from illness, the mechanisms of the formation of symptoms, etc., have come to enjoy increasing recognition and have won notice even from those who are in general opposed to our views. That part of the theory, however, which lies on the frontiers of biology and the foundations of which are contained in this little work is still faced with undiminished contradiction. It has even led some who for a time took a very active interest in psycho-analysis to abandon it and to adopt fresh views which were intended to restrict once more the part played by the factor of sexuality in normal and pathological mental life.

Nevertheless I cannot bring myself to accept the idea that this part of psycho-analytic theory can be very much more distant than the rest from the reality which it is its business to discover. My recollections, as well as a constant re-examination of the material, assure me that this part of the theory is based upon equally careful and impartial observation. There is, moreover, no difficulty in finding an explanation of this discrepancy in the general acceptance of my views. In the first place, the beginnings of human sexual life which are here described can only be confirmed by investigators who have enough patience and technical skill to trace back an analysis to the first years of a patient's childhood. And there is often no possibility of doing this, since medical treatment demands that an illness should, at least in appearance, be dealt with more rapidly. None, however, but physicians who practise psycho-analysis can have any access whatever to this sphere of knowledge or any possibility of forming a judgement that is uninfluenced by their own dislikes and prejudices. If mankind had been able to learn from a direct observation of children, these three essays could have remained unwritten.

It must also be remembered, however, that some of what this book contains—its insistence on the importance of sexuality in all human achievements and the attempt that it makes at enlarging the concept of sexuality—has from the first provided the strongest motives for the resistance against psycho-analysis. People have gone so far in their search for high-sounding catch-words as to talk of the 'pan-sexualism' of psycho-analysis and to raise the senseless charge against it of explaining 'everything' by sex. We might be astonished at this, if we ourselves could forget the way in which emotional factors make people confused and forgetful. For it is some time since Arthur Schopenhauer, the philosopher, showed mankind the extent to which their activities are determined by sexual impulses—in the ordinary sense of the word. It should surely have been impossible for a whole world of readers to banish such a startling piece of information so completely from their minds. And as for the 'stretching' of the concept of sexuality which has been necessitated by the analysis of children and what are called perverts, anyone who looks down with contempt upon psycho-analysis from a superior vantage-point should remember how closely the enlarged sexuality of psycho-analysis coincides with the Eros of the divine Plato. (Cf. Nachmansohn, 1915.)

VIENNA, *May* 1920

INTRODUCTION

STEVEN MARCUS

In 1905 Freud published three works of major importance. The first of these, "Fragment of an Analysis of a Case of Hysteria," destined to be known as the case of Dora, had been originally drafted in 1901; however, for reasons which still remain unclear, Freud returned it to a drawer. Four years later, he took it up again, revised it and sent it forth into the medical world; it appeared in the *Monatschrift für Psychiatrie und Neurologie* during the autumn. Earlier in the year he published a volume called *Jokes and Their Relation to the Unconscious*, one of the several larger spin-offs, derivatives, or subsidiary consequences that the monumental *The Interpretation of Dreams* had left residually in its wake. The third publication was a small paper-covered book, *Three Essays on the Theory of Sexuality*. Freud had written this work simultaneously with the book on jokes. He kept the two manuscripts on adjoining tables and moved freely back and forth between them according to his mood.[1] Although it took more than four years to sell the thousand copies that were printed of the first edition, it was not very long before the exceptional importance of the *Three Essays* began to be recognized. Today it is by common consent regarded, along with *The Interpretation of Dreams*, as Freud's most fundamental and original work.

Freud himself was aware of this circumstance, and one of his ways of registering that awareness was by returning to this text repeatedly during the next twenty years in order to revise, correct, amend, alter, clarify, and add to its substance. As a result, as the reader of the present edition will quickly see, the text of the *Three Essays* is something of a palimpsest. Moreover, it is a peculiar kind of palimpsest. Not only is the visible surface or layer of writing difficult, sometimes obscure and frequently problematical. As we, so to say, peel away the surface and retrieve the hidden earlier layers, versions, or

[1] Ernest Jones, *The Life and Work of Sigmund Freud*, 3 vols. (New York, 1953–57), Vol. 2, p. 286.

formulations, the difficulty, obscurity and problematicality tend to deepen. Indeed if one consults the first German edition of 1905 or the first English translation made by A. A. Brill in 1910 from the second German edition, it is difficult to know what an original generation of readers could have made out of the formidable darknesses that involve so many parts of this work. Freud was manifestly sensitive to these difficulties. He ends the text with a sentence of complaint that the "unsatisfactory conclusion . . . that emerges from these investigations . . . is that we know far too little . . . to be able to construct from our fragmentary information a theory adequate to the understanding alike of normal and of pathological conditions." He returns to this complaint in the preface to the second edition: "the author is under no illusions as to the deficiencies and obscurities of this little work," is the way he characteristically puts it. He is still at it in his preface to the fourth edition of 1920: "that part of the theory," he writes, "which lies on the frontiers of biology and the foundations of which are contained in this little work is still faced with undiminished contradiction." And the reader will have no difficulty in picking up similar remarks throughout the text and in the additions and notes to it made up until 1924.

I am suggesting that we have before us—as is usual with Freud—is something that cannot be thought of as an innocent text. This suggestion should come as no surprise, since it was Freud as much as anyone else in the history of the modern world who taught us to suspect the claim to, or the appearance of, innocence of any kind.[2] The *Three Essays* are innocent in neither form, substance, nor intention. Indeed from the outset one of the overt aims of this work was to declare the end of a historical innocence. In its disclosure to the world of the universality and normality of infantile and childhood sexuality in all its polymorphously perverse impulsiveness, the *Three Essays* was bringing to a close that epoch of cultural innocence in which infancy and childhood were regarded as themselves innocent, as special preserves of our lives untouched by desires, strivings after selfish pleasure,

---

[2] About the only kind of innocence that Freud allowed of was a small class of "innocent jokes."

twinges of demonic perversity, drives toward carnal satis-
factions. Some considerable measure of the odium that was
attached for years to Freud's name has to be understood in
this light. In the name of truth and reality, he undertook
to deprive Western culture of one of its sanctified myths.
Cultures do not as a rule take kindly to such demythologiz-
ings, and it should come as no surprise that of all of Freud's
findings those that have to do with infantile and childhood
sexuality were resisted with the most persistency.

If we turn to the form of the *Three Essays*, the evidence
of Freud's complex intentionality is immediately in view.
Each of the essays is divided into a number of sections, each
of which is given a title. These sections are in turn further
divided into smaller subsections, to each of which another
substantive heading is also attached. The work as a whole
is composed out of these small juxtaposed blocks of material.
If the *Three Essays* resemble a palimpsest in the dimension
of historical time, then they resemble a mosaic in either the
dimension of printed space or in the dimension of the experiential time that any single reading of them requires. In contrast to the grand expository sweep that we usually associate
with Freud's writing, the discourse of the *Three Essays* is
made up of these fragments that are both connected and
easy to separate, manipulate, revise, or delete. They function
as movable parts of a system, and Freud's complex intentionality in this text includes the explicit intentionality of being
systematic, of setting forth a coherent, systematic theory.
Freud is explicitly conscious of the circumstance that he is
on this occasion setting forth a theory that as a *psychology*
has to stand up in point of comprehensiveness, depth, systematic integrity, and heuristic value to the demands of what
a theory should be.

A second question of form has to do with the large structure of these essays. Why, it may be asked, did Freud begin
the way he does? Why did he start out with an essay on "The
Sexual Aberrations" and move on from these to essays on
"Infantile Sexuality" and "The Transformations of Puberty"?
His strategy in this context is not difficult to understand. In
starting out with the sexual aberrations he was seeking to
deal in the first place with certain forms of adult sexual
behavior; in addition, the sexual practices in question were

familiar and recognizable to whatever limited audience he might in 1905 think he was addressing. Such behaviors were, moreover, aggregated wholes, and Freud's procedure in the opening essay is to take these aggregated phenomena and arrange them in such a way that they can be disaggregated and decomposed. A further pertinence of this device of working backward begins to be revealed when we see Freud regarding these adult manifestations of sexual behavior as being on one level integrated forms of sexual activity and at the same time on another level failures of integration, developmental outcomes in which the various component drives of the sexual instinct have not been put together in a fully integrated way. In addition to the relative familiarity of this material, however, a further strategic consideration vis-à-vis his audience may have been guiding him. The explosive material of this book is to be found in the second essay; it would have been imprudent in the most elementary sense to begin straightaway with that material. A groundwork in the familiar and paradoxically less inflammatory subject of the sexual aberrations had first to be put down before Freud could proceed to the unsettling question of infantile sexuality.

In this connection, it may be useful to note that in the *Three Essays* Freud is writing with a model somewhere in his mind. That model is Darwin, and the *Three Essays* is Freud's most truly Darwinian work. It occupies the boundary that both separates and connects the biological and the psychological realms of existence, and it touches unavoidably upon the complex relations that obtain between phylogenesis and ontogenesis. It is about "origins" in more ways than one, and is written from a consistently evolutionary point of view. Like Darwin, Freud is concerned with the "variations" in form and structure that the sexual instinct takes, and he is interested in arranging or classifying these "variations" in such a way that both their resemblances and differences be rendered in full account. Thus in enumerating the various kinds of homosexual activities, Freud remarks that though there are certainly distinctions and differences among them, it is nonetheless "impossible to overlook the existence of numerous intermediate examples of every type, so that we are driven to conclude that we are dealing with a connected series." At the same time, he is concerned to discover "the general conditions under which mere variations of the sexual instinct pass over into pathological aberrations." This double interest is clearly analogous to the interest in Darwin of tracing both the relations of variations within a species to one another and discovering the point or points at which variations subtly pass over into new or different species. And just as the principal theme of Darwin's work was the "transmutation" of species, so the fundamental preoccupation of the *Three Essays* is with "the transformation[s] of the sexual instinct." Yet each time that he works out such a transformation, Freud hastens to remind us "that an unbroken chain bridges the gap between the neuroses in all their manifestations and normality." The distinctions between variation and species or the normal and the pathological are never simple, nor are they ever held simply. The purpose of Freud's taxonomy is not merely to create new distinctions and classifications; its purpose is to understand how all the distinctions are related to one another, and how one is created out of the transformation of another.

Freud also reminds us of Darwin in some of his larger statements and speculations. The penultimate paragraph of the section on "Deviations in Respect of the Sexual Object" reads as follows:

> The very remarkable relation which thus holds between sexual variations and the descending scale from health to insanity gives us plenty of material for thought. I am inclined to believe that it may be explained by the fact that the impulses of sexual life are among those which, even normally, are the least controlled by the higher activities of the mind. In my experience anyone who is in any way, whether socially or ethically, abnormal mentally is invariably abnormal also in his sexual life. But many people are abnormal in their sexual life who in every other respect approximate to the average, and have, along with the rest, passed through the process of human cultural development, in which sexuality remains the weak spot. [p. 15]

What Freud is saying in this passage among other things is that in human cultural evolution—which the species as a whole has undergone, and which each individual recapitulates in his own development—sexuality remains the "weak spot." That is to say it is the part of us that is most recalcitrant to civilized constraints and does not undergo evolution smoothly. Hence individual development is precarious, and the achievement of "normal" heterosexual maturity is in fact something that has to be achieved. Nothing about it is assured or inevitable; it is contingent upon almost everything else.[3] In a similar sense, Freud regards the childhood of each person as a "primeval period, which falls within the lifetime of the individual himself," and he goes on to remark of infantile amnesia that it "turns everyone's childhood into something like a prehistoric epoch and conceals from him the beginnings of his own sexual life." Although Freud, like Darwin, was rigorously antiteleological in his formal point of view, there are some moments in this text when the evidence of structure, design, and a coherent and meaningful sequence of developments seem so overwhelming that he (like Darwin again) wrote passages that can only be construed in a teleological way. One of these he later excised.

Darwin mulled over his material for two decades before he sent it into print. (And even then he only did so because Alfred Russell Wallace had in the meantime also discovered the principle of natural selection.) Freud had been dealing with much of the material in the *Three Essays* for almost ten years, and he too, living in his self-styled "splendid isolation," was in no great hurry to publish his theoretical findings. Darwin was a confirmed empiricist who was at the same time capable of pursuing a grand theoretical hypothesis with originality and ingenuity and thus introduce a successful scientific revolution. A similar though not the same assertion may be made about Freud. Freud parts company with Darwin at the point at which empirical evidence on the one

[3] At the end of the text Freud offers the following related observation: "in consequence of the inverse relation holding between civilization and the free development of sexuality, of which the consequences can be followed far into the structure of our existences, the course taken by the sexual life of a child is just as unimportant for later life where the cultural or social level is relatively low as it is important where that level is relatively high." Whatever one may wish to make of the last part of this statement, the opposition between civilization and "the free development of sexuality" is a notion that Freud obdurately held to throughout his life; behind this notion is a further idea that human cultural evolution is founded on a deep-seated set of contradictions.

hand and speculation and inferential boldness of thought on the other meet. How beforehand in his boldness Freud can be is revealed in two critical footnotes which he almost casually sets down. The first of these is the first footnote in the first essay. In its original form Freud says that the information on homosexuality and the adult perversions on which the first two-thirds of the essay are based is derived from the "well-known writings" of Krafft-Ebing, Havelock Ellis, et al. In other words, Freud went through these large volumes of medical and psychiatric case summaries and drew from them the material on which he based his analysis. What goes without saying, and what does not quite get said, is that in 1905 Freud had as yet had no direct psychoanalytic experience of either homosexual patients or adults who practiced some form of perverse sexual behavior.[4] This lack of first-hand empirical evidence appears to have been in no way a deterrent to Freud's theoretical inclinations and energies. A similar circumstance occurs in the second essay on infantile sexuality. In a footnote added in 1910, Freud writes: "When the account which I have given above of infantile sexuality was first published in 1905, it was founded for the most part on the results of psycho-analytic research upon adults. At that time it was impossible to make full use of direct observation on children: only isolated hints and some valuable pieces of confirmation came from that source." In their original form, therefore, the first two essays have the character of grand inferential constructions that happen somehow—almost incidentally, one might say—to coincide with or catch up a good deal of the truth. Based on experience of some kind, they are nonetheless not primarily empirical in nature but are systematic and relatively coherent reworkings of glimpses into, intuitions of, and insights about hidden truths which still remain partly hidden.

II

In order to gain some sense of how this work might have affected its early readers, let us reconstitute in a general

---

[4] In a footnote situated further on in the 1905 text, he did make the admission in respect to homosexuals.

way part of the argument of the text of 1905. (I will of course refer to later additions and revisions when it seems appropriate.) Freud begins the first essay on "The Sexual Aberrations" by making an axial distinction. He divides all sexual behavior into two categories. One has to do with the "sexual object," the person toward whom sexual activity is directed or sexual desire felt. The second has to do with the "sexual aim," the act toward which the sexual instinct inclines. Both of these categories contain numerous deviations, and Freud classifies these deviations by means of this first distinction. The first class of aberrations contains those sexual activities that are deviant in respect of the sexual object. The most important and largest population in this class consists of adults whose sexual object has been "inverted." These inverts, or homosexuals as they are ordinarily called, "vary greatly in their behavior in several respects." Freud divides such behavior according to exclusiveness at one end of a scale and contingency at the other. He also notes variations that have to do with the subjective views of inverts toward their own behavior and with the date of onset and persistency of such behavior. Although the range of variation is great, the variations seem nonetheless connected, and he is forced to conclude that they form "a connected series." If there is a totality here it is organized heterogeneously.

When he turns to contemporary explanations of this aberration, he finds that the explanations explain very little. As for the currently popular medical ascription that inversion is "an innate indication of nervous degeneracy," Freud rejects both parts of the diagnosis as inadequate in classificatory precision and explanatory value. Inversion occurs among too many otherwise normal and indeed gifted and highly developed people to be regarded as a sign of some kind of organic degeneration. As for the argument about whether homosexuality is "innate" or "acquired," Freud refuses to choose exclusively between the two opposed alternatives. He then turns to certain theories of bisexuality. He cannot accept those explanations of homosexuality that ascribe it to either somatic or psychical hermaphroditism, nor does he think that it can be traced to certain localized centers of the brain. Nevertheless, partly because of the evolutionary evidence in normal human anatomy that points toward "an originally bisexual disposition," Freud accepts the notion that this disposition "is somehow concerned in inversion, though we do not know in what that disposition exists, beyond anatomical structure." Along with this, which explains nothing, he accepts the hypothesis that in confronting inversion "we have to deal with disturbances that affect the sexual instinct in the course of its development," which is a little better.

He turns next to homosexuals' attitudes toward their sexual objects and demonstrates that there is no uniformity of attitude to be found. And the same variety exists in respect of sexual aim—a whole array of activities characterizes homosexual behavior, not any exclusive kind of activity. What Freud is doing here is refusing to accept homosexuality as a simple or single entity; indeed he does the opposite. He stresses its complexity and hints that it may consist of more than one entity. And he continued to place stress in this direction. In 1915, he added as part of a long footnote the following reflection:

> Psycho-analytic research is most decidedly opposed to any attempts at separating off homosexuals from the rest of mankind as a group of a special character. By studying sexual excitations other than those that are manifestly displayed, it has found that all human beings are capable of making a homosexual object-choice and have in fact made one in their unconscious. . . . Thus from the point of view of psycho-analysis the exclusive sexual interest felt by men for women is also a problem that needs elucidation and is not a self-evident fact based upon an attraction that is ultimately of a chemical nature. [p. 11]

In refusing to separate out homosexuals from other "normal" human beings, Freud was emphasizing the continuity and relatedness that exists between both groups—or between pathology and nonpathology, if you will. And in adding that heterosexual normality is itself problematical, unelucidated, and not self-evident, he was drawing attention to the uncertain and complex character of what we ordinarily take to be the natural human norm.

Freud concludes this section by remarking that the present state of knowledge does not provide a position on which to base "a satisfactory explanation of the origin of inversion."

Nevertheless, his "investigation" of the material before him has led him to discover that the connection between the sexual instinct and the sexual object is not as intimate as is commonly supposed.

> Experience of the cases that are considered abnormal has shown us that in them the sexual instinct and the sexual object are merely soldered together—a fact which we have been in danger of overlooking in consequence of the uniformity of the normal picture, where the object appears to form part and parcel of the instinct. We are thus warned to loosen the bond that exists in our thoughts between instinct and object. It seems probable that the sexual instinct is in the first instance independent of its object; nor is its origin likely to be due to its object's attraction. [p. 14]

In this passage of speculative flight Freud is making a number of theoretical proposals. He is suggesting that the sexual instinct is plastic and labile, that it can be displaced, that it is not entirely dependent upon its object—or the object world—and that it may indeed be at first independent and without an object. All of these suggestions will lead to momentous consequences later on.[5]

Deviations in respect to the sexual aim comprise those practices that are known as "perversions." They begin for Freud with activities in which the mouth is brought into contact with the genitals of another person. Such practices, Freud remarks, "have no doubt been common among mankind from primeval times." And those who condemn these acts as perversions "are giving way to an unmistakable feeling of *disgust,* which protects them from accepting sexual aims of the kind. The limits of such disgust are, however, often purely conventional." In other words, preversions are commonly known or recognized by the subjective feeling of disgust that their contemplation elicits; moreover, this subjective sign is for Freud in part a historical and conventional

---

[5] One of them is to be found in a footnote that he added in 1910. "The most striking distinction between the erotic life of antiquity and our own no doubt lies in the fact that the ancients laid the stress upon the instinct itself, whereas we emphasize its object. The ancients glorified the instinct and were prepared on its account to honour even an inferior object; while we despise the instinctual activity itself, and find excuses for it only in the merits of the object."

circumstance. It is in some measure a socially induced force, and its action leads "to a restriction of the sexual aim." Nevertheless, Freud wryly adds, "the sexual instinct in its strength enjoys overriding this disgust." The same holds true for those activities which make sexual use of the anal orifice.

The sexual instinct extends its interest to other parts of the body as well, and in those activities described as fetishism we see one such extension. These activities can extend to inanimate objects as well, such as "a piece of clothing or underlinen." What is interesting about such practices—and about all the other perversions as well—is that they are in some degree "habitually present in normal love," especially in its preliminary aims. And Freud regards them as pathological only when they take the place of the normal sexual aims and object "in *all* circumstances," when they take on the "characteristics of exclusiveness and fixation." Such characteristics apply as well to the perversions that have to do with looking and being looked at, namely voyeurism and exhibitionism. These connected symptoms occur in both active and passive forms, which leads Freud on to the "the most common and the most significant of all the perversions," sadism and masochism. He finds the roots of sadism in the "element of *aggressiveness*" that is usually part of the sexuality of most male human beings. In sadism, the "aggressive component of the sexual instinct . . . has become independent and exaggerated and, by displacement, has usurped the leading position." Masochism is a more complex and mysterious phenomenon, and in 1905 Freud had to content himself with the remark that "no satisfactory explanation of this perversion has been put forward and . . . it seems possible that a number of mental impulses are combined in it to produce a single resultant."

Yet sadism and masochism have a further interest because both are "habitually found to occur together in the same individual." This copresence of opposites, Freud remarks, has "a high theoretical significance," and he proceeds to connect these opposites "with the opposing masculinity and femininity which are combined in bisexuality—a contrast which often has to be replaced in psychoanalysis by that between activity and passivity." At this point even a casual reader cannot escape the sense that a large theoretical design is beginning to take shape.

As he moves toward a conclusion of this section, Freud notes once again that the sexual life of healthy adults is rarely without perverse constituents in it, and he repeats his admonition that when it comes to the sphere of sexuality "we are brought up against peculiar and, indeed, insoluble difficulties as soon as we try to draw a sharp line to distinguish mere variations within the range of what is physiological from pathological symptoms." This "most unruly of all the instincts" can lead people whose behavior is in other respects normal to activities of the most astonishing and repulsive kind. In such activities, Freud observes, it is impossible to overlook the important role played by the mind in the transformations of the sexual instinct. "It is impossible to deny that in their case a piece of mental work has been performed which, in spite of its horrifying result, is the equivalent of an idealization of the instinct." It was the ancients, one recalls, that Freud describes as idealizing the instinct; and the inference must follow that in the perversions the past survives in the present, and that there is something archaic about these expressions of sexuality in which the highest and the lowest intersect and are joined. Indeed some perversions are intelligible only if we assume such a convergence. "If such perversions admit of analysis," Freud concludes, "that is, if they can be taken to pieces, then they must be of a composite nature. This gives us a hint that perhaps the sexual instinct itself may be no simple thing, but put together from components which have come apart again in the perversions." The obscure circularity of this chain of reasoning may be interpreted as follows. The sexual instinct is not a single or unitary entity. It is made up of different components that are brought together—amalgamated, aggregated, or synthesized—in normal adult sexual activity. In the perversions, however, we see that the components have come apart again; they have decomposed, and some of them have been recomposed to form these alternate kinds of behavior. The disaggregation and decomposition that Freud had chosen as the analytic and expository form in which to treat the sexual aberrations is now revealed to be an essential attribute in the formation and structure of those aberrations themselves. The fit between form and content or analytic intellectual style and material structure is very snug indeed.

At this point, Freud abruptly shifts gears and begins without warning or transition a new section entitled "The Sexual Instinct in Neurotics." At once the reader becomes aware that the territory has been shifted as well, as has the pitch of explanatory discourse. Persons who suffer from such complaints as hysteria or obsessional neuroses, Freud begins, are approximately closer to the normal than the aberrants with whom he has just finished his preliminary dealings. Nevertheless, psychoanalytic investigation has determined that the sexual instinct is fundamental in the maintenance of neurotic symptoms; it provides the most important "source of energy" of the neuroses, and as a consequence the sexual life of neurotics tends in varying degree to be expressed in their symptoms. Indeed, Freud continues, "the symptoms constitute the sexual activity of the patient." The symptoms are in fact substitutes—"transcriptions as it were"—for certain highly charged wishes and desires which have undergone the peculiar and unexplained mental process called repression and have as a result been lost to consciousness. They have not, however, lost their force, and since they cannot be discharged by conscious mental representation, they find expression in "somatic phenomena." By means of another mysterious process called "conversion," they appear as the somatic symptoms—the paralyses, tics, convulsions, blindnessess—of hysteria. Hysteria is thus an embodiment or exemplification of the mind-body problem, one expression of that apparently insoluble—and indissoluble—relation. Moreover, hysterics are excessively civilized persons. In them the restrictive forces of "shame, disgust and morality," which are overridden in the perversions, act with decisive power against sexual desire. Yet their excessive aversion to sexuality is regularly combined with a characterizing opposite, an "exaggerated sexual craving," although this craving is also fated to become at some point unconscious. Torn between sexual strivings and his aversion to sexuality, the hysteric chooses illness as a means of escaping his conflict. Unfortunately illness "does not solve his conflict, but seeks to evade it by transforming his libidinal impulses into symptoms."

At the same time, it would be misleading to assert that

such symptoms originate either solely or exclusively at the cost of normal adult sexuality—though that, Freud notes, is what he is commonly taken to be saying. Neurotic symptoms also express perverse or abnormal sexual instincts and ideas and are formed in part out of them. Hence, Freud concludes, rising to his large formulation, *"neuroses are, so to say, the negative of perversions."* Inversion, all the perversions, and all the "component instincts" in their paired opposites—including sadism and masochism—appear "without exception" in the "unconscious mental life" of neurotics. We suddenly see what Freud is doing. In a bewilderingly brief few pages on the neuroses he has recapitulated the entire structure of the earlier part of the essay, which was, one recalls, about actually perverse sexual behavior. But the recapitulation is now on the level of the neurotic symptom, of unconscious mental life, of fantasies, ideas, and mental representations. It is, in other words, on the level of theory. Just as for Marx political economy was the theory of capitalism, so for Freud the neuroses contain the theory of sexual behavior in both its normal and aberrant modes of expression. They contain that theory, and with Freud's help they will contain it in an integrated form. Having decomposed the perversions into component parts, he has at once recomposed them in the neuroses. In the neuroses the language of sexuality begins to speak articulately, coherently, and theoretically.[6]

But Freud is not content with letting the neuroses speak just yet. Instead he begins to speak himself about "Component Instincts and Erotogenic Zones," and of the linkage of the two in both perversions and psychoneuroses. He reminds us again of the role played by perverse impulses in both the neuroses and normal life, and of the unbroken series of gradients that connect "the neuroses in all their manifestations and normality." He reaches the conclusion that "there is indeed something innate lying behind the perversions but that it is something innate in *everyone*, though as a disposition it may vary in its intensity and may be increased by the influences of actual life." He is speaking about the democracy of instinctual, biological life; and what is at stake are the

---

[6] Some years later Freud remarked that "the theory of the neuroses is psychoanalysis itself." *Introductory Lectures on Psychoanalysis* (1916–17), *Standard Edition*, Vol. 16, p. 379.

"innate constitutional roots of the sexual instinct." In one class of persons—those with perversions—these roots "may grow into the actual vehicles of sexual activity." In another —the neurotics—they have undergone insufficient repression and persist as symptoms. And in "the most favorable cases" they have undergone such restrictions and modifications that somehow "what is known as normal sexual life" is brought about or achieved. In addition, he remarks, these roots and this constitution will only be demonstrable in children.

> A formula begins to take shape which lays it down that the sexuality of neurotics has remained in, or been brought back to, an infantile state. Thus our interest turns to the sexual life of children, and we will now proceed to trace the play of influences which govern the evolution of infantile sexuality till its outcome in perversion, neurosis or normal sexual life. [p. 38]

The recomposition that was summarily demonstrated in the neuroses has now been displaced in historical time. In order to make the full demonstration of recomposition Freud is going back to the very beginning. The theory will exist in fully integrated coherence only after—having first disassembled the perversions—Freud has been able to take the fragments and components of infantile sexual life and show how they develop historically and emerge in adulthood into integrated coherence themselves—or into the deformed coherences of the neuroses and sexual aberrations. Once again the discursive form taken by the theoretical structure is inseparable from the experiential form taken by the material content of which that structure is the theory.

III

Freud begins the essay on infantile sexuality by noting that as far as he is aware "not a single author has clearly recognized the regular existence of a sexual instinct in childhood." He is indeed so struck by the boldness of this assertion that he has gone through the literature on the subject yet once more to test its validity. It remains valid.[7] What Freud means is that no one before him had unequivocally recognized the pleasure seeking activities of infancy and childhood as both sexual and normal. There was in fact a wealth of literature on childhood sexuality published during the Victorian period, but that literature tended almost uniformly to regard the sexual experiences or activities of children as pathological, abnormal, and deplorable. In the growing literature that was concerned with the development of the child, sexuality was not included as part of that development, nor did it have a special development in childhood itself. Freud sets out to repair this neglect, this cultural amnesia that is the counterpart to the personal infantile amnesia in which we all cloak this decisive period of life.

We cannot follow Freud in any detail as he develops his exposition—and as it additionally develops in the much-revised text across a period of twenty years. In brief, Freud sees both the occurrence of sexuality in childhood and the building up of restrictions against it and inhibitions of it in a double sense. Both the sexuality and the constraining structures are in the first instance organically determined and arise endogenously or endosomatically in the course of normal growth. At the same time both sexual impulses and the constraining structures are open to influences from the outside, are affected by experience and education; and the final form which they will take will bear upon it the marks of such influences.

Freud begins with the phenomenon of thumb-sucking or sensual sucking. This early behavior itself refers back to a still earlier one, and is a search for a pleasure that is remembered. The child's "first and most vital activity, his sucking at his mother's breast" is also his first experience of pleasure. This first experience arises out of and is associated with a vital organic function; moreover, the membranes of the lips and mouth of the child function as an erogenous zone. The experience is exemplary and determinative. "No one," writes Freud, in one of his most famous remarks, "who has seen a

[7] Some slight modifications of this claim have to be made. See Stephen Kern, "Freud and the Discovery of Child Sexuality," *History of Childhood Quarterly,* 1 (Summer 1973), 117–141, in which a number of partial anticipations of certain of Freud's findings are mentioned.

baby sinking back satiated from the breast and falling asleep with flushed cheeks and a blissful smile can escape the reflection that this picture persists as a prototype of the expression of sexual satisfaction in later life." Later on, or when the mother is not present, the child's need to repeat this pleasure becomes "detached from the need for taking nourishment." The child then can take a part of its own body—his thumb—to suck on and recapture the pleasure. The pleasure is therefore autoerotic, which leads Freud to remark that at first the sexual instinct in childhood is without an object—a speculative construction of considerable theoretical depth and resonance.

The oral phase is followed by activities at the other end of the alimentary canal. The anal zone is the second area of erotegenic pleasure. The sexual excitements of this zone are both active and passive and involve both the stimulation of the mucous membrane and the control (and release) of the sphincter muscle. As with the oral phase, the persistence of significance into later life of the erotogenic importance of this zone has a determining influence on what character or personality will be like. The third erotogenic zone in children is the genitals. This zone is also connected with a vital function, urination. Although it is not the site or vehicle of the oldest sexual impulses, it is "destined to great things in the future." It is easily and regularly stimulated, and "it is scarcely possible to avoid the conclusion that the foundations for the future primacy over sexual activity exercised by this erotogenic zone are established by early infantile masturbation, which scarcely a single individual escapes." Freud also distinguishes two kinds of infantile masturbation—that which is associated with early infancy and that which revives during the later-named phallic and Oedipal phases.

It should be noted that although Freud represented infantile sexuality from the very beginning as a matter of overlapping periodicities and interlocking phases, in 1905 he was not yet able to particularize with full concreteness what those periodicities and phases are and when they specifically occur. One corollary of this uncertainty was that he put his theoretical system together in such a way that revisions of, deletions from, and additions to it could be conveniently and easily made. This combination of openness to new experience

and material with genuine systematic coherence at a high
level of abstract theoretical generality is one of the identifying qualities of Freud's thinking. As is the similar alliance
in him of a simultaneous commitment to the idea of the
determination, and overdetermination, of all events and
developments in mental and sexual life along with the idea
that such events and developments are also contingent upon
accidents of both disposition and experience. An essential
part of the distinction of this text is to be found in the poised
equilibrium in it of the open-ended and the systematic, the
.concrete and the abstract, and the contingent and the determined—and in the delicacy with which that equilibrium is
sustained.[8] It is what leads Freud to emphasize repeatedly,
for example, that "persons who remain normal may have
had the same experiences in their childhood" as those who
become neurotic or perverse later on. In other words, there
is no single causal or developmental scenario that leads to a
particular adult outcome. Different scenarios may in fact
lead to the same outcome in maturity. And the converse is
also possible and demonstrable: a single scenario may lead
in different persons to different adult outcomes. Hence, although it is true that "under the influence of seduction
children can become polymorphously perverse, and can be

[8] On a later occasion, Freud addressed this difficult subject directly.
"So long as we trace the development from its final outcome backwards,
the chain of events appears continuous, and we feel we have gained an
insight which is completely satisfactory or even exhaustive. But if we
proceed the reverse way, if we start from the premises inferred from
the analysis and try to follow these up to the final result, then we no
longer get the impression of an inevitable sequence of events which
could not have been otherwise determined. We notice at once that
there might have been another result, and that we might have been
just as well able to understand and explain the latter. The synthesis
is thus not so satisfactory as the analysis; in other words, from a knowledge of the premises we could not have foretold the nature of the
result. . . . But we never know beforehand which of the determining
factors will prove the weaker or the stronger. We only say at the end
that those which succeeded must have been the stronger. Hence the
chain of causation can always be recognized with certainty if we follow
the line of analysis, whereas to predict it along the line of synthesis is
impossible." *The Psychogenesis of a Case of Homosexuality in a
Woman* (1920), *Standard Edition*, Vol. 18, pp. 167–168. Such a passage
suggests Freud's awareness that psychoanalytic theory, like the modern
theory of evolution, is essentially a historical theory; its powers are
explanatory rather than predictive.

led into all possible kinds of sexual irregularities," it is equally true that: (1) "seduction is not required in order to arouse a child's sexual life; that can also come about spontaneously from internal causes"; and (2) it is "impossible not to recognize that this same disposition to perversions of every kind is a general and fundamental human characteristic."

Freud proceeds with his recapitulation of the first essay and his recomposition of the adult aberrations out of the normal development of sexuality in childhood. He turns to those component instincts in childhood "which from the very first involve other people as sexual objects." These are scopophilia, exhibitionism and cruelty. Freud followed the discussion of these developments by adding in 1915 two entirely new sections on the sexual researches of childhood and the phases of development of the sexual organization in which the "pregenital organizations" of childhood are brought into full explicitness. He closes the essay with a section in which he brings forward some additional sources in childhood of sexual stimulation, excitation, and satisfaction.

With the arrival of puberty a further series of transformations take place. New objects appear along with a new sexual aim. And the component instincts must now be brought together, assembled, integrated and subordinated to "the primary of the genital zone."[9] Freud rehearses in his customary, compact style the three sources of stimuli that impinge on the developing organism. These are stimuli that come from the external world, from the organic interior, and from mental life, "which is itself a storehouse for external impressions and a receiving post for internal excitations." He takes up for a second time the puzzling and many-sided problem of the nature of sexual tension or excitation and its relation to pleasure, describes how the erotogenic zones "fit themselves into the new arrangements" as forepleasures, and relates once again these forepleasures to the mechanism of the perversions. He passes on to the extremely complex question of the differentiation between men and women, a differentiation in which the notion of bisexuality makes an important return. In

[9] In addition, "the sexual instinct is now subordinated to the reproductive function; it becomes, so to say, altruistic." This is at the other extreme from the archaic or primitive or perverse arrangements in which the instinct itself is idealized.

addition, this transformation involves for women a further change. In little girls, genital sexuality is experienced on a phallic model or prototype, with the clitoris as the organ of stimulation and pleasure. When a girl turns into a woman, this organ both enlarges and relinquishes a part of its function: "When at last the sexual act is permitted and the clitoris itself becomes excited, it still retains a function: the task namely, of transmitting the excitation to the adjacent female sexual parts, just as—to use a simile—pine shavings can be kindled to set a log of harder wood on fire." In view of the tragicomedy that so much subsequent discussion of female sexuality has turned out to be, it is appropriate to bring forward this early and largely neglected remark, including the homely and half-inappropriate metaphor that Freud enlists to illustrate it. The clitoris does not altogether give up its excitability;[10] what it does is to transfer "susceptability to stimulation" to "the vaginal orifice." It ceases to be the exclusive or leading zone for female sexual activity. For 1905 that is not an altogether condemnable formulation.

Yet we cannot let the matter rest there. In the first essay there is an important theoretical subsection on the "overvaluation of the sexual object," which contains the following passage:

> The significance of the factor of sexual overvaluation can be best studied in men, for their erotic life alone has become accessible to research. That of women—partly owing to the stunting effect of civilized conditions and partly owing to their conventional secretiveness and insincerity—is still veiled in an impenetrable obscurity. [p. 17]

If we juxtapose these remarks with those taken from the third essay, we are left with a series of questions. Where did Freud get the information that he construes into the theoretical construction of the third essay, information which, in addition, he denies having access to in the first? From the street? from folklore? from experience? out of his ear? from the observations he said he was unable to make? from unconscious hints let drop by his patients? Are the two passages compatible or incompatible? It is quite impossible to say,

---

[10] Freud is in this text undecided about the degree to which the clitoris has to "abandon its excitability," and the passage is ambiguous on this score.

and the matter remains veiled in impenetrable obscurity.[11]

Nevertheless, along with the establishment of genital primacy at puberty, there takes place as well the completion of the process that permits the organism to seek and find a sexual object. Here too psychical preparations have been made from a very early date. "At a time at which the first beginnings of sexual satisfaction are still linked with the taking of nourishment, the sexual instinct has a sexual object outside the infant's body in the shape of his mother's breast. It is only later that the instinct loses that object, just at the time, perhaps, when the child is able to form a total idea of the person to whom the organ that is giving him satisfaction belongs." It is then, Freud writes inconsistently, that the instinct becomes autoerotic, and not until latency has been passed through is it ready to resume and restore the original relation. The inconsistency has to do with his earlier statement that at first, at its origin, the sexual instinct in infants has no object. And since he is making conjectural inferences about such occluded matters as the origin and formation of object relations—matters about which reliable data are still today very hard to come by—one can understand his lack of certitude and oscillation. His conclusion, however, has a sturdy coherence to it. "There are thus good reasons," he wrote, "why a child sucking at its mother's breast has

---

[11] One can add as a piece of crowning confusion the following leap in the dark from the second essay. In his discussion of the polymorphous perverse sexuality of children, Freud pauses for an illustration: "In this respect children behave in the same kind of way as an average uncultivated woman in whom the same polymorphous perverse disposition persists. Under ordinary conditions she may remain normal sexually, but if she is led on by a clever seducer she will find every sort of perversion to her taste, and will retain them as part of her own sexual activities. Prostitutes exploit the same polymorphous, that is, infantile, disposition for the purposes of their profession; and, considering the immense number of women who are prostitutes or who must be supposed to have an aptitude for prostitution without becoming engaged in it, it becomes impossible not to recognize that this same disposition to perversions of every kind is a general and fundamental human characteristic." One doesn't know where to look for a handle to these remarks. It is even difficult to frame a context that might make discussion of them pertinent. Perhaps we can do no better than repeat the waggish observation that it is very difficult to know the meaning of a statement about Freud being right or wrong since he is always both.

become the prototype of every relation of love. The finding of an object is in fact a refinding of it." The past is the prehistory of the present in the sense that it is the necessary precondition of present existence. And history repeats and recapitulates prehistory, though at a further stage of organization and development.

Hence the child's relations with those who care for it—especially its mother—are sexual in character. And the mother in turn regards the child "with feelings that are derived from her own sexual life," as she mothers and nurses and nurtures it. There is nothing to be horrified at in recognizing the sexual nature of this relation, Freud quickly adds. Moreover, "if the mother understood more of the high importance of the part played by instincts in mental life as a whole—in all its ethical and psychical achievements—she would spare herself any self-reproaches even after her enlightenment. She is only fulfilling her task in teaching the child to love." Although love takes many forms, the kind of love Freud has ideally in mind is associated with the idea of a vigorous and autonomous adult human being.

This autonomy is a goal that cannot be reached directly. For the object that is found in adult life cannot be the identical refound object of infancy and early childhood. The Oedipal experience must be gone through and resolved. The barrier against incest—"a cultural demand made by society"—must be internalized, along with other prohibitions and restraints. When at puberty the incestuous fantasies are rearoused, they must again be overcome and repudiated. If this work is gone through successfully, "one of the most significant, but also one of the most painful, psychical achievements of the pubertal period is completed: detachment from parental authority, a process that alone makes possible the opposition, which is so important for the progress of civilization, between the new generation and the old." In view of the widespread tendency to regard Freud's thinking as essentially classical and conservative in affinity, it is helpful to be reminded of such a remark. Freud is also one of the last great legatees of the Romantic tradition in European thought. His theories are grounded in the idea of conflict, and this conflict exists in the realm of the normal as much as it does in the pathological. Even his conceptions of integration are touched by it. He sees integration as falling within the larger contexts of conflict and of incompatible needs, contradictory aims, and implacably opposed demands. Such integration as he finds is never complete, rarely adequate, and more often than not unstable. He never envisages the human or the social world as composing now or in the future to some harmonious order. There is the recognition and remembrance of bliss and satisfaction in his world, but there is no music of the spheres. In his world men and women go through a long development of striving for autonomy, but the achievement of such autonomy is arduous, unpredictable, and easily subverted.

At this point Freud closes his exposition. He adds to it a "Summary" in which the arguments of the three separate essays are rehearsed together and a few further theoretical observations put down. He closes with a reminder of the importance for all later development of the experiences of childhood, "a period which is regarded as being devoid of sexuality." After writing this text Freud was to live for more than thirty years. During that period he would continue to write and develop his ideas. But with the *Three Essays* now fitted in alongside of *The Interpretation of Dreams*, the new theoretical paradigm—and the new vision of human existence—that he was to introduce into the consciousness of the western world was there in its essentials. He and his followers would go on filling in new details, adding observations, plugging up gaps, throwing out new explanatory epicycles. They would, in short, begin to operate—as they are operating today—on the analogy of normal science. But the fundamental theory was there in 1905. That it was a theory fully deserving of the name is in part suggested to us in the circumstance that nothing has come along in seventy years that remotely resembles it in explanatory power, coherence, and integrity. No intellectually serious challenges to it have taken or lasted. The superseders of it that have been regularly announced have just as regularly fallen away. And Freud's own followers continue working on the boundaries of knowledge, about four inches ahead of where Freud left off. Such a circumstance is no discredit to them; it is one more illustration of how rarely genius of revolutionary proportions occurs in both science and other theoretical disciplines. And it illustrates as well how when such a genius occurs the world changes.

THREE ESSAYS ON THE
THEORY OF SEXUALITY

I

THE SEXUAL ABERRATIONS [1]

THE fact of the existence of sexual needs in human beings and animals is expressed in biology by the assumption of a 'sexual instinct', on the analogy of the instinct of nutrition, that is of hunger. Everyday language possesses no counterpart to the word 'hunger', but science makes use of the word 'libido' for that purpose. [2]

Popular opinion has quite definite ideas about the nature and characteristics of this sexual instinct. It is generally understood to be absent in childhood, to set in at the time of puberty in connection with the process of coming to maturity and to be revealed in the manifestations of an irresistible attraction exercised by one sex upon the other; while its aim is presumed to be sexual union, or at all events actions leading in that direction. We have every reason to believe, however, that these views give a very false picture of the true situation. If we look into them more closely we shall find that they contain a number of errors, inaccuracies and hasty conclusions.

I shall at this point introduce two technical terms. Let us call the person from whom sexual attraction proceeds the *sexual*

---

[1] The information contained in this first essay is derived from the well-known writings of Krafft-Ebing, Moll, Moebius, Havelock Ellis, Schrenck-Notzing, Löwenfeld, Eulenburg, Bloch and Hirschfeld, and from the *Jahrbuch für sexuelle Zwischenstufen*, published under the direction of the last-named author. Since full bibliographies of the remaining literature of the subject will be found in the works of these writers, I have been able to spare myself the necessity for giving detailed references. [*Added* 1910:] The data obtained from the psycho-analytic investigation of inverts are based upon material supplied to me by I. Sadger and upon my own findings.

[2] [*Footnote added* 1910:] The only appropriate word in the German language, '*Lust*', is unfortunately ambiguous, and is used to denote the experience both of a need and of a gratification. [Unlike the English 'lust' it can mean either 'desire' or 'pleasure'. See footnote page 78.]

1

object and the act towards which the instinct tends the *sexual aim*. Scientifically sifted observation, then, shows that numerous deviations occur in respect of both of these—the sexual object and the sexual aim. The relation between these deviations and what is assumed to be normal requires thorough investigation.

(1) DEVIATIONS IN RESPECT OF THE SEXUAL OBJECT

The popular view of the sexual instinct is beautifully reflected in the poetic fable which tells how the original human beings were cut up into two halves—man and woman—and how these are always striving to unite again in love.[1] It comes as a great surprise therefore to learn that there are men whose sexual object is a man and not a woman, and women whose sexual object is a woman and not a man. People of this kind are described as having 'contrary sexual feelings', or better, as being 'inverts', and the fact is described as 'inversion'. The number of such people is very considerable, though there are difficulties in establishing it precisely.[2]

(A) INVERSION

BEHAVIOUR   Such people vary greatly in their behaviour in
OF INVERTS   several respects.

(*a*) They may be *absolute* inverts. In that case their sexual objects are exclusively of their own sex. Persons of the opposite sex are never the object of their sexual desire, but leave them cold, or even arouse sexual aversion in them. As a consequence of this aversion, they are incapable, if they are men, of carrying out the sexual act, or else they derive no enjoyment from it.

(*b*) They may be *amphigenic* inverts, that is psychosexual hermaphrodites. In that case their sexual objects may equally well be of their own or of the opposite sex. This kind of inversion thus lacks the characteristic of exclusiveness.

---

[1] [This is no doubt an allusion to the theory expounded by Aristophanes in Plato's *Symposium*. Freud recurred to this much later, at the end of Chapter VI of *Beyond the Pleasure Principle* (1920g).]

[2] On these difficulties and on the attempts which have been made to arrive at the proportional number of inverts, see Hirschfeld (1904).

(c) They may be *contingent* inverts. In that case, under certain external conditions—of which inaccessibility of any normal sexual object and imitation are the chief—they are capable of taking as their sexual object someone of their own sex and of deriving satisfaction from sexual intercourse with him.

Again, inverts vary in their views as to the peculiarity of their sexual instinct. Some of them accept their inversion as something in the natural course of things, just as a normal person accepts the direction of *his* libido, and insist energetically that inversion is as legitimate as the normal attitude; others rebel against their inversion and feel it as a pathological compulsion.[1]

Other variations occur which relate to questions of time. The trait of inversion may either date back to the very beginning, as far back as the subject's memory reaches, or it may not have become noticeable till some particular time before or after puberty.[2] It may either persist throughout life, or it may go into temporary abeyance, or again it may constitute an episode on the way to a normal development. It may even make its first appearance late in life after a long period of normal sexual activity. A periodic oscillation between a normal and an inverted sexual object has also sometimes been observed. Those cases are of particular interest in which the libido changes over to an inverted sexual object after a distressing experience with a normal one.

As a rule these different kinds of variations are found side by side independently of one another. It is, however, safe to assume that the most extreme form of inversion will have been present from a very early age and that the person concerned will feel at one with his peculiarity.

Many authorities would be unwilling to class together all

[1] The fact of a person struggling in this way against a compulsion towards inversion may perhaps determine the possibility of his being influenced by suggestion [*added* 1910:] or psycho-analysis.

[2] Many writers have insisted with justice that the dates assigned by inverts themselves for the appearance of their tendency to inversion are untrustworthy, since they may have repressed the evidence of their heterosexual feelings from their memory. [*Added* 1910:] These suspicions have been confirmed by psycho-analysis in those cases of inversion to which it has had access; it has produced decisive alterations in their anamnesis by filling in their infantile amnesia.—[In the first edition (1905) the place of this last sentence was taken by the following one: 'A decision on this point could be arrived at only by a psycho-analytic investigation of inverts.']

the various cases which I have enumerated and would prefer to lay stress upon their differences rather than their resemblances, in accordance with their own preferred view of inversion. Nevertheless, though the distinctions cannot be disputed, it is impossible to overlook the existence of numerous intermediate examples of every type, so that we are driven to conclude that we are dealing with a connected series.

NATURE OF INVERSION   The earliest assessments regarded inversion as an innate indication of nervous degeneracy. This corresponded to the fact that medical observers first came across it in persons suffering, or appearing to suffer, from nervous diseases. This characterization of inversion involves two suppositions, which must be considered separately: that it is innate and that it is degenerate.

DEGENERACY   The attribution of degeneracy in this connection is open to the objections which can be raised against the indiscriminate use of the word in general. It has become the fashion to regard any symptom which is not obviously due to trauma or infection as a sign of degeneracy. Magnan's classification of degenerates is indeed of such a kind as not to exclude the possibility of the concept of degeneracy being applied to a nervous system whose general functioning is excellent. This being so, it may well be asked whether an attribution of 'degeneracy' is of any value or adds anything to our knowledge. It seems wiser only to speak of it where

(1) several serious deviations from the normal are found together, and

(2) the capacity for efficient functioning and survival seem to be severely impaired.[1]

Several facts go to show that in this legitimate sense of the word inverts cannot be regarded as degenerate:

(1) Inversion is found in people who exhibit no other serious deviations from the normal.

---

[1] Moebius (1900) confirms the view that we should be chary in making a diagnosis of degeneracy and that it has very little practical value: 'If we survey the wide field of degeneracy upon which some glimpses of revealing light have been thrown in these pages, it will at once be clear that there is small value in ever making a diagnosis of degeneracy.'

(2) It is similarly found in people whose efficiency is unimpaired, and who are indeed distinguished by specially high intellectual development and ethical culture.[1]

(3) If we disregard the patients we come across in our medical practice, and cast our eyes round a wider horizon, we shall come in two directions upon facts which make it impossible to regard inversion as a sign of degeneracy:

(*a*) Account must be taken of the fact that inversion was a frequent phenomenon—one might almost say an institution charged with important functions—among the peoples of antiquity at the height of their civilization.

(*b*) It is remarkably widespread among many savage and primitive races, whereas the concept of degeneracy is usually restricted to states of high civilization (cf. Bloch); and, even amongst the civilized peoples of Europe, climate and race exercise the most powerful influence on the prevalence of inversion and upon the attitude adopted towards it.[2]

INNATE
CHARACTER

As may be supposed, innateness is only attributed to the first, most extreme, class of inverts, and the evidence for it rests upon assurances given by them that at no time in their lives has their sexual instinct shown any sign of taking another course. The very existence of the two other classes, and especially the third [the 'contingent' inverts], is difficult to reconcile with the hypothesis of the innateness of inversion. This explains why those who support this view tend to separate out the group of absolute inverts from all the rest, thus abandoning any attempt at giving an account of inversion which shall have universal application. In the view of these authorities inversion is innate in one group of cases, while in others it may have come about in other ways.

The reverse of this view is represented by the alternative one that inversion is an acquired character of the sexual

[1] It must be allowed that the spokesmen of 'Uranism' are justified in asserting that some of the most prominent men in all recorded history were inverts and perhaps even absolute inverts.

[2] The pathological approach to the study of inversion has been displaced by the anthropological. The merit for bringing about this change is due to Bloch (1902–3), who has also laid stress on the occurrence of inversion among the civilizations of antiquity.

instinct. This second view is based on the following considerations:

(1) In the case of many inverts, even absolute ones, it is possible to show that very early in their lives a sexual impression occurred which left a permanent after-effect in the shape of a tendency to homosexuality.

(2) In the case of many others, it is possible to point to external influences in their lives, whether of a favourable or inhibiting character, which have led sooner or later to a fixation of their inversion. (Such influences are exclusive relations with persons of their own sex, comradeship in war, detention in prison, the dangers of heterosexual intercourse, celibacy, sexual weakness, etc.)

(3) Inversion can be removed by hypnotic suggestion, which would be astonishing in an innate characteristic.

In view of these considerations it is even possible to doubt the very existence of such a thing as innate inversion. It can be argued (cf. Havelock Ellis [1915]) that, if the cases of allegedly innate inversion were more closely examined, some experience of their early childhood would probably come to light which had a determining effect upon the direction taken by their libido. This experience would simply have passed out of the subject's conscious recollection, but could be recalled to his memory under appropriate influence. In the opinion of these writers inversion can only be described as a frequent variation of the sexual instinct, which can be determined by a number of external circumstances in the subject's life.

The apparent certainty of this conclusion is, however, completely countered by the reflection that many people are subjected to the same sexual influences (e.g. to seduction or mutual masturbation, which may occur in early youth) without becoming inverted or without remaining so permanently. We are therefore forced to a suspicion that the choice between 'innate' and 'acquired' is not an exclusive one or that it does not cover all the issues involved in inversion.

EXPLANATION   The nature of inversion is explained neither
OF INVERSION   by the hypothesis that it is innate nor by the
               alternative hypothesis that it is acquired. In the
former case we must ask in what respect it is innate, unless we are to accept the crude explanation that everyone is born with

his sexual instinct attached to a particular sexual object. In the latter case it may be questioned whether the various accidental influences would be sufficient to explain the acquisition of inversion without the co-operation of something in the subject himself. As we have already shown, the existence of this last factor is not to be denied.

BISEXUALITY   A fresh contradiction of popular views is involved in the considerations put forward by Lydston [1889], Kiernan [1888] and Chevalier [1893] in an endeavour to account for the possibility of sexual inversion. It is popularly believed that a human being is either a man or a woman. Science, however, knows of cases in which the sexual characters are obscured, and in which it is consequently difficult to determine the sex. This arises in the first instance in the field of anatomy. The genitals of the individuals concerned combine male and female characteristics. (This condition is known as hermaphroditism.) In rare cases both kinds of sexual apparatus are found side by side fully developed (true hermaphroditism); but far more frequently both sets of organs are found in an atrophied condition.[1]

The importance of these abnormalities lies in the unexpected fact that they facilitate our understanding of normal development. For it appears that a certain degree of anatomical hermaphroditism occurs normally. In every normal male or female individual, traces are found of the apparatus of the opposite sex. These either persist without function as rudimentary organs or become modified and take on other functions.

These long-familiar facts of anatomy lead us to suppose that an originally bisexual physical disposition has, in the course of evolution, become modified into a unisexual one, leaving behind only a few traces of the sex that has become atrophied.

It was tempting to extend this hypothesis to the mental sphere and to explain inversion in all its varieties as the expression of a psychical hermaphroditism. All that was required further in order to settle the question was that inversion should be regularly accompanied by the mental and somatic signs of hermaphroditism.

[1] For the most recent descriptions of somatic hermaphroditism, see Taruffi (1903), and numerous papers by Neugebauer in various volumes of the *Jahrbuch für sexuelle Zwischenstufen.*

But this expectation was disappointed. It is impossible to demonstrate so close a connection between the hypothetical psychical hermaphroditism and the established anatomical one. A general lowering of the sexual instinct and a slight anatomical atrophy of the organs is found frequently in inverts (cf. Havelock Ellis, 1915). Frequently, but by no means regularly or even usually. The truth must therefore be recognized that inversion and somatic hermaphroditism are on the whole independent of each other.

A great deal of importance, too, has been attached to what are called the secondary and tertiary sexual characters and to the great frequency of the occurrence of those of the opposite sex in inverts (cf. Havelock Ellis, 1915). Much of this, again, is correct; but it should never be forgotten that in general the secondary and tertiary sexual characters of one sex occur very frequently in the opposite one. They are indications of hermaphroditism, but are not attended by any change of sexual object in the direction of inversion.

Psychical hermaphroditism would gain substance if the inversion of the sexual object were at least accompanied by a parallel change-over of the subject's other mental qualities, instincts and character traits into those marking the opposite sex. But it is only in inverted women that character-inversion of this kind can be looked for with any regularity. In men the most complete mental masculinity can be combined with inversion. If the belief in psychical hermaphroditism is to be persisted in, it will be necessary to add that its manifestations in various spheres show only slight signs of being mutually determined. Moreover the same is true of somatic hermaphroditism: according to Halban (1903),[1] occurrences of individual atrophied organs and of secondary sexual characters are to a considerable extent independent of one another.

The theory of bisexuality has been expressed in its crudest form by a spokesman of the male inverts: 'a feminine brain in a masculine body'. But we are ignorant of what characterizes a feminine brain. There is neither need nor justification for replacing the psychological problem by the anatomical one. Krafft-Ebing's attempted explanation seems to be more exactly framed than that of Ulrichs but does not differ from it in essentials. According to Krafft-Ebing (1895, 5), every indi-

[1] His paper includes a bibliography of the subject.

vidual's bisexual disposition endows him with masculine and feminine brain centres as well as with somatic organs of sex; these centres develop only at puberty, for the most part under the influence of the sex-gland, which is independent of them in the original disposition. But what has just been said of masculine and feminine brains applies equally to masculine and feminine 'centres'; and incidentally we have not even any grounds for assuming that certain areas of the brain ('centres') are set aside for the functions of sex, as is the case, for instance, with those of speech.[1]

Nevertheless, two things emerge from these discussions. In the first place, a bisexual disposition is somehow concerned in

[1] It appears (from a bibliography given in the sixth volume of the *Jahrbuch für sexuelle Zwischenstufen*) that E. Gley was the first writer to suggest bisexuality as an explanation of inversion. As long ago as in January, 1884, he published a paper, 'Les aberrations de l'instinct sexuel', in the *Revue Philosophique*. It is, moreover, noteworthy that the majority of authors who derive inversion from bisexuality bring forward that factor not only in the case of inverts, but also for all those who have grown up to be normal, and that, as a logical consequence, they regard inversion as the result of a disturbance in development. Chevalier (1893) already writes in this sense. Krafft-Ebing (1895, 10) remarks that there are a great number of observations 'which prove at least the virtual persistence of this second centre (that of the subordinated sex)'. A Dr. Arduin (1900) asserts that 'there are masculine and feminine elements in every human being (cf. Hirschfeld, 1899); but one set of these—according to the sex of the person in question—is incomparably more strongly developed than the other, so far as heterosexual individuals are concerned. . . .' Herman (1903) is convinced that 'masculine elements and characteristics are present in every woman and feminine ones in every man', etc. [*Added* 1910:] Fliess (1906) subsequently claimed the idea of bisexuality (in the sense of *duality of sex*) as his own. [*Added* 1924:] In lay circles the hypothesis of human bisexuality is regarded as being due to O. Weininger, the philosopher, who died at an early age, and who made the idea the basis of a somewhat unbalanced book (1903). The particulars which I have enumerated above will be sufficient to show how little justification there is for the claim.

[Freud's own realization of the importance of bisexuality owed much to Fliess (cf. p. 86 *n*.), and his forgetfulness of this fact on one occasion provided him with an example in his *Psychopathology of Everyday Life*, 1901*b*, Chapter VII (11). He did not, however, accept Fliess's view that bisexuality provided the explanation of repression. See Freud's discussion of this in 'A Child is Being Beaten' (1919*e*, half-way through Section VI). The whole question is gone into in detail by Kris in Section IV of his introduction to the Fliess correspondence (Freud, 1950*a*).]

inversion, though we do not know in what that disposition consists, beyond anatomical structure. And secondly, we have to deal with disturbances that affect the sexual instinct in the course of its development.

SEXUAL OBJECT   The theory of psychical hermaphroditism
OF INVERTS   presupposes that the sexual object of an invert
        is the opposite of that of a normal person. An
inverted man, it holds, is like a woman in being subject to the
charm that proceeds from masculine attributes both physical
and mental: he feels he is a woman in search of a man.

But however well this applies to quite a number of inverts, it is, nevertheless, far from revealing a universal characteristic of inversion. There can be no doubt that a large proportion of male inverts retain the mental quality of masculinity, that they possess relatively few of the secondary characters of the opposite sex and that what they look for in their sexual object are in fact feminine mental traits. If this were not so, how would it be possible to explain the fact that male prostitutes who offer themselves to inverts—to-day just as they did in ancient times— imitate women in all the externals of their clothing and behaviour? Such imitation would otherwise inevitably clash with the ideal of the inverts. It is clear that in Greece, where the most masculine men were numbered among the inverts, what excited a man's love was not the *masculine* character of a boy, but his physical resemblance to a woman as well as his feminine mental qualities—his shyness, his modesty and his need for instruction and assistance. As soon as the boy became a man he ceased to be a sexual object for men and himself, perhaps, became a lover of boys. In this instance, therefore, as in many others, the sexual object is not someone of the same sex but someone who combines the characters of both sexes; there is, as it were, a compromise between an impulse that seeks for a man and one that seeks for a woman, while it remains a paramount condition that the object's body (i.e. genitals) shall be masculine. Thus the sexual object is a kind of reflection of the subject's own bisexual nature.[1]

[1] [This last sentence was added in 1915.—*Footnote added* 1910:] It is true that psycho-analysis has not yet produced a complete explanation of the origin of inversion; nevertheless, it has discovered the psychical mechanism of its development, and has made essential contributions to

The position in the case of women is less ambiguous; for among them the active inverts exhibit masculine characteristics, both physical and mental, with peculiar frequency and look for femininity in their sexual objects—though here again a closer knowledge of the facts might reveal greater variety.

SEXUAL AIM   The important fact to bear in mind is that no
OF INVERTS   one single aim can be laid down as applying in
              cases of inversion. Among men, intercourse *per anum* by no means coincides with inversion; masturbation is quite as frequently their exclusive aim, and it is even true that

the statement of the problems involved. In all the cases we have examined we have established the fact that the future inverts, in the earliest years of their childhood, pass through a phase of very intense but short-lived fixation to a woman (usually their mother), and that, after leaving this behind, they identify themselves with a woman and take *themselves* as their sexual object. That is to say, they proceed from a narcissistic basis, and look for a young man who resembles themselves and whom *they* may love as their mother loved *them*. Moreover, we have frequently found that alleged inverts have been by no means insusceptible to the charms of women, but have continually transposed the excitation aroused by women on to a male object. They have thus repeated all through their lives the mechanism by which their inversion arose. Their compulsive longing for men has turned out to be determined by their ceaseless flight from women.

[At this point the footnote proceeded as follows in the 1910 edition only: 'It must, however, be borne in mind that hitherto only a single type of invert has been submitted to psycho-analysis—persons whose sexual activity is in general stunted and the residue of which is manifested as inversion. The problem of inversion is a highly complex one and includes very various types of sexual activity and development. A strict conceptual distinction should be drawn between different cases of inversion according to whether the sexual character of the *object* or that of the *subject* has been inverted.']

[*Added* 1915:] Psycho-analytic research is most decidedly opposed to any attempt at separating off homosexuals from the rest of mankind as a group of a special character. By studying sexual excitations other than those that are manifestly displayed, it has found that all human beings are capable of making a homosexual object-choice and have in fact made one in their unconscious. Indeed, libidinal attachments to persons of the same sex play no less a part as factors in normal mental life, and a greater part as a motive force for illness, than do similar attachments to the opposite sex. On the contrary, psycho-analysis considers that a choice of an object independently of its sex—freedom to range equally over male and female objects—as it is found in childhood, in primitive states of society and early periods of history, is the original basis from

restrictions of sexual aim—to the point of its being limited to simple outpourings of emotion—are commoner among them than among heterosexual lovers. Among women, too, the sexual aims of inverts are various: there seems to be a special preference for contact with the mucous membrane of the mouth.

CONCLUSION   It will be seen that we are not in a position to base a satisfactory explanation of the origin of inversion upon the material at present before us. Nevertheless our investigation has put us in possession of a piece of knowledge

which, as a result of restriction in one direction or the other, both the normal and the inverted types develop. Thus from the point of view of psycho-analysis the exclusive sexual interest felt by men for women is also a problem that needs elucidating and is not a self-evident fact based upon an attraction that is ultimately of a chemical nature. A person's final sexual attitude is not decided until after puberty and is the result of a number of factors, not all of which are yet known; some are of a constitutional nature but others are accidental. No doubt a few of these factors may happen to carry so much weight that they influence the result in their sense. But in general the multiplicity of determining factors is reflected in the variety of manifest sexual attitudes in which they find their issue in mankind. In inverted types, a predominance of archaic constitutions and primitive psychical mechanisms is regularly to be found. Their most essential characteristics seem to be a coming into operation of narcissistic object-choice and a retention of the erotic significance of the anal zone. There is nothing to be gained, however, by separating the most extreme types of inversion from the rest on the basis of constitutional peculiarities of that kind. What we find as an apparently sufficient explanation of these types can be equally shown to be present, though less strongly, in the constitution of transitional types and of those whose manifest attitude is normal. The differences in the end-products may be of a qualitative nature, but analysis shows that the differences between their determinants are only quantitative. Among the accidental factors that influence object-choice we have found that frustration (in the form of an early deterrence, by fear, from sexual activity) deserves attention, and we have observed that the presence of both parents plays an important part. The absence of a strong father in childhood not infrequently favours the occurrence of inversion. Finally, it may be insisted that the concept of inversion in respect of the sexual object should be sharply distinguished from that of the occurrence in the subject of a mixture of sexual characters. In the relation between these two factors, too, a certain degree of reciprocal independence is unmistakably present.

[*Added* 1920:] Ferenczi (1914) has brought forward a number of interesting points on the subject of inversion. He rightly protests that, because they have in common the symptom of inversion, a large number

which may turn out to be of greater importance to us than the solution of that problem. It has been brought to our notice that we have been in the habit of regarding the connection between the sexual instinct and the sexual object as more intimate than

of conditions, which are very different from one another and which are of unequal importance both in organic and psychical respects, have been thrown together under the name of 'homosexuality' (or, to follow him in giving it a better name, 'homo-erotism'). He insists that a sharp distinction should at least be made between two types: 'subject homo-erotics', who feel and behave like women, and 'object homo-erotics', who are completely masculine and who have merely exchanged a female for a male object. The first of these two types he recognizes as true 'sexual intermediates' in Hirschfeld's sense of the word; the second he describes, less happily, as obsessional neurotics. According to him, it is only in the case of object homo-erotics that there is any question of their struggling against their inclination to inversion or of the possibility of their being influenced psychologically. While granting the existence of these two types, we may add that there are many people in whom a certain quantity of subject homo-erotism is found in combination with a proportion of object homo-erotism.

During the last few years work carried out by biologists, notably by Steinach, has thrown a strong light on the organic determinants of homo-erotism and of sexual characters in general. By carrying out experimental castration and subsequently grafting the sex-glands of the opposite sex, it was possible in the case of various species of mammals to transform a male into a female and vice versa. The transformation affected more or less completely both the somatic sexual characters and the psychosexual attitude (that is, both subject and object erotism). It appeared that the vehicle of the force which thus acted as a sex-determinant was not the part of the sex-gland which forms the sex-cells but what is known as its interstitial tissue (the 'puberty-gland'). In one case this transformation of sex was actually effected in a man who had lost his testes owing to tuberculosis. In his sexual life he behaved in a feminine manner, as a passive homosexual, and exhibited very clearly-marked feminine sexual characters of a secondary kind (e.g. in regard to growth of hair and beard and deposits of fat on the breasts and hips). After an undescended testis from another male patient had been grafted into him, he began to behave in a masculine manner and to direct his libido towards women in a normal way. Simultaneously his somatic feminine characters disappeared. (Lipschütz, 1919, 356–7.)

It would be unjustifiable to assert that these interesting experiments put the theory of inversion on a new basis, and it would be hasty to expect them to offer a universal means of 'curing' homosexuality. Fliess has rightly insisted that these experimental findings do not invalidate the theory of the general bisexual disposition of the higher animals. On the contrary, it seems to me probable that further research of a similar kind will produce a direct confirmation of this presumption of bisexuality.

it in fact is. Experience of the cases that are considered abnormal has shown us that in them the sexual instinct and the sexual object are merely soldered together—a fact which we have been in danger of overlooking in consequence of the uniformity of the normal picture, where the object appears to form part and parcel of the instinct. We are thus warned to loosen the bond that exists in our thoughts between instinct and object. It seems probable that the sexual instinct is in the first instance independent of its object; nor is its origin likely to be due to its object's attractions.

(b) Sexually Immature Persons and Animals as Sexual Objects

People whose sexual objects belong to the normally inappropriate sex—that is, inverts—strike the observer as a collection of individuals who may be quite sound in other respects. On the other hand, cases in which sexually immature persons (children) are chosen as sexual objects are instantly judged as sporadic aberrations. It is only exceptionally that children are the exclusive sexual objects in such a case. They usually come to play that part when someone who is cowardly or has become impotent adopts them as a substitute, or when an urgent instinct (one which will not allow of postponement) cannot at the moment get possession of any more appropriate object. Nevertheless, a light is thrown on the nature of the sexual instinct by the fact that it permits of so much variation in its objects and such a cheapening of them—which hunger, with its far more energetic retention of its objects, would only permit in the most extreme instances. A similar consideration applies to sexual intercourse with animals, which is by no means rare, especially among country people, and in which sexual attraction seems to override the barriers of species.

One would be glad on aesthetic grounds to be able to ascribe these and other severe aberrations of the sexual instinct to insanity; but that cannot be done. Experience shows that disturbances of the sexual instinct among the insane do not differ from those that occur among the healthy and in whole races or occupations. Thus the sexual abuse of children is found with uncanny frequency among school teachers and child attendants, simply because they have the best opportunity for it. The insane merely exhibit any such aberration to an intensified degree; or, what is particularly significant, it may become exclusive and replace normal sexual satisfaction entirely.

The very remarkable relation which thus holds between sexual variations and the descending scale from health to insanity gives us plenty of material for thought. I am inclined to believe that it may be explained by the fact that the impulses of sexual life are among those which, even normally, are the least controlled by the higher activities of the mind. In my experience anyone who is in any way, whether socially or ethically, abnormal mentally is invariably abnormal also in his sexual life. But many people are abnormal in their sexual life who in every other respect approximate to the average, and have, along with the rest, passed through the process of human cultural development, in which sexuality remains the weak spot.

The most general conclusion that follows from all these discussions seems, however, to be this. Under a great number of conditions and in surprisingly numerous individuals, the nature and importance of the sexual object recedes into the background. What is essential and constant in the sexual instinct is something else.[1]

(2) DEVIATIONS IN RESPECT OF THE SEXUAL AIM

The normal sexual aim is regarded as being the union of the genitals in the act known as copulation, which leads to a release of the sexual tension and a temporary extinction of the sexual instinct—a satisfaction analogous to the sating of hunger. But even in the most normal sexual process we may detect rudiments which, if they had developed, would have led to the deviations described as 'perversions'. For there are certain intermediate relations to the sexual object, such as touching and looking at it, which lie on the road towards copulation and are recognized as being preliminary sexual aims. On the one hand these

[1] [*Footnote added* 1910:] The most striking distinction between the erotic life of antiquity and our own no doubt lies in the fact that the ancients laid the stress upon the instinct itself, whereas we emphasize its object. The ancients glorified the instinct and were prepared on its account to honour even an inferior object; while we despise the instinctual activity in itself, and find excuses for it only in the merits of the object.

activities are themselves accompanied by pleasure, and on the
other hand they intensify the excitation, which should persist
until the final sexual aim is attained. Moreover, the kiss, one
particular contact of this kind, between the mucous membrane
of the lips of the two people concerned, is held in high sexual
esteem among many nations (including the most highly civilized
ones), in spite of the fact that the parts of the body involved do
not form part of the sexual apparatus but constitute the
entrance to the digestive tract. Here, then, are factors which
provide a point of contact between the perversions and normal
sexual life and which can also serve as a basis for their classification. Perversions are sexual activities which either (a) extend, in
an anatomical sense, beyond the regions of the body that are
designed for sexual union, or (b) linger over the intermediate
relations to the sexual object which should normally be
traversed rapidly on the path towards the final sexual aim.

(A) ANATOMICAL EXTENSIONS

OVERVALUATION   It is only in the rarest instances that the
OF THE SEXUAL   psychical valuation that is set on the sexual
OBJECT   object, as being the goal of the sexual in-
                      stinct, stops short at its genitals. The apprecia-
tion extends to the whole body of the sexual object and tends
to involve every sensation derived from it. The same overvaluation spreads over into the psychological sphere: the subject
becomes, as it were, intellectually infatuated (that is, his powers
of judgement are weakened) by the mental achievements and
perfections of the sexual object and he submits to the latter's
judgements with credulity. Thus the credulity of love becomes
an important, if not the most fundamental, source of *authority*.[1]
    This sexual overvaluation is something that cannot be easily
reconciled with a restriction of the sexual aim to union of the

---

[1] In this connection I cannot help recalling the credulous submissive-
ness shown by a hypnotized subject towards his hypnotist. This leads
me to suspect that the essence of hypnosis lies in an unconscious fixation
of the subject's libido to the figure of the hypnotist, through the medium
of the masochistic components of the sexual instinct. [*Added* 1910:]
Ferenczi (1909) has brought this characteristic of suggestibility into
relation with the 'parental complex'.—[The relation of the subject to
the hypnotist was discussed by Freud much later, in Chapter VIII of
his *Group Psychology* (1921c). See also 1905b, *S.E.*, **7**, 294 ff.]

actual genitals and it helps to turn activities connected with other parts of the body into sexual aims.[1]

The significance of the factor of sexual overvaluation can be best studied in men, for their erotic life alone has become accessible to research. That of women—partly owing to the stunting effect of civilized conditions and partly owing to their conventional secretiveness and insincerity—is still veiled in an impenetrable obscurity.[2]

SEXUAL USE OF THE MUCOUS MEMBRANE OF THE LIPS AND MOUTH   The use of the mouth as a sexual organ is regarded as a perversion if the lips (or tongue) of one person are brought into contact with the genitals of another, but not if the mucous membranes of the lips of both of them come together. This exception is the point of contact with what is normal. Those who condemn the other practices (which have no doubt been common among mankind from primaeval times) as being perversions, are giving way to an unmistakable feeling of *disgust*, which protects them from accepting sexual aims of the kind. The limits of such disgust are, however, often purely conventional: a man who will kiss a pretty girl's lips passionately, may perhaps be disgusted at the idea of

[1] [In the editions earlier than 1920 this paragraph ended with the further sentence: 'The emergence of these extremely various anatomical extensions clearly implies a need for variation, and this has been described by Hoche as "craving for stimulation".' The first two sentences of the footnote which follows were added in 1915, before which date it had begun with the sentence: 'Further consideration leads me to conclude that I. Bloch has over-estimated the theoretical importance of the factor of craving for stimulation.' The whole footnote and the paragraph in the text above were recast in their present form in 1920:] It must be pointed out, however, that sexual overvaluation is not developed in the case of *every* mechanism of object-choice. We shall become acquainted later on with another and more direct explanation of the sexual role assumed by the other parts of the body. The factor of 'craving for stimulation' has been put forward by Hoche and Bloch as an explanation of the extension of sexual interest to parts of the body other than the genitals; but it does not seem to me to deserve such an important place. The various channels along which the libido passes are related to each other from the very first like inter-communicating pipes, and we must take the phenomenon of collateral flow into account. [See p. 36.]

[2] [*Footnote added* 1920:] In typical cases women fail to exhibit any sexual overvaluation towards men; but they scarcely ever fail to do so towards their own children.

using her tooth-brush, though there are no grounds for supposing that his own oral cavity, for which he feels no disgust, is any cleaner than the girl's. Here, then, our attention is drawn to the factor of disgust, which interferes with the libidinal overvaluation of the sexual object but can in turn be overridden by libido. Disgust seems to be one of the forces which have led to a restriction of the sexual aim. These forces do not as a rule extend to the genitals themselves. But there is no doubt that the genitals of the opposite sex can in themselves be an object of disgust and that such an attitude is one of the characteristics of all hysterics, and especially of hysterical women. The sexual instinct in its strength enjoys overriding this disgust. (See below [p. 22 f.].)

SEXUAL USE OF THE   Where the anus is concerned it be-
ANAL ORIFICE   comes still clearer that it is disgust which
                                      stamps that sexual aim as a perversion.
I hope, however, I shall not be accused of partisanship when I assert that people who try to account for this disgust by saying that the organ in question serves the function of excretion and comes in contact with excrement—a thing which is disgusting in itself—are not much more to the point than hysterical girls who account for their disgust at the male genital by saying that it serves to void urine.

The playing of a sexual part by the mucous membrane of the anus is by no means limited to intercourse between men: preference for it is in no way characteristic of inverted feeling. On the contrary, it seems that *paedicatio* with a male owes its origin to an analogy with a similar act performed with a woman; while mutual masturbation is the sexual aim most often found in intercourse between inverts.

SIGNIFICANCE   The extension of sexual interest to other re-
OF OTHER   gions of the body, with all its variations, offers
REGIONS OF   us nothing that is new in principle; it adds
THE BODY   nothing to our knowledge of the sexual instinct,
                               which merely proclaims its intention in this way
of getting possession of the sexual object in every possible direction. But these anatomical extensions inform us that, besides sexual overvaluation, there is a second factor at work which is strange to popular knowledge. Certain regions of the body, such as the mucous membrane of the mouth and anus,

which are constantly appearing in these practices, seem, as it were, to be claiming that they should themselves be regarded and treated as genitals. We shall learn later that this claim is justified by the history of the development of the sexual instinct and that it is fulfilled in the symptomatology of certain pathological states.

UNSUITABLE SUB-
STITUTES FOR THE
SEXUAL OBJECT—
FETISHISM

There are some cases which are quite specially remarkable—those in which the normal sexual object is replaced by another which bears some relation to it, but is entirely unsuited to serve the normal sexual aim. From the point of view of classification, we should no doubt have done better to have mentioned this highly interesting group of aberrations of the sexual instinct among the deviations in respect of the sexual *object*. But we have postponed their mention till we could become acquainted with the factor of sexual overvaluation, on which these phenomena, being connected with an abandonment of the sexual aim, are dependent.

What is substituted for the sexual object is some part of the body (such as the foot or hair) which is in general very inappropriate for sexual purposes, or some inanimate object which bears an assignable relation to the person whom it replaces and preferably to that person's sexuality (e.g. a piece of clothing or underlinen). Such substitutes are with some justice likened to the fetishes in which savages believe that their gods are embodied.

A transition to those cases of fetishism in which the sexual aim, whether normal or perverse, is entirely abandoned is afforded by other cases in which the sexual object is required to fulfil a fetishistic condition—such as the possession of some particular hair-colouring or clothing, or even some bodily defect— if the sexual aim is to be attained. No other variation of the sexual instinct that borders on the pathological can lay so much claim to our interest as this one, such is the peculiarity of the phenomena to which it gives rise. Some degree of diminution in the urge towards the normal sexual aim (an executive weakness of the sexual apparatus) seems to be a necessary precondition in every case.[1] The point of contact with the normal

---

[1] [*Footnote added* 1915:] This weakness would represent the *constitutional* precondition. Psycho-analysis has found that the phenomenon can also

is provided by the psychologically essential overvaluation of the sexual object, which inevitably extends to everything that is associated with it. A certain degree of fetishism is thus habitually present in normal love, especially in those stages of it in which the normal sexual aim seems unattainable or its fulfilment prevented:

> Schaff' mir ein Halstuch von ihrer Brust,
> Ein Strumpfband meiner Liebeslust![1]

The situation only becomes pathological when the longing for the fetish passes beyond the point of being merely a necessary condition attached to the sexual object and actually *takes the place* of the normal aim, and, further, when the fetish becomes detached from a particular individual and becomes the *sole* sexual object. These are, indeed, the general conditions under which mere variations of the sexual instinct pass over into pathological aberrations.

Binet (1888) was the first to maintain (what has since been confirmed by a quantity of evidence) that the choice of a fetish is an after-effect of some sexual impression, received as a rule in early childhood. (This may be brought into line with the proverbial durability of first loves: *on revient toujours à ses premiers amours.*) This derivation is particularly obvious in cases where there is merely a fetishistic condition attached to the sexual object. We shall come across the importance of early sexual impressions again in another connection [p. 108].[2]

be *accidentally* determined, by the occurrence of an early deterrence from sexual activity owing to fear, which may divert the subject from the normal sexual aim and encourage him to seek a substitute for it.

[1] [Get me a kerchief from her breast,
   A garter that her knee has pressed.
          Goethe, *Faust*, Part I, Scene 7. (*Trans.* Bayard Taylor.)]

[2] [*Footnote added* 1920:] Deeper-going psycho-analytic research has raised a just criticism of Binet's assertion. All the observations dealing with this point have recorded a first meeting with the fetish at which it already aroused sexual interest without there being anything in the accompanying circumstances to explain the fact. Moreover, all of these 'early' sexual impressions relate to a time after the age of five or six, whereas psycho-analysis makes it doubtful whether fresh pathological fixations can occur so late as this. The true explanation is that behind the first recollection of the fetish's appearance there lies a submerged and forgotten phase of sexual development. The fetish, like a 'screen-memory', represents this phase and is thus a remnant and precipitate of it. The fact that this early infantile phase turns in the direction of

In other cases the replacement of the object by a fetish is determined by a symbolic connection of thought, of which the person concerned is usually not conscious. It is not always possible to trace the course of these connections with certainty. (The foot, for instance, is an age-old sexual symbol which occurs even in mythology;[1] no doubt the part played by fur as a fetish owes its origin to an association with the hair of the *mons Veneris*.) None the less even symbolism such as this is not always unrelated to sexual experiences in childhood.[2]

(B) Fixations of Preliminary Sexual Aims

APPEARANCE   Every external or internal factor that hinders
OF NEW AIMS   or postpones the attainment of the normal
                       sexual aim (such as impotence, the high price
of the sexual object or the danger of the sexual act) will

fetishism, as well as the choice of the fetish itself, are constitutionally determined.

    [1] [*Footnote added* 1910:] The shoe or slipper is a corresponding symbol of the *female* genitals.

    [2] [*Footnote added* 1910:] Psycho-analysis has cleared up one of the remaining gaps in our understanding of fetishism. It has shown the importance, as regards the choice of a fetish, of a coprophilic pleasure in smelling which has disappeared owing to repression. Both the feet and the hair are objects with a strong smell which have been exalted into fetishes after the olfactory sensation has become unpleasurable and been abandoned. Accordingly, in the perversion that corresponds to foot-fetishism, it is only dirty and evil-smelling feet that become sexual objects. Another factor that helps towards explaining the fetishistic preference for the foot is to be found among the sexual theories of children (see below p. 61): the foot represents a woman's penis, the absence of which is deeply felt. [*Added* 1915:] In a number of cases of foot-fetishism it has been possible to show that the scopophilic instinct, seeking to reach its object (originally the genitals) from underneath, was brought to a halt in its pathway by prohibition and repression. For that reason it became attached to a fetish in the form of a foot or shoe, the female genitals (in accordance with the expectations of childhood) being imagined as male ones.—[The importance of the repression of pleasure in smell had been indicated by Freud in two letters to Fliess of January 11 and November 14, 1897 (Freud, 1950a, Letters 55 and 75). He returned to the subject at the end of his analysis of the 'Rat Man' (Freud, 1909d), and discussed it at considerable length in two long footnotes to Chapter IV of *Civilization and its Discontents* (1930a). The topic of fetishism was further considered in Freud's paper on that subject (1927e) and again still later in a posthumously published fragment on the splitting of the ego (1940e [1938]) and at the end of Chapter VIII of his *Outline of Psycho-Analysis* (1940a [1938]).]

evidently lend support to the tendency to linger over the preparatory activities and to turn them into new sexual aims that can take the place of the normal one. Attentive examination always shows that even what seem to be the strangest of these new aims are already hinted at in the normal sexual process.

TOUCHING AND LOOKING   A certain amount of touching is indispensable (at all events among human beings) before the normal sexual aim can be attained. And everyone knows what a source of pleasure on the one hand and what an influx of fresh excitation on the other is afforded by tactile sensations of the skin of the sexual object. So that lingering over the stage of touching can scarcely be counted a perversion, provided that in the long run the sexual act is carried further.

The same holds true of seeing—an activity that is ultimately derived from touching. Visual impressions remain the most frequent pathway along which libidinal excitation is aroused; indeed, natural selection counts upon the accessibility of this pathway—if such a teleological form of statement is permissible [1]—when it encourages the development of beauty in the sexual object. The progressive concealment of the body which goes along with civilization keeps sexual curiosity awake. This curiosity seeks to complete the sexual object by revealing its hidden parts. It can, however, be diverted ('sublimated') in the direction of art, if its interest can be shifted away from the genitals on to the shape of the body as a whole.[2] It is usual for most normal people to linger to some extent over the inter-

[1] [The words in this parenthesis were added in 1915. Cf. footnote 1, p. 54.]

[2] [This seems to be Freud's first published use of the term 'sublimate', though it occurs as early as May 2, 1897, in the Fliess correspondence (Freud, 1950a, Letter 61). It also appears in the 'Dora' case history, 1905e, actually published later than the present work (S.E., 7, pp. 50 and 116) though drafted in 1901. The concept is further discussed below on p. 44.—Footnote added 1915:] There is to my mind no doubt that the concept of 'beautiful' has its roots in sexual excitation and that its original meaning was 'sexually stimulating'. [There is an allusion in the original to the fact that the German word 'Reiz' is commonly used both as the technical term for 'stimulus' and, in ordinary language, as an equivalent to the English 'charm' or 'attraction'.] This is related to the fact that we never regard the genitals themselves, which produce the strongest sexual excitation, as really 'beautiful'.

mediate sexual aim of a looking that has a sexual tinge to it; indeed, this offers them a possibility of directing some proportion of their libido on to higher artistic aims. On the other hand, this pleasure in looking [scopophilia] becomes a perversion (*a*) if it is restricted exclusively to the genitals, or (*b*) if it is connected with the overriding of disgust (as in the case of *voyeurs* or people who look on at excretory functions), or (*c*) if, instead of being *preparatory* to the normal sexual aim, it supplants it. This last is markedly true of exhibitionists, who, if I may trust the findings of several analyses,[1] exhibit their own genitals in order to obtain a reciprocal view of the genitals of the other person.[2]

In the perversions which are directed towards looking and being looked at, we come across a very remarkable characteristic with which we shall be still more intensely concerned in the aberration that we shall consider next: in these perversions the sexual aim occurs in two forms, an *active* and a *passive* one.

The force which opposes scopophilia, but which may be overridden by it (in a manner parallel to what we have previously seen in the case of disgust), is *shame*.

SADISM AND   The most common and the most significant of
MASOCHISM   all the perversions—the desire to inflict pain upon the sexual object, and its reverse—received from Krafft-Ebing the names of 'sadism' and 'masochism' for its active and passive forms respectively. Other writers [e.g. Schrenck-Notzing (1899)] have preferred the narrower term 'algolagnia'. This emphasizes the pleasure in *pain*, the cruelty; whereas the names chosen by Krafft-Ebing bring into prominence the pleasure in any form of humiliation or subjection.

As regards active algolagnia, sadism, the roots are easy to detect in the normal. The sexuality of most male human beings contains an element of *aggressiveness*—a desire to subjugate; the

---

[1] [In the editions before 1924 this read 'of a single analysis'.]

[2] [*Footnote added* 1920:] Under analysis, these perversions—and indeed most others—reveal a surprising variety of motives and determinants. The compulsion to exhibit, for instance, is also closely dependent on the castration complex: it is a means of constantly insisting upon the integrity of the subject's own (male) genitals and it reiterates his infantile satisfaction at the absence of a penis in those of women. [Cf. p. 61.]

biological significance of it seems to lie in the need for over-coming the resistance of the sexual object by means other than the process of wooing. Thus sadism would correspond to an aggressive component of the sexual instinct which has become independent and exaggerated and, by displacement, has usurped the leading position.[1]

In ordinary speech the connotation of sadism oscillates between, on the one hand, cases merely characterized by an active or violent attitude to the sexual object, and, on the other hand, cases in which satisfaction is entirely conditional on the humiliation and maltreatment of the object. Strictly speaking, it is only this last extreme instance which deserves to be des-cribed as a perversion.

Similarly, the term masochism comprises any passive attitude towards sexual life and the sexual object, the extreme instance of which appears to be that in which satisfaction is conditional upon suffering physical or mental pain at the hands of the sexual object. Masochism, in the form of a perversion, seems to be further removed from the normal sexual aim than its counter-part; it may be doubted at first whether it can ever occur as a primary phenomenon or whether, on the contrary, it may not invariably arise from a transformation of sadism.[2] It can often be shown that masochism is nothing more than an extension of sadism turned round upon the subject's own self, which thus, to begin with, takes the place of the sexual object. Clinical analysis of extreme cases of masochistic perversion show that a great number of factors (such as the castration complex and the sense of guilt) have combined to exaggerate and fixate the original passive sexual attitude.

[1] [In the editions of 1905 and 1910 the following two sentences appeared in the text at this point: 'One at least of the roots of masochism can be inferred with equal certainty. It arises from sexual overvaluation as a necessary psychical consequence of the choice of a sexual object.' From 1915 onwards these sentences were omitted and the next two paragraphs were inserted in their place.]

[2] [Footnote added 1924:] My opinion of masochism has been to a large extent altered by later reflection, based upon certain hypotheses as to the structure of the apparatus of the mind and the classes of instincts operating in it. I have been led to distinguish a primary or erotogenic masochism, out of which two later forms, feminine and moral masochism, have developed. Sadism which cannot find employment in actual life is turned round upon the subject's own self and so produces a secondary masochism, which is superadded to the primary kind. (Cf. Freud, 1924c.)

Pain, which is overridden in such cases, thus falls into line with disgust and shame as a force that stands in opposition and resistance to the libido.[1]

Sadism and masochism occupy a special position among the perversions, since the contrast between activity and passivity which lies behind them is among the universal characteristics of sexual life.

The history of human civilization shows beyond any doubt that there is an intimate connection between cruelty and the sexual instinct; but nothing has been done towards explaining the connection, apart from laying emphasis on the aggressive factor in the libido. According to some authorities this aggressive element of the sexual instinct is in reality a relic of cannibalistic desires—that is, it is a contribution derived from the apparatus for obtaining mastery, which is concerned with the satisfaction of the other and, ontogenetically, the older of the great instinctual needs.[2] It has also been maintained that every pain contains in itself the possibility of a feeling of pleasure. All that need be said is that no satisfactory explanation of this perversion has been put forward and that it seems possible that a number of mental impulses are combined in it to produce a single resultant.[3]

But the most remarkable feature of this perversion is that its active and passive forms are habitually found to occur together in the same individual. A person who feels pleasure in producing pain in someone else in a sexual relationship is also capable of enjoying as pleasure any pain which he may himself derive from sexual relations. A sadist is always at the same time a masochist, although the active or the passive aspect of the perversion may be the more strongly developed in him and may represent his predominant sexual activity.[4]

---

[1] [This short paragraph was in the first edition (1905), but the last two, as well as the next one, were only added in 1915.]

[2] [*Footnote added* 1915:] Cf. my remarks below [p. 64] on the pregenital phases of sexual development, which confirm this view.

[3] [*Footnote added* 1924:] The enquiry mentioned above [in footnote 2 on p. 24] has led me to assign a peculiar position, based upon the origin of the instincts, to the pair of opposites constituted by sadism and masochism, and to place them outside the class of the remaining 'perversions'.

[4] Instead of multiplying the evidence for this statement, I will quote a passage from Havelock Ellis (1913, 119): 'The investigation of histories

We find, then, that certain among the impulses to perversion occur regularly as pairs of opposites; and this, taken in conjunction with material which will be brought forward later, has a high theoretical significance.[1] It is, moreover, a suggestive fact that the existence of the pair of opposites formed by sadism and masochism cannot be attributed merely to the element of aggressiveness. We should rather be inclined to connect the simultaneous presence of these opposites with the opposing masculinity and femininity which are combined in bisexuality— a contrast which often has to be replaced in psycho-analysis by that between activity and passivity.[2]

(3) THE PERVERSIONS IN GENERAL

VARIATION   It is natural that medical men, who first
AND DISEASE studied perversions in outstanding examples and
             under special conditions, should have been inclined to regard them, like inversion, as indications of degeneracy or disease. Nevertheless, it is even easier to dispose of that view in this case than in that of inversion. Everyday experience has shown that most of these extensions, or at any rate the less severe of them, are constituents which are rarely absent from the sexual life of healthy people, and are judged by them no differently from other intimate events. If circumstances favour such an occurrence, normal people too can substitute a perversion of this kind for the normal sexual aim for quite a time, or can find place for the one alongside the other. No healthy person, it appears, can fail to make some addition that might be called perverse to the normal sexual aim; and the universality of this finding is in itself enough to show how inappropriate it is to use the word perversion as a term of reproach. In the sphere of sexual life we are brought up against

of sadism and masochism, even those given by Krafft-Ebing (as indeed Colin Scott and Féré have already pointed out), constantly reveals traces of both groups of phenomena in the same individual.'

[1] [Footnote added 1915:] Cf. my discussion of 'ambivalence' below [p. 65].

[2] [The last clause did not occur in the 1905 or 1910 editions. In 1915 the following clause was added: 'a contrast whose significance is reduced in psycho-analysis to that between activity and passivity.' This was replaced in 1924 by the words now appearing in the text.]

peculiar and, indeed, insoluble difficulties as soon as we try to draw a sharp line to distinguish mere variations within the range of what is physiological from pathological symptoms.

Nevertheless, in some of these perversions the quality of the new sexual aim is of a kind to demand special examination. Certain of them are so far removed from the normal in their content that we cannot avoid pronouncing them 'pathological'. This is especially so where (as, for instance, in cases of licking excrement or of intercourse with dead bodies) the sexual instinct goes to astonishing lengths in successfully overriding the resistances of shame, disgust, horror or pain. But even in such cases we should not be too ready to assume that people who act in this way will necessarily turn out to be insane or subject to grave abnormalities of other kinds. Here again we cannot escape from the fact that people whose behaviour is in other respects normal can, under the domination of the most unruly of all the instincts, put themselves in the category of sick persons in the single sphere of sexual life. On the other hand, manifest abnormality in the other relations of life can invariably be shown to have a background of abnormal sexual conduct.

In the majority of instances the pathological character in a perversion is found to lie not in the *content* of the new sexual aim but in its relation to the normal. If a perversion, instead of appearing merely *alongside* the normal sexual aim and object, and only when circumstances are unfavourable to *them* and favourable to *it*—if, instead of this, it ousts them completely and takes their place in *all* circumstances—if, in short, a perversion has the characteristics of exclusiveness and fixation—then we shall usually be justified in regarding it as a pathological symptom.

THE MENTAL FACTOR IN THE PERVERSIONS   It is perhaps in connection precisely with the most repulsive perversions that the mental factor must be regarded as playing its largest part in the transformation of the sexual instinct. It is impossible to deny that in their case a piece of mental work has been performed which, in spite of its horrifying result, is the equivalent of an idealization of the instinct. The omnipotence of love is perhaps never more strongly proved than in such of its aberrations as these. The highest and the lowest are always closest to each other in the sphere of sexuality: 'vom Himmel durch die Welt zur Hölle.' [1]

TWO   Our study of the perversions has shown us that
CONCLUSIONS   the sexual instinct has to struggle against certain
              mental forces which act as resistances, and of
which shame and disgust are the most prominent. It is permissible to suppose that these forces play a part in restraining that instinct within the limits that are regarded as r ɔrmal; and if they develop in the individual before the sexual instinct has reached its full strength, it is no doubt they that will determine the course of its development.[2]

In the second place we have found that some of the perversions which we have examined are only made intelligible if we assume the convergence of several motive forces. If such perversions admit of analysis, that is, if they can be taken to pieces, then they must be of a composite nature. This gives us a hint that perhaps the sexual instinct itself may be no simple thing, but put together from components which have come apart again in the perversions. If this is so, the clinical observation of these abnormalities will have drawn our attention to amalgamations which have been lost to view in the uniform behaviour of normal people.[3]

    [1] ['From Heaven, across the world, to Hell.'
    Goethe, *Faust*, Prelude in the Theatre. (*Trans.* Bayard Taylor.)
In a letter to Fliess of January 3, 1897 (Freud 1950a, Letter 54), Freud suggests the use of this same quotation as the motto for a chapter on 'Sexuality' in a projected volume. This letter was written at a time when he was beginning to turn his attention to the perversions. His first reference to them in the Fliess correspondence dates from January 1, 1896 (Draft K).]
    [2] [*Footnote added* 1915:] On the other hand, these forces which act like dams upon sexual development—disgust, shame and morality—must also be regarded as historical precipitates of the external inhibitions to which the sexual instinct has been subjected during the psychogenesis of the human race. We can observe the way in which, in the development of individuals, they arise at the appropriate moment, as though spontaneously, when upbringing and external influence give the signal.
    [3] [*Footnote added* 1920:] As regards the origin of the perversions, I will add a word in anticipation of what is to come. There is reason to suppose that, just as in the case of fetishism, abortive beginnings of normal sexual development occur before the perversions become fixated. Analytic investigation has already been able to show in a few cases that perversions are a residue of development towards the Oedipus complex and that

(4) THE SEXUAL INSTINCT IN NEUROTICS

PSYCHO-ANALYSIS An important addition to our knowledge of the sexual instinct in certain people who at least approximate to the normal can be obtained from a source which can only be reached in one particular way. There is only one means of obtaining exhaustive information that will not be misleading about the sexual life of the persons known as 'psychoneurotics'—sufferers from hysteria, from obsessional neurosis, from what is wrongly described as neurasthenia, and, undoubtedly, from dementia praecox and paranoia was well.[1] They must be subjected to psycho-analytic investigation, which is employed in the therapeutic procedure introduced by Josef Breuer and myself in 1893 and known at that time as 'catharsis'.

I must first explain—as I have already done in other writings—that all my experience shows that these psychoneuroses are based on sexual instinctual forces. By this I do not merely mean that the energy of the sexual instinct makes a contribution to the forces that maintain the pathological manifestations (the symptoms). I mean expressly to assert that that contribution is the most important and only constant source of energy of the neurosis and that in consequence the sexual life of the persons in question is expressed—whether exclusively or principally or only partly—in these symptoms. As I have put it elsewhere [1905e, Postscript; S.E., 7, p. 115], the symptoms constitute the sexual activity of the patient. The evidence for this assertion is derived from the ever-increasing number of psycho-analyses of hysterical and other neurotics which I have carried out during the last 25 years [2] and of whose findings I have given (and shall continue to give) a detailed account in other publications.[3]

after the repression of that complex the components of the sexual instinct which are strongest in the disposition of the individual concerned emerge once more.

[1] [Before 1915 the words 'probably paranoia' take the place of the last eight words of this sentence.]

[2] [In 1905 '10 years', the figure being increased with each edition up to and including 1920.]

[3] [Footnote added 1920:] It implies no qualification of the above assertion, but rather an amplification of it, if I restate it as follows: neurotic symptoms are based on the one hand on the demands of the libidinal instincts and on the other hand on those made by the ego by way of reaction to them.

The removal of the symptoms of hysterical patients by psycho-analysis proceeds on the supposition that those symptoms are substitutes—transcriptions as it were—for a number of emotionally cathected mental processes, wishes and desires, which, by the operation of a special psychical procedure (repression), have been prevented from obtaining discharge in psychical activity that is admissible to consciousness. These mental processes, therefore, being held back in a state of unconsciousness, strive to obtain an expression that shall be appropriate to their emotional importance—to obtain discharge; and in the case of hysteria they find such an expression (by means of the process of 'conversion') in somatic phenomena, that is, in hysterical symptoms. By systematically turning these symptoms back (with the help of a special technique) into emotionally cathected ideas—ideas that will now have become conscious—it is possible to obtain the most accurate knowledge of the nature and origin of these formerly unconscious psychical structures.

FINDINGS OF PSYCHO-ANALYSIS   In this manner the fact has emerged that symptoms represent a substitute for impulses the source of whose strength is derived from the sexual instinct. What we know about the nature of hysterics before they fall ill—and they may be regarded as typical of all psychoneurotics—and about the occasions which precipitate their falling ill, is in complete harmony with this view. The character of hysterics shows a degree of sexual repression in excess of the normal quantity, an intensification of resistance against the sexual instinct (which we have already met with in the form of shame, disgust and morality), and what seems like an instinctive aversion on their part to any intellectual consideration of sexual problems. As a result of this, in especially marked cases, the patients remain in complete ignorance of sexual matters right into the period of sexual maturity.[1]

On a cursory view, this trait, which is so characteristic of hysteria, is not uncommonly screened by the existence of a second constitutional character present in hysteria, namely the

[1] Breuer [in the second paragraph of the first case history, Breuer and Freud, 1895] writes of the patient in connection with whom he first adopted the cathartic method: 'The factor of sexuality was astonishingly undeveloped in her.'

predominant development of the sexual instinct. Psycho-analysis, however, can invariably bring the first of these factors to light and clear up the enigmatic contradiction which hysteria presents, by revealing the pair of opposites by which it is characterized—exaggerated sexual craving and excessive aversion to sexuality.

In the case of anyone who is predisposed to hysteria, the onset of his illness is precipitated when, either as a result of his own progressive maturity or of the external circumstances of his life, he finds himself faced by the demands of a real sexual situation. Between the pressure of the instinct and his antagonism to sexuality, illness offers him a way of escape. It does not solve his conflict, but seeks to evade it by transforming his libidinal impulses into symptoms.[1] The exception is only an *apparent* one when a hysteric—a male patient it may be—falls ill as a result of some trivial emotion, some conflict which does not centre around any sexual interest. In such cases psychoanalysis is regularly able to show that the illness has been made possible by the sexual component of the conflict, which has prevented the mental processes from reaching a normal issue.

NEUROSIS AND PERVERSION   There is no doubt that a large part of the opposition to these views of mine is due to the fact that sexuality, to which I trace back psychoneurotic symptoms, is regarded as though it coincided with the normal sexual instinct. But psycho-analytic teaching goes further than this. It shows that it is by no means only at the cost of the so-called *normal* sexual instinct that these symptoms originate —at any rate such is not exclusively or mainly the case; they also give expression (by conversion) to instincts which would be described as *perverse* in the widest sense of the word if they could be expressed directly in phantasy and action without being diverted from consciousness. Thus symptoms are formed in part at the cost of *abnormal* sexuality; *neuroses are, so to say, the negative of perversions.*[2]

[1] [This theme was elaborated by Freud in his paper on the different types of onset of neurosis (1912c).]

[2] [This idea had been expressed by Freud in precisely these terms in a letter to Fliess of January 24, 1897 (Freud, 1950a, Letter 57). But it had already been implied in the letters of December 6, 1896, and January 11, 1897 (Letters 52 and 55). It will also be found in the case history of 'Dora' (1905e, S.E., 7, 50).] The contents of the clearly conscious

The sexual instinct of psychoneurotics exhibits all the aberrations which we have studied as variations of normal, and as manifestations of abnormal, sexual life.

(*a*) The unconscious mental life of all neurotics (without exception) shows inverted impulses, fixation of their libido upon persons of their own sex. It would be impossible without deep discussion to give any adequate appreciation of the importance of this factor in determining the form taken by the symptoms of the illness. I can only insist that an unconscious tendency to inversion is never absent and is of particular value in throwing light upon hysteria in men.[1]

(*b*) It is possible to trace in the unconscious of psycho-neurotics tendencies to every kind of anatomical extension of sexual activity and to show that those tendencies are factors in the formation of symptoms. Among them we find occurring with particular frequency those in which the mucous membrane of the mouth and anus are assigned the role of genitals.

(*c*) An especially prominent part is played as factors in the formation of symptoms in psychoneuroses by the component instincts,[2] which emerge for the most part as pairs of opposites and which we have met with as introducing new sexual aims—the scopophilic instinct and exhibitionism and the active and passive forms of the instinct for cruelty. The contribution made by the last of these is essential to the understanding of the fact that symptoms involve *suffering*, and it almost invariably dominates a part of the patient's social behaviour. It is also through the

phantasies of perverts (which in favourable circumstances can be transformed into manifest behaviour), of the delusional fears of paranoics (which are projected in a hostile sense on to other people) and of the unconscious phantasies of hysterics (which psycho-analysis reveals behind their symptoms)—all of these coincide with one another even down to their details. [See Addenda, p. 112.]

[1] Psychoneuroses are also very often associated with *manifest* inversion. In such cases the heterosexual current of feeling has undergone complete suppression. It is only fair to say that my attention was first drawn to the necessary universality of the tendency to inversion in psychoneurotics by Wilhelm Fliess of Berlin, after I had discussed its presence in individual cases.—[*Added* 1920:] This fact, which has not been sufficiently appreciated, cannot fail to have a decisive influence on any theory of homosexuality.

[2] [The term 'component instinct' here makes its first appearance in Freud's published works, though the *concept* has already been introduced above on p. 28.]

medium of this connection between libido and cruelty that the transformation of love into hate takes place, the transformation of affectionate into hostile impulses, which is characteristic of a great number of cases of neurosis, and indeed, it would seem, of paranoia in general.

The interest of these findings is still further increased by certain special facts.[1]

(a) Whenever we find in the unconscious an instinct of this sort which is capable of being paired off with an opposite one, this second instinct will regularly be found in operation as well. Every active perversion is thus accompanied by its passive counterpart: anyone who is an exhibitionist in his unconscious is at the same time a *voyeur*; in anyone who suffers from the consequences of repressed sadistic impulses there is sure to be another determinant of his symptoms which has its source in masochistic inclinations. The complete agreement which is here shown with what we have found to exist in the corresponding 'positive' perversions is most remarkable, though in the actual symptoms one or other of the opposing tendencies plays the predominant part.

(β) In any fairly marked case of psychoneurosis it is unusual for only a single one of these perverse instincts to be developed. We usually find a considerable number and as a rule traces of them all. The degree of development of each particular instinct is, however, independent of that of the others. Here, too, the study of the 'positive' perversions provides an exact counterpart.

(5) COMPONENT INSTINCTS AND EROTOGENIC ZONES [2]

If we put together what we have learned from our investigation of positive and negative perversions, it seems plausible to

[1] [In the editions before 1920 *three* such 'special facts' were enumerated. The first, which was subsequently omitted, ran as follows: 'Among the unconscious trains of thought found in neuroses there is nothing corresponding to a tendency to fetishism—a circumstance which throws light on the psychological peculiarity of this well-understood perversion.']

[2] [This appears to be the first published occurrence of the term 'erotogenic zone'. Freud had already used it in a letter to Fliess on December 6, 1896 (Freud, 1950a, Letter 52). It also occurs in a passage (*S.E.*, **7**, 52) in Section I of the case history of 'Dora' (1905e),

trace them back to a number of 'component instincts', which, however, are not of a primary nature, but are susceptible to further analysis.[1] By an 'instinct' is provisionally to be understood the psychical representative of an endosomatic, continuously flowing source of stimulation, as contrasted with a 'stimulus', which is set up by *single* excitations coming from *without*. The concept of instinct is thus one of those lying on the frontier between the mental and the physical. The simplest and likeliest assumption as to the nature of instincts would seem to be that in itself an instinct is without quality, and, so far as mental life is concerned, is only to be regarded as a measure of the demand made upon the mind for work. What distinguishes the instincts from one another and endows them with specific qualities is their relation to their somatic sources and to their aims. The source of an instinct is a process of excitation occurring in an organ and the immediate aim of the instinct lies in the removal of this organic stimulus.[2]

There is a further provisional assumption that we cannot escape in the theory of the instincts. It is to the effect that excitations of two kinds arise from the somatic organs, based upon differences of a chemical nature. One of these kinds of excitation we describe as being specifically sexual, and we speak of the organ concerned as the 'erotogenic zone' of the sexual component instinct arising from it.[3]

presumably written in 1901. It was evidently constructed on the analogy of the term 'hysterogenic zone' which was already in common use.]

[1] [The passage from this point till the end of the paragraph dates from 1915. In the first two editions (1905 and 1910) the following sentences appeared instead: 'We can distinguish in them [the component instincts] (in addition to an 'instinct' which is not itself sexual and which has its source in motor impulses) a contribution from an organ capable of receiving stimuli (e.g. the skin, the mucous membrane or a sense organ). An organ of this kind will be described in this connection as an "erotogenic zone"—as being the organ whose excitation lends the instinct a sexual character.'—The revised version dates from the period of Freud's paper on 'Instincts and their Vicissitudes' (1915c), where the whole topic is examined at length.]

[2] [*Footnote added* 1924:] The theory of the instincts is the most important but at the same time the least complete portion of psychoanalytic theory. I have made further contributions to it in my later works *Beyond the Pleasure Principle* (1920g) and *The Ego and the Id* (1923b).

[3] [*Footnote added* 1915:] It is not easy in the present place to justify these assumptions, derived as they are from the study of a particular

The part played by the erotogenic zones is immediately obvious in the case of those perversions which assign a sexual significance to the oral and anal orifices. These behave in every respect like a portion of the sexual apparatus. In hysteria these parts of the body and the neighbouring tracts of mucous membrane become the seat of new sensations and of changes in innervation—indeed, of processes that can be compared to erection [1]—in just the same way as do the actual genitalia under the excitations of the normal sexual processes.

The significance of the erotogenic zones as apparatuses subordinate to the genitals and as substitutes for them is, among all the psychoneuroses, most clearly to be seen in hysteria; but this does not imply that that significance is any the less in the other forms of illness. It is only that in them it is less recognizable, because in their case (obsessional neurosis and paranoia) the formation of the symptoms takes place in regions of the mental apparatus which are more remote from the particular centres concerned with somatic control. In obsessional neurosis what is more striking is the significance of those impulses which create new sexual aims and seem independent of erotogenic zones. Nevertheless, in scopophilia and exhibitionism the eye corresponds to an erotogenic zone; while in the case of those components of the sexual instinct which involve pain and cruelty the same role is assumed by the skin—the skin, which in particular parts of the body has become differentiated into sense organs or modified into mucous membrane, and is thus the erotogenic zone *par excellence*.[2]

class of neurotic illness. But on the other hand, if I omitted all mention of them, it would be impossible to say anything of substance about the instincts.

[1] [The phrase in parenthesis was added in 1920.]

[2] We are reminded at this point of Moll's analysis of the sexual instinct into an instinct of 'contrectation' and an instinct of 'detumescence'. Contrectation represents a need for contact with the skin. [The instinct of detumescence was described by Moll (1898) as an impulse for the spasmodic relief of tension of the sexual organs, and the instinct of contrectation as an impulse to come into contact with another person. He believed that the latter impulse arose later than the first in the individual's development. (See also below, p. 46, *n.* 2.)—The following additional sentence appeared at the end of this footnote in 1905 and 1910, but was afterwards omitted: 'Strohmayer has very rightly inferred from a case under his observation that obsessive self-reproaches originate from suppressed sadistic impulses.']

(6) REASONS FOR THE APPARENT PREPONDERANCE OF PERVERSE SEXUALITY IN THE PSYCHONEUROSES

The preceding discussion may perhaps have placed the sexuality of psychoneurotics in a false light. It may have given the impression that, owing to their disposition, psychoneurotics approximate closely to perverts in their sexual behaviour and are proportionately remote from normal people. It may indeed very well be that the constitutional disposition of these patients (apart from their exaggerated degree of sexual repression and the excessive intensity of their sexual instinct) includes an unusual tendency to perversion, using that word in its widest sense. Nevertheless, investigation of comparatively slight cases shows that this last assumption is not absolutely necessary, or at least that in forming a judgement on these pathological developments there is a factor to be considered which weighs in the other direction. Most psychoneurotics only fall ill after the age of puberty as a result of the demands made upon them by normal sexual life. (It is most particularly against the latter that repression is directed.) Or else illnesses of this kind set in later, when the libido fails to obtain satisfaction along normal lines. In both these cases the libido behaves like a stream whose main bed has become blocked. It proceeds to fill up collateral channels which may hitherto have been empty. Thus, in the same way, what appears to be the strong tendency (though, it is true, a negative one) of psychoneurotics to perversion may be collaterally determined, and must, in any case, be collaterally intensified. The fact is that we must put sexual repression as an internal factor alongside such external factors as limitation of freedom, inaccessibility of a normal sexual object, the dangers of the normal sexual act, etc., which bring about perversions in persons who might perhaps otherwise have remained normal.

In this respect different cases of neurosis may behave differently: in one case the preponderating factor may be the innate strength of the tendency to perversion, in another it may be the collateral increase of that tendency owing to the libido being forced away from a normal sexual aim and sexual object. It would be wrong to represent as opposition what is in fact a co-operative relation. Neurosis will always produce its greatest effects when constitution and experience work together in the same direction. Where the constitution is a marked one it will perhaps not require the support of actual experiences; while a great shock in real life will perhaps bring about a neurosis even in an average constitution. (Incidentally, this view of the relative aetiological importance of what is innate and what is accidentally experienced applies equally in other fields.)

If we prefer to suppose, nevertheless, that a particularly strongly developed tendency to perversion is among the characteristics of psychoneurotic constitutions, we have before us the prospect of being able to distinguish a number of such constitutions according to the innate preponderance of one or the other of the erotogenic zones or of one or the other of the component instincts. The question whether a special relation holds between the perverse disposition and the particular form of illness adopted, has, like so much else in this field, not yet been investigated.

(7) INTIMATION OF THE INFANTILE CHARACTER OF SEXUALITY

By demonstrating the part played by perverse impulses in the formation of symptoms in the psychoneuroses, we have quite remarkably increased the number of people who might be regarded as perverts. It is not only that neurotics in themselves constitute a very numerous class, but it must also be considered that an unbroken chain bridges the gap between the neuroses in all their manifestations and normality. After all, Moebius could say with justice that we are all to some extent hysterics. Thus the extraordinarily wide dissemination of the perversions forces us to suppose that the disposition to perversions is itself of no great rarity but must form a part of what passes as the normal constitution.

It is, as we have seen, debatable whether the perversions go back to innate determinants or arise, as Binet assumed was the case with fetishism [p. 20], owing to chance experiences. The conclusion now presents itself to us that there is indeed something innate lying behind the perversions but that it is something innate in *everyone*, though as a disposition it may vary in its intensity and may be increased by the influences of actual life. What is in question are the innate constitutional roots of the sexual instinct. In one class of cases (the perversions) these roots may grow into the actual vehicles of sexual activity; in others they may be submitted to an insufficient suppression (repression) and thus be able in a roundabout way to attract a considerable proportion of sexual energy to themselves as symptoms; while in the most favourable cases, which lie between these two extremes, they may by means of effective restriction and other kinds of modification bring about what is known as normal sexual life.

We have, however, a further reflection to make. This postulated constitution, containing the germs of all the perversions, will only be demonstrable in *children*, even though in them it is only with modest degrees of intensity that any of the instincts can emerge. A formula begins to take shape which lays it down that the sexuality of neurotics has remained in, or been brought back to, an infantile state. Thus our interest turns to the sexual life of children, and we will now proceed to trace the play of influences which govern the evolution of infantile sexuality till its outcome in perversion, neurosis or normal sexual life.

II

INFANTILE SEXUALITY

NEGLECT OF
THE INFANTILE
FACTOR

One feature of the popular view of the sexual instinct is that it is absent in childhood and only awakens in the period of life described as puberty. This, however, is not merely a simple error but one that has had grave consequences, for it is mainly to this idea that we owe our present ignorance of the fundamental conditions of sexual life. A thorough study of the sexual manifestations of childhood would probably reveal the essential characters of the sexual instinct and would show us the course of its development and the way in which it is put together from various sources.

It is noticeable that writers who concern themselves with explaining the characteristics and reactions of the adult have devoted much more attention to the primaeval period which is comprised in the life of the individual's ancestors—have, that is, ascribed much more influence to heredity—than to the other primaeval period, which falls within the lifetime of the individual himself—that is, to childhood. One would surely have supposed that the influence of this latter period would be easier to understand and could claim to be considered before that of heredity.[1] It is true that in the literature of the subject one occasionally comes across remarks upon precocious sexual activity in small children—upon erections, masturbation and even activities resembling coitus. But these are always quoted only as exceptional events, as oddities or as horrifying instances of precocious depravity. So far as I know, not a single author has clearly recognized the regular existence of a sexual instinct in childhood; and in the writings that have become so numerous on the development of children, the chapter on 'Sexual Development' is as a rule omitted.[2]

[1] [*Footnote added* 1915:] Nor is it possible to estimate correctly the part played by heredity until the part played by childhood has been assessed.

[2] The assertion made in the text has since struck me myself as being so bold that I have undertaken the task of testing its validity by looking through the literature once more. The outcome of this is that I have

INFANTILE   The reason for this strange neglect is to be sought,
AMNESIA   I think, partly in considerations of propriety, which
the authors obey as a result of their own upbring-
ing, and partly in a psychological phenomenon which has itself
hitherto eluded explanation. What I have in mind is the peculiar
amnesia which, in the case of most people, though by no means
all, hides the earliest beginnings of their childhood up to their
sixth or eighth year. Hitherto it has not occurred to us to feel
any astonishment at the fact of this amnesia, though we might
have had good grounds for doing so. For we learn from other
people that during these years, of which at a later date we retain
nothing in our memory but a few unintelligible and fragmentary
recollections, we reacted in a lively manner to impressions, that
we were capable of expressing pain and joy in a human fashion,
that we gave evidence of love, jealousy and other passionate
feelings by which we were strongly moved at the time, and even
that we gave utterance to remarks which were regarded by
adults as good evidence of our possessing insight and the be-

allowed my statement to stand unaltered. The scientific examination of
both the physical and mental phenomena of sexuality in childhood is
still in its earliest beginnings. One writer, Bell (1902, 327), remarks:
'I know of no scientist who has given a careful analysis of the emotion
as it is seen in the adolescent.' Somatic sexual manifestations from the
period before puberty have only attracted attention in connection with
phenomena of degeneracy and as indications of degeneracy. In none of
the accounts which I have read of the psychology of this period of life
is a chapter to be found on the erotic life of children; and this applies
to the well-known works of Preyer [1882], Baldwin (1898), Pérez (1886),
Strümpell (1899), Groos (1904), Heller (1904), Sully (1895) and others.
We can obtain the clearest impression of the state of things in this field
to-day from the periodical *Die Kinderfehler* from 1896 onwards. Nevertheless the conviction is borne in upon us that the existence of love in
childhood stands in no need of discovery. Pérez (1886, 272 ff.) argues
in favour of its existence. Groos (1899, 326) mentions as a generally
recognized fact that 'some children are already accessible to sexual
impulses at a very early age and feel an urge to have contact with the
opposite sex'. The earliest instance of the appearance of 'sex-love'
recorded by Bell (1902, 330) concerns a child in the middle of his third
year. On this point compare further Havelock Ellis (1913, Appendix B).
   [*Added* 1910:] This judgement upon the literature of infantile sexuality
need no longer be maintained since the appearance of Stanley Hall's
exhaustive work (1904). No such modification is necessitated by Moll's
recent book (1909). See, on the other hand, Bleuler (1908). [*Added* 1915:]
Since this was written, a book by Hug-Hellmuth (1913) has taken the
neglected sexual factor fully into account.

ginnings of a capacity for judgement. And of all this we, when we are grown up, have no knowledge of our own! Why should our memory lag so far behind the other activities of our minds? We have, on the contrary, good reason to believe that there is no period at which the capacity for receiving and reproducing impressions is greater than precisely during the years of childhood.[1]

On the other hand we must assume, or we can convince ourselves by a psychological examination of other people, that the very same impressions that we have forgotten have none the less left the deepest traces on our minds and have had a determining effect upon the whole of our later development. There can, therefore, be no question of any real abolition of the impressions of childhood, but rather of an amnesia similar to that which neurotics exhibit for later events, and of which the essence consists in a simple witholding of these impressions from consciousness, viz., in their repression. But what are the forces which bring about this repression of the impressions of childhood? Whoever could solve this riddle would, I think, have explained *hysterical* amnesia as well.

Meanwhile we must not fail to observe that the existence of infantile amnesia provides a new point of comparison between the mental states of children and psychoneurotics. We have already [p. 38] come across another such point in the formula to which we were led, to the effect that the sexuality of psychoneurotics has remained at, or been carried back to, an infantile stage. Can it be, after all, that infantile amnesia, too, is to be brought into relation with the sexual impulses of childhood?

Moreover, the connection between infantile and hysterical amnesia is more than a mere play upon words. Hysterical amnesia, which occurs at the bidding of repression, is only explicable by the fact that the subject is already in possession of a store of memory-traces which have been withdrawn from conscious disposal, and which are now, by an associative link, attracting to themselves the material which the forces of repression are engaged in repelling from consciousness.[2] It may be

[1] I have attempted to solve one of the problems connected with the earliest memories of childhood in a paper on 'Screen Memories' (1899a). [*Added* 1924:] See also Chapter IV of my *Psychopathology of Everyday Life* (1901b).

[2] [*Footnote added* 1915:] The mechanism of repression cannot be understood unless account is taken of *both* of these two concurrent

said that without infantile amnesia there would be no hysterical amnesia. [See Addenda, p. 112.]

I believe, then, that infantile amnesia, which turns everyone's childhood into something like a prehistoric epoch and conceals from him the beginnings of his own sexual life, is responsible for the fact that in general no importance is attached to childhood in the development of sexual life. The gaps in our knowledge which have arisen in this way cannot be bridged by a single observer. As long ago as in the year 1896[1] I insisted on the significance of the years of childhood in the origin of certain important phenomena connected with sexual life, and since then I have never ceased to emphasize the part played in sexuality by the infantile factor.

[1] THE PERIOD OF SEXUAL LATENCY IN CHILDHOOD AND ITS INTERRUPTIONS

The remarkably frequent reports of what are described as irregular and exceptional sexual impulses in childhood, as well as the uncovering in neurotics of what have hitherto been unconscious memories of childhood, allow us to sketch out the sexual occurrences of that period in some such way as this.[2]

There seems no doubt that germs of sexual impulses are already present in the new-born child and that these continue to develop for a time, but are then overtaken by a progressive process of suppression; this in turn is itself interrupted by periodical advances in sexual development or may be held up by individual peculiarities. Nothing is known for certain concerning the regularity and periodicity of this oscillating course of development. It seems, however, that the sexual life of

processes. They may be compared with the manner in which tourists are conducted to the top of the Great Pyramid of Giza by being pushed from one direction and pulled from the other. [Cf. Freud's paper on 'Repression' (1915d).]

[1] [E.g. in the last paragraph of Section I of his paper on the aetiology of hysteria (1896c).]

[2] We are able to make use of the second of these two sources of material since we are justified in expecting that the early years of children who are later to become neurotic are not likely in this respect to differ *essentially* from those of children who are to grow up into normal adults, [*added* 1915:] but only in the intensity and clarity of the phenomena involved.

children usually emerges in a form accessible to observation round about the third or fourth year of life.[1]

SEXUAL   It is during this period of total or only partial
INHIBITIONS   latency that are built up the mental forces which
              are later to impede the course of the sexual instinct
and, like dams, restrict its flow—disgust, feelings of shame and the claims of aesthetic and moral ideals. One gets an impression from civilized children that the construction of these dams is a product of education, and no doubt education has much to do with it. But in reality this development is organically determined and fixed by heredity, and it can occasionally occur without any

---

[1] There is a possible anatomical analogy to what I believe to be the course of development of the infantile sexual function in Bayer's discovery (1902) that the internal sexual organs (i.e. the uterus) are as a rule larger in new-born children than in older ones. It is not certain, however, what view we should take of this involution that occurs after birth (which has been shown by Halban to apply also to other portions of the genital apparatus). According to Halban (1904) the process of involution comes to an end after a few weeks of extra-uterine life. [*Added* 1920:] Those authorities who regard the interstitial portion of the sex-gland as the organ that determines sex have on their side been led by anatomical researches to speak of infantile sexuality and a period of sexual latency. I quote a passage from Lipschütz's book (1919, 168), which I mentioned on p. 13 *n.*: 'We shall be doing more justice to the facts if we say that the maturation of the sexual characters which is accomplished at puberty is only due to a great acceleration which occurs at that time of processes which began much earlier—in my view as early as during intra-uterine life.' 'What has hitherto been described in a summary way as puberty is probably only a second major phase of puberty which sets in about the middle of the second decade of life . . . Childhood, from birth until the beginning of this second major phase, might be described as "the intermediate phase of puberty" ' (ibid., 170). Attention was drawn to this coincidence between anatomical findings and psychological observation in a review [of Lipschütz's book] by Ferenczi (1920). The agreement is marred only by the fact that the 'first peak' in the development of the sexual organ occurs during the early intra-uterine period, whereas the early efflorescence of infantile sexual life must be ascribed to the third and fourth years of life. There is, of course, no need to expect that anatomical growth and psychical development must be exactly simultaneous. The researches in question were made on the sex-glands of human beings. Since a period of latency in the psychological sense does not occur in animals, it would be very interesting to know whether the anatomical findings which have led these writers to assume the occurrence of two peaks in sexual development are also demonstrable in the higher animals.

help at all from education. Education will not be trespassing beyond its appropriate domain if it limits itself to following the lines which have already been laid down organically and to impressing them somewhat more clearly and deeply.

REACTION-   What is it that goes to the making of these
FORMATION   constructions which are so important for the
AND   growth of a civilized and normal individual?
SUBLIMATION   They probably emerge at the cost of the infantile
                 sexual impulses themselves. Thus the activity of
those impulses does not cease even during this period of latency, though their energy is diverted, wholly or in great part, from their sexual use and directed to other ends. Historians of civilization appear to be at one in assuming that powerful components are acquired for every kind of cultural achievement by this diversion of sexual instinctual forces from sexual aims and their direction to new ones—a process which deserves the name of 'sublimation'. To this we would add, accordingly, that the same process plays a part in the development of the individual and we would place its beginning in the period of sexual latency of childhood.[1]

It is possible further to form some idea of the mechanism of this process of sublimation. On the one hand, it would seem, the sexual impulses cannot be utilized during these years of childhood, since the reproductive functions have been deferred —a fact which constitutes the main feature of the period of latency. On the other hand, these impulses would seem in themselves to be perverse—that is, to arise from erotogenic zones and to derive their activity from instincts which, in view of the direction of the subject's development, can only arouse unpleasurable feelings. They consequently evoke opposing mental forces (reacting impulses) which, in order to suppress this unpleasure effectively, build up the mental dams that I have already mentioned—disgust, shame and morality.[2]

[1] Once again, it is from Fliess that I have borrowed the term 'period of sexual latency'.

[2] [*Footnote added* 1915:] In the case which I am here discussing, the sublimation of sexual instinctual forces takes place along the path of reaction-formation. But in general it is possible to distinguish the concepts of sublimation and reaction-formation from each other as two different processes. Sublimation can also take place by other and simpler

INTERRUPTIONS OF   We must not deceive ourselves as to the
THE LATENCY   hypothetical nature and insufficient clarity
PERIOD   of our knowledge concerning the processes
of the infantile period of latency or defer-
ment; but we shall be on firmer ground in pointing out that
such an application of infantile sexuality represents an educa-
tional ideal from which individual development usually diverges
at some point and often to a considerable degree. From time to
time a fragmentary manifestation of sexuality which has evaded
sublimation may break through; or some sexual activity may
persist through the whole duration of the latency period until
the sexual instinct emerges with greater intensity at puberty. In
so far as educators pay any attention at all to infantile sexuality,
they behave exactly as though they shared our views as to the
construction of the moral defensive forces at the cost of sexuality,
and as though they knew that sexual activity makes a child
ineducable: for they stigmatize every sexual manifestation by
children as a 'vice', without being able to do much against it.
We, on the other hand, have every reason for turning our
attention to these phenomena which are so much dreaded by
education, for we may expect them to help us to discover the
original configuration of the sexual instincts.

[2] THE MANIFESTATIONS OF INFANTILE
SEXUALITY

THUMB-SUCKING   For reasons which will appear later, I shall
take thumb-sucking (or sensual sucking) as a
sample of the sexual manifestations of childhood. (An excellent study of this subject has been made by the Hungarian
paediatrician, Lindner, 1879.)[1]

Thumb-sucking appears already in early infancy and may
continue into maturity, or even persist all through life. It consists in the rhythmic repetition of a sucking contact by the

mechanisms. [Further theoretical discussions of sublimation will be
found in Section III of Freud's paper on narcissism (1914c) and at
several points in *The Ego and the Id* (1923b, Chapters III, IV and V).]

[1] [There seems to be no nursery word in English equivalent to the
German '*lutschen*' and '*ludeln*', used by Freud alongside '*wonnesaugen*'
('sensual sucking'). Conrad in *Struwwelpeter* was a '*Lutscher*'; but, as will
be seen from the context, 'suck-a-thumbs' and 'thumb-sucking' have in
fact too narrow a connotation for the present purpose.]

mouth (or lips). There is no question of the purpose of this procedure being the taking of nourishment. A portion of the lip itself, the tongue, or any other part of the skin within reach—even the big toe—may be taken as the object upon which this sucking is carried out. In this connection a grasping-instinct may appear and may manifest itself as a simultaneous rhythmic tugging at the lobes of the ears or a catching hold of some part of another person (as a rule the ear) for the same purpose. Sensual sucking involves a complete absorption of the attention and leads either to sleep or even to a motor reaction in the nature of an orgasm.[1] It is not infrequently combined with rubbing some sensitive part of the body such as the breast or the external genitalia. Many children proceed by this path from sucking to masturbation.

Lindner himself [2] clearly recognized the sexual nature of this activity and emphasized it without qualification. In the nursery, sucking is often classed along with the other kinds of sexual 'naughtiness' of children. This view has been most energetically repudiated by numbers of paediatricians and nerve-specialists, though this is no doubt partly due to a confusion between 'sexual' and 'genital'. Their objection raises a difficult question and one which cannot be evaded: what is the general characteristic which enables us to recognize the sexual manifestations of children? The concatenation of phenomena into which we have been given an insight by psycho-analytic investigation justifies us, in my opinion, in regarding thumb-sucking as a sexual mani-

---

[1] Thus we find at this early stage, what holds good all through life, that sexual satisfaction is the best soporific. Most cases of nervous insomnia can be traced back to lack of sexual satisfaction. It is well known that unscrupulous nurses put crying children to sleep by stroking their genitals. [Cf. Freud, 1905e, Section III, S.E., 7, 98, n. 1.]

[2] [This paragraph was added in 1915. In its place the following paragraph appears in the editions of 1905 and 1910 only: 'No observer has felt any doubt as to the sexual nature of this activity. Nevertheless, the best theories formed by adults in regard to this example of the sexual behaviour of children leave us in the lurch. Consider Moll's [1898] analysis of the sexual instinct into an instinct of detumescence and an instinct of contrectation. [See above p. 35, n. 2.] The first of these factors cannot be concerned in our present instance, and the second one can only be recognized with difficulty, since, according to Moll, it emerges later than the instinct of detumescence and is directed towards other people.'—In 1910 the following footnote was attached to the first sentence of this cancelled paragraph: 'With the exception of Moll (1909).']

festation and in choosing it for our study of the essential features of infantile sexual activity.[1]

AUTO-EROTISM   We are in duty bound to make a thorough examination of this example. It must be insisted that the most striking feature of this sexual activity is that the instinct is not directed towards other people, but obtains satisfaction from the subject's own body. It is 'auto-erotic', to call it by a happily chosen term introduced by Havelock Ellis (1910).[2]

Furthermore, it is clear that the behaviour of a child who indulges in thumb-sucking is determined by a search for some pleasure which has already been experienced and is now remembered. In the simplest case he proceeds to find this satisfaction by sucking rhythmically at some part of the skin or mucous membrane. It is also easy to guess the occasions on which the child had his first experiences of the pleasure which he is now striving to renew. It was the child's first and most vital activity, his sucking at his mother's breast, or at substitutes for it, that must have familiarized him with this pleasure. The child's lips, in our view, behave like an erotogenic zone, and no doubt stimulation by the warm flow of milk is the cause of the pleasurable sensation. The satisfaction of the erotogenic zone is associated, in the first instance, with the satisfaction of the need for

[1] [Footnote added 1920:] In 1919, a Dr. Galant published, under the title of 'Das Lutscherli', the confession of a grown-up girl who had never given up this infantile sexual activity and who represents the satisfaction to be gained from sucking as something completely analogous to sexual satisfaction, particularly when this is obtained from a lover's kiss: 'Not every kiss is equal to a "Lutscherli"—no, no, not by any means! It is impossible to describe what a lovely feeling goes through your whole body when you suck; you are right away from this world. You are absolutely satisfied, and happy beyond desire. It is a wonderful feeling; you long for nothing but peace—uninterrupted peace. It is just unspeakably lovely: you feel no pain and no sorrow, and ah! you are carried into another world.'

[2] [Footnote added 1920:] Havelock Ellis, it is true, uses the word 'auto-erotic' in a somewhat different sense, to describe an excitation which is not provoked from outside but arises internally. What psychoanalysis regards as the essential point is not the genesis of the excitation, but the question of its relation to an object.—[In all editions before 1920 this footnote read as follows: 'Havelock Ellis, however, has spoilt the meaning of the term he invented by including the whole of hysteria and all the manifestations of masturbation among the phenomena of autoerotism.']

nourishment. To begin with, sexual activity attaches itself to functions serving the purpose of self-preservation and does not become independent of them until later.[1] No one who has seen a baby sinking back satiated from the breast and falling asleep with flushed cheeks and a blissful smile can escape the reflection that this picture persists as a prototype of the expression of sexual satisfaction in later life. The need for repeating the sexual satisfaction now becomes detached from the need for taking nourishment—a separation which becomes inevitable when the teeth appear and food is no longer taken in only by sucking, but is also chewed up. The child does not make use of an extraneous body for his sucking, but prefers a part of his own skin because it is more convenient, because it makes him independent of the external world, which he is not yet able to control, and because in that way he provides himself, as it were, with a second erotogenic zone, though one of an inferior kind. The inferiority of this second region is among the reasons why at a later date he seeks the corresponding part—the lips—of another person. ('It's a pity I can't kiss myself', he seems to be saying.)

It is not every child who sucks in this way. It may be assumed that those children do so in whom there is a constitutional intensification of the erotogenic significance of the labial region. If that significance persists, these same children when they are grown up will become epicures in kissing, will be inclined to perverse kissing, or, if males, will have a powerful motive for drinking and smoking. If, however, repression ensues, they will feel disgust at food and will produce hysterical vomiting. The repression extends to the nutritional instinct owing to the dual purpose served by the labial zone. Many[2] of my women patients who suffer from disturbances of eating, *globus hystericus*, constriction of the throat and vomiting, have indulged energetically in sucking during their childhood.

Our study of thumb-sucking or sensual sucking has already given us the three essential characterisitics of an infantile sexual manifestation. At its origin it attaches itself to one of the vital somatic functions;[3] it has as yet no sexual object, and is thus auto-erotic; and its sexual aim is dominated by an erotogenic

---

[1] [This sentence was added in 1915. Cf. Section II of Freud's paper on narcissism (1914c).]   [2] [In the first edition only this reads 'all'.]

[3] [This clause was added in 1915; and in the earlier editions the word 'three' in the last sentence is replaced by 'two'.]

zonc. It is to be anticipated that these characteristics will be found to apply equally to most of the other activities of the infantile sexual instincts.

[3] THE SEXUAL AIM OF INFANTILE SEXUALITY

CHARACTERISTICS
OF EROTOGENIC
ZONES

The example of thumb-sucking shows us still more about what constitutes an erotogenic zone. It is a part of the skin or mucous membrane in which stimuli of a certain sort evoke a feeling of pleasure possessing a particular quality. There can be no doubt that the stimuli which produce the pleasure are governed by special conditions, though we do not know what those are. A rhythmic character must play a part among them and the analogy of tickling is forced upon our notice. It seems less certain whether the character of the pleasurable feeling evoked by the stimulus should be described as a 'specific' one—a 'specific' quality in which the sexual factor would precisely lie. Psychology is still so much in the dark in questions of pleasure and unpleasure that the most cautious assumption is the one most to be recommended. We may later come upon reasons which seem to support the idea that the pleasurable feeling does in fact possess a specific quality.

The character of erotogenicity can be attached to some parts of the body in a particularly marked way. There are predestined erotogenic zones, as is shown by the example of sucking. The same example, however, also shows us that any other part of the skin or mucous membrane can take over the functions of an erotogenic zone, and must therefore have some aptitude in that direction. Thus the quality of the stimulus has more to do with producing the pleasurable feeling than has the nature of the part of the body concerned. A child who is indulging in sensual sucking searches about his body and chooses some part of it to suck—a part which is afterwards preferred by him from force of habit; if he happens to hit upon one of the predestined regions (such as the nipples or genitals) no doubt it retains the preference. A precisely analogous tendency to displacement is also found in the symptomatology of hysteria. In that neurosis repression affects most of all the actual genital zones and these transmit their susceptibility to stimulation to other erotogenic zones (normally neglected in adult life), which then behave exactly like genitals. But besides this, precisely as in the case of sucking, any other part of the body can acquire the same susceptibility to stimulation as is possessed by the genitals and can become an erotogenic zone. Erotogenic and hysterogenic zones show the same characteristics.[1]

THE INFANTILE SEXUAL AIM   The sexual aim of the infantile instinct consists in obtaining satisfaction by means of an appropriate stimulation of the erotogenic zone which has been selected in one way or another. This satisfaction must have been previously experienced in order to have left behind a need for its repetition; and we may expect that Nature will have made safe provisions so that this experience of satisfaction shall not be left to chance.[2] We have already learnt what the contrivance is that fulfils this purpose in the case of the labial zone: it is the simultaneous connection which links this part of the body with the taking in of food. We shall come across other, similar contrivances as sources of sexuality. The state of being in need of a repetition of the satisfaction reveals itself in two ways: by a peculiar feeling of tension, possessing, rather, the character of unpleasure, and by a sensation of itching or stimulation which is centrally conditioned and projected on to the peripheral erotogenic zone. We can therefore formulate a sexual aim in another way: it consists in replacing the projected sensation of stimulation in the erotogenic zone by an external stimulus which removes that sensation by producing a feeling of satisfaction. This external stimulus will usually consist in some kind of manipulation that is analogous to the sucking.[3]

---

[1] [*Footnote added* 1915:] After further reflection and after taking other observations into account, I have been led to ascribe the quality of erotogenicity to all parts of the body and to all the internal organs. Cf. also in this connection what is said below on narcissism [p. 83 f.]. [In the 1910 edition only, the following footnote appeared at this point: 'The biological problems relating to the hypothesis of erotogenic zones have been discussed by Alfred Adler (1907).']

[2] [*Footnote added* 1920:] In biological discussions it is scarcely possible to avoid a teleological way of thinking, even though one is aware that in any particular instance one is not secure against error. [Cf. footnote 1, p. 54.]

[3] [This account of the way in which a particular sexual desire becomes established on the basis of an 'experience of satisfaction' is only a special application of Freud's general theory of the mechanism of wishes, as explained in Section C of Chapter VII of *The Interpretation of Dreams*

The fact that the need can also be evoked peripherally, by a real modification of the erotogenic zone, is in complete harmony with our physiological knowledge. This strikes us as somewhat strange only because, in order to remove one stimulus, it seems necessary to adduce a second one at the same spot.

[4] MASTURBATORY SEXUAL MANIFESTATIONS [1]

It must come as a great relief to find that, when once we have understood the nature of the instinct arising from a single one of the erotogenic zones, we shall have very little more to learn of the sexual activity of children. The clearest distinctions as between one zone and another concern the nature of the contrivance necessary for satisfying the instinct; in the case of the labial zone it consisted of sucking, and this has to be replaced by other muscular actions according to the position and nature of the other zones.

ACTIVITY OF THE ANAL ZONE   Like the labial zone, the anal zone is well suited by its position to act as a medium through which sexuality may attach itself to other somatic functions. It is to be presumed that the erotogenic significance of this part of the body is very great from the first. We learn with some astonishment from psycho-analysis of the transmutations normally undergone by the sexual excitations arising from this zone and of the frequency with which it retains a considerable amount of susceptibility to genital stimulation throughout life.[2] The intestinal disturbances which are so common in childhood see to it that the zone shall not

(1900a, Standard Ed., 5, 565 f.). This theory had already been sketched out by him in his posthumously published 'Project for a Scientific Psychology' (Freud, 1950a, Appendix, Part I, Section 16). In both these passages the example chosen as an illustration is in fact that of an infant at the breast. The whole topic links up with Freud's views on 'reality-testing', as discussed, for instance, in his paper on 'Negation' (1925h).]

[1] Cf. the very copious literature on the subject of masturbation, which for the most part, however, is at sea upon the main issues, e.g. Rohleder (1899). [Added 1915:] See also the report of the discussion on the subject in the Vienna Psycho-Analytical Society (Diskussionen, 1912)—[and especially Freud's own contributions to it (1912f)].

[2] [Footnote added 1910:] Cf. my papers on 'Character and Anal Erotism' (1908b) [added 1920:] and 'On Transformations of Instinct as Exemplified in Anal Erotism' (1917c).

lack intense excitations. Intestinal catarrhs at the tenderest age make children 'nervy', as people say, and in cases of later neurotic illness they have a determining influence on the symptoms in which the neurosis is expressed, and they put at its disposal the whole range of intestinal disturbances. If we bear in mind the erotogenic significance of the outlet of the intestinal canal, which persists, at all events in a modified form, we shall not be inclined to scoff at the influence of haemorrhoids, to which old-fashioned medicine used to attach so much importance in explaining neurotic conditions.

Children who are making use of the susceptibility to erotogenic stimulation of the anal zone betray themselves by holding back their stool till its accumulation brings about violent muscular contractions and, as it passes through the anus, is able to produce powerful stimulation of the mucous membrane. In so doing it must no doubt cause not only painful but also highly pleasurable sensations. One of the clearest signs of subsequent eccentricity or nervousness is to be seen when a baby obstinately refuses to empty his bowels when he is put on the pot—that is, when his nurse wants him to—and holds back that function till he himself chooses to exercise it. He is naturally not concerned with dirtying the bed, he is only anxious not to miss the subsidiary pleasure attached to defaecating. Educators are once more right when they describe children who keep the process back as 'naughty'.

The contents of the bowels,[1] which act as a stimulating mass upon a sexually sensitive portion of mucous membrane, behave like forerunners of another organ, which is destined to come into action after the phase of childhood. But they have other important meanings for the infant. They are clearly treated as a part of the infant's own body and represent his first 'gift': by producing them he can express his active compliance with his environment and, by witholding them, his disobedience. From being a 'gift' they later come to acquire the meaning of 'baby'—for babies, according to one of the sexual theories of children [see below, p. 62], are acquired by eating and are born through the bowels.

The retention of the faecal mass, which is thus carried out intentionally by the child to begin with, in order to serve, as it

[1] [This paragraph was added in 1915. Its contents were expanded in one of the papers (1917c) mentioned in the last footnote.]

were, as a masturbatory stimulus upon the anal zone or to be employed in his relation to the people looking after him, is also one of the roots of the constipation which is so common among neuropaths. Further, the whole significance of the anal zone is reflected in the fact that few neurotics are to be found without their special scatological practices, ceremonies, and so on, which they carefully keep secret.[1]

Actual masturbatory stimulation of the anal zone by means of the finger, provoked by a centrally determined or peripherally maintained sensation of itching, is by no means rare among older children.

ACTIVITY OF THE
GENITAL ZONES

Among the erotogenic zones that form part of the child's body there is one which certainly does not play the opening part, and which cannot be the vehicle of the oldest sexual impulses, but which is destined to great things in the future. In both male and female children it is brought into connection with micturition (in the glans and clitoris) and in the former is enclosed in a pouch of mucous membrane, so that there can be no lack of stimulation of it by secretions which may give an early start to sexual excitation. The sexual activities of this erotogenic zone, which forms part of the sexual organs proper, are the beginning of what is later to become 'normal' sexual life. The anatomical situation of this region, the secretions in which it is bathed, the washing and rubbing to which it is subjected in the course of a child's toilet, as well as accidental stimulation (such as the

---

[1] [*Footnote added* 1920:] Lou Andreas-Salomé (1916), in a paper which has given us a very much deeper understanding of the significance of anal erotism, has shown how the history of the first prohibition which a child comes across—the prohibition against getting pleasure from anal activity and its products—has a decisive effect on his whole development. This must be the first occasion on which the infant has a glimpse of an environment hostile to his instinctual impulses, on which he learns to separate his own entity from this alien one and on which he carries out the first 'repression' of his possibilities for pleasure. From that time on, what is 'anal' remains the symbol of everything that is to be repudiated and excluded from life. The clear-cut distinction between anal and genital processes which is later insisted upon is contradicted by the close anatomical and functional analogies and relations which hold between them. The genital apparatus remains the neighbour of the cloaca, and actually [to quote Lou Andreas-Salomé] 'in the case of women is only taken from it on lease'.

movement of intestinal worms in the case of girls), make it inevitable that the pleasurable feeling which this part of the body is capable of producing should be noticed by children even during their earliest infancy, and should give rise to a need for its repetition. If we consider this whole range of contrivances and bear in mind that both making a mess and measures for keeping clean are bound to operate in much the same way, it is scarcely possible to avoid the conclusion that the foundations for the future primacy over sexual activity exercised by this erotogenic zone are established by early infantile masturbation, which scarcely a single individual escapes.[1] The action which disposes of the stimulus and brings about satisfaction consists in a rubbing movement with the hand or in the application of pressure (no doubt on the lines of a pre-existing reflex) either from the hand or by bringing the thighs together. This last method is by far the more common in the case of girls. The preference for the hand which is shown by boys is already evidence of the important contribution which the instinct for mastery is destined to make to masculine sexual activity.[2]

It will be in the interests of clarity[3] if I say at once that three

[1] [In the editions of 1905 and 1910 the last part of this sentence read: 'it is difficult to overlook Nature's purpose of establishing the future primacy over sexual activity exercised by this erotogenic zone by means of early infantile masturbation, which scarcely a single individual escapes.' The teleological nature of this argument in favour of the universality of infantile masturbation was sharply criticized by Rudolf Reitler in the course of the discussions on that topic in the Vienna Psycho-Analytical Society in 1912 (*Diskussionen*, 1912, 92 f.). In his own contribution to the discussion (ibid., 134; = Freud, 1912*f*), Freud agreed that the phrasing he had used was unfortunate, and undertook to alter it in later reprints. The present version of the sentence was accordingly substituted in 1915. Cf. pp. 22 and 50.]

[2] [*Footnote added* 1915:] Unusual techniques in carrying out masturbation in later years seem to point to the influence of a prohibition against masturbation which has been overcome.

[3] [This paragraph was added in 1915. In the edition of that year there were also added the title of the next paragraph and the parenthesis 'as a rule before the fourth year' in its second sentence. Moreover, in the first sentence of the same paragraph the words 'after a short time' were substituted for the words 'at the onset of the latency period' which had appeared in 1905 and 1910. Finally, in those first two editions, the *following* paragraph began with the words 'During the years of childhood (it has not yet been possible to generalize as to the chronology)

phases of infantile masturbation are to be distinguished. The first of these belongs to early infancy, and the second to the brief efflorescence of sexual activity about the fourth year of life; only the third phase corresponds to pubertal masturbation, which is often the only kind taken into account.

SECOND PHASE OF INFANTILE MASTURBATION The masturbation of early infancy seems to disappear after a short time; but it may persist uninterruptedly until puberty, and this would constitute the first great deviation from the course of development laid down for civilized men. At some point of childhood after early infancy, as a rule before the fourth year, the sexual instinct belonging to the genital zone usually revives and persists again for a time until it is once more suppressed, or it may continue without interruption. This second phase of infantile sexual activity may assume a variety of different forms which can only be determined by a precise analysis of individual cases. But all its details leave behind the deepest (unconscious) impressions in the subject's memory, determine the development of his character, if he is to remain healthy, and the symptomatology of his neurosis, if he is to fall ill after puberty.[1] In the latter case we find that this sexual period has been forgotten and that the conscious memories that bear witness to it have been displaced. (I have already mentioned that I am also inclined to relate normal infantile amnesia to this infantile sexual activity.) Psycho-analytic investigation enables us to make what has been forgotten conscious and thus do away with a compulsion that arises from the unconscious psychical material.

the sexual excitation of early infancy returns . . .' The motive for all these changes made in 1915 was evidently to distinguish more sharply between the second and first phases of infantile sexual activity and to assign a more precise date—'about the fourth year'—to the second phase.]

[1] [*Footnote added* 1915:] The problem of why the sense of guilt of neurotics is, as Bleuler [1913] recently recognized, regularly attached to the memory of some masturbatory activity, usually at puberty, still awaits an exhaustive analytic explanation. [*Added* 1920:] The most general and most important factor concerned must no doubt be that masturbation represents the executive agency of the whole of infantile sexuality and is, therefore, able to take over the sense of guilt attaching to it.

RETURN OF   During the years of childhood with which
EARLY INFANTILE   I am now dealing, the sexual excitation of
MASTURBATION   early infancy returns, either as a centrally
                  determined tickling stimulus which seeks
satisfaction in masturbation, or as a process in the nature of
a nocturnal emission which, like the nocturnal emissions of
adult years, achieves satisfaction without the help of any action
by the subject. The latter case is the more frequent with
girls and in the second half of childhood; its determinants
are not entirely intelligible and often, though not invariably, it
seems to be conditioned by a period of earlier *active* masturbation. The symptoms of these sexual manifestations are scanty;
they are mostly displayed on behalf of the still undeveloped
sexual apparatus by the *urinary* apparatus, which thus acts, as it
were, as the former's trustee. Most of the so-called bladder disorders of this period are sexual disturbances: nocturnal enuresis,
unless it represents an epileptic fit, corresponds to a nocturnal
emission.

The reappearance of sexual activity is determined by internal
causes and external contingencies, both of which can be guessed
in cases of neurotic illness from the form taken by their symptoms and can be discovered with certainty by psycho-analytic
investigation. I shall have to speak presently of the internal
causes; great and lasting importance attaches at this period to
the accidental *external* contingencies. In the foreground we find
the effects of seduction, which treats a child as a sexual object
prematurely and teaches him, in highly emotional circumstances, how to obtain satisfaction from his genital zones, a
satisfaction which he is then usually obliged to repeat again
and again by masturbation. An influence of this kind may
originate either from adults or from other children. I cannot
admit that in my paper on 'The Aetiology of Hysteria' (1896c)
I exaggerated the frequency or importance of that influence,
though I did not then know that persons who remain normal
may have had the same experiences in their childhood, and
though I consequently overrated the importance of seduction in
comparison with the factors of sexual constitution and development.[1] Obviously seduction is not required in order to arouse

---

[1] [See Freud's detailed discussion of this in his second paper on
the part played by sexuality in the neuroses (1906a; *S.E.*, **7**, 274).]
Havelock Ellis [1913, Appendix B] has published a number of auto-

a child's sexual life; that can also come about spontaneously from internal causes.

POLYMORPHOUSLY PERVERSE DISPOSITION   It is an instructive fact that under the influence of seduction children can become polymorphously perverse, and can be led into all possible kinds of sexual irregularities. This shows that an aptitude for them is innately present in their disposition. There is consequently little resistance towards carrying them out, since the mental dams against sexual excesses—shame, disgust and morality—have either not yet been constructed at all or are only in course of construction, according to the age of the child. In this respect children behave in the same kind of way as an average uncultivated woman in whom the same polymorphously perverse disposition persists. Under ordinary conditions she may remain normal sexually, but if she is led on by a clever seducer she will find every sort of perversion to her taste, and will retain them as part of her own sexual activities. Prostitutes exploit the same polymorphous, that is, infantile, disposition for the purposes of their profession; and, considering the immense number of women who are prostitutes or who must be supposed to have an aptitude for prostitution without becoming engaged in it, it becomes impossible not to recognize that this same disposition to perversions of every kind is a general and fundamental human characteristic.

COMPONENT INSTINCTS   Moreover, the effects of seduction do not help to reveal the early history of the sexual instinct; they rather confuse our view of it by presenting children prematurely with a sexual object for which the infantile sexual instinct at first shows no need. It must, however, be admitted that infantile sexual life, in spite of the preponderating

biographical narratives written by people who remained predominantly normal in later life and describing the first sexual impulses of their childhood and the occasions which gave rise to them. These reports naturally suffer from the fact that they omit the prehistoric period of the writers' sexual lives, which is veiled by infantile amnesia and which can only be filled in by psycho-analysis in the case of an individual who has developed a neurosis. In more than one respect, nevertheless, the statements are valuable, and similar narratives were what led me to make the modification in my aetiological hypotheses which I have mentioned in the text.

dominance of erotogenic zones, exhibits components which from the very first involve other people as sexual objects. Such are the instincts of scopophilia, exhibitionism and cruelty, which appear in a sense independently of erotogenic zones; these instincts do not enter into intimate relations with genital[1] life until later, but are already to be observed in childhood as independent impulses, distinct in the first instance from erotogenic sexual activity. Small children are essentially without shame, and at some periods of their earliest years show an unmistakable satisfaction in exposing their bodies, with especial emphasis on the sexual parts. The counterpart of this supposedly perverse inclination, curiosity to see other people's genitals, probably does not become manifest until somewhat later in childhood, when the obstacle set up by a sense of shame has already reached a certain degree of development.[2] Under the influence of seduction the scopophilic perversion can attain great importance in the sexual life of a child. But my researches into the early years of normal people, as well as of neurotic patients, force me to the conclusion that scopophilia can also appear in children as a spontaneous manifestation. Small children whose attention has once been drawn—as a rule by masturbation—to their own genitals usually take the further step without help from outside and develop a lively interest in the genitals of their playmates. Since opportunities for satisfying curiosity of this kind usually occur only in the course of satisfying the two kinds of need for excretion, children of this kind turn into *voyeurs*, eager spectators of the processes of micturition and defaecation. When repression of these inclinations sets in, the desire to see other people's genitals (whether of their own or the opposite sex) persists as a tormenting compulsion, which in some cases of neurosis later affords the strongest motive force for the formation of symptoms.

The cruel component of the sexual instinct develops in childhood even more independently of the sexual activities that are attached to erotogenic zones. Cruelty in general comes easily

[1] ['Sexual' in 1905 and 1910.]

[2] [In the first (1905) edition this sentence read: 'The counterpart . . . does not join in until later in childhood, when. . . .' In 1910 the word 'probably' was inserted; in 1915 'join in' was replaced by 'become manifest'; and in 1920 'somewhat' was inserted before 'later'.—The subject of exhibitionism in young children had been discussed at some length by Freud in his *Interpretation of Dreams*, Chapter V, Section D (α) (Standard Ed., **4**, 224 f.).]

to the childish nature, since the obstacle that brings the instinct for mastery to a halt at another person's pain—namely a capacity for pity—is developed relatively late. The fundamental psychological analysis of this instinct has, as we know, not yet been satisfactorily achieved. It may be assumed that the impulse of cruelty arises from the instinct for mastery and appears at a period of sexual life at which the genitals have not yet taken over their later role. It then dominates a phase of sexual life which we shall later describe as a pregenital organization.[1] Children who distinguish themselves by special cruelty towards animals and playmates usually give rise to a just suspicion of an intense and precocious sexual activity arising from erotogenic zones; and, though all the sexual instincts may display simultaneous precocity, *erotogenic* sexual activity seems, nevertheless, to be the primary one. The absence of the barrier of pity brings with it a danger that the connection between the cruel and the erotogenic instincts, thus established in childhood, may prove unbreakable in later life. Ever since Jean Jacques Rousseau's *Confessions*, it has been well known to all educationalists that the painful stimulation of the skin of the buttocks is one of the erotogenic roots of the *passive* instinct of cruelty (masochism). The conclusion has rightly been drawn by them that corporal punishment, which is usually applied to this part of the body, should not be inflicted upon any children whose libido is liable to be forced into collateral channels by the later demands of cultural education.[2]

[1] [The last two sentences were given their present form in 1915. In 1905 and 1910 they read as follows: 'It may be assumed that the impulses of cruelty arise from sources which are in fact independent of sexuality, but may become united with it at an early stage owing to an anastomosis [cross-connection] near their points of origin. Observation teaches us, however, that sexual development and the development of the instinct of scopophilia and cruelty are subject to mutual influences which limit this presumed independence of the two sets of instincts.']

[2] [*Footnote added* 1910:] When the account which I have given above of infantile sexuality was first published in 1905, it was founded for the most part on the results of psycho-analytic research upon adults. At that time it was impossible to make full use of direct observation on children: only isolated hints and some valuable pieces of confirmation came from that source. Since then it has become possible to gain direct insight into infantile psycho-sexuality by the analysis of some cases of neurotic illness during the early years of childhood. It is gratifying to be able to report that direct observation has fully confirmed the conclusions

[5] THE SEXUAL RESEARCHES OF CHILDHOOD [1]

THE INSTINCT   At about the same time as the sexual life
FOR KNOWLEDGE   of children reaches its first peak, between
                              the ages of three and five, they also begin to
show signs of the activity which may be ascribed to the instinct
for knowledge or research. This instinct cannot be counted
among the elementary instinctual components, nor can it be
classed as exclusively belonging to sexuality. Its activity corresponds on the one hand to a sublimated manner of obtaining
mastery, while on the other hand it makes use of the energy of
scopophilia. Its relations to sexual life, however, are of particular
importance, since we have learnt from psycho-analysis that the
instinct for knowledge in children is attracted unexpectedly
early and intensively to sexual problems and is in fact possibly
first aroused by them.

THE RIDDLE OF   It is not by theoretical interests but by
THE SPHINX   practical ones that activities of research are
                              set going in children. The threat to the bases
of a child's existence offered by the discovery or the suspicion

arrived at by psycho-analysis—which is incidentally good evidence of
the trustworthiness of that method of research. In addition to this, the
'Analysis of a Phobia in a Five-Year-Old Boy' (1909*b*) has taught us
much that is new for which we have not been prepared by psycho-
analysis: for instance, the fact that sexual symbolism—the representation of what is sexual by non-sexual objects and relations—extends back
into the first years of possession of the power of speech. I was further
made aware of a defect in the account I have given in the text, which,
in the interests of lucidity, describes the conceptual distinction between
the two phases of auto-erotism and object-love as though it were also a
separation in time. But the analyses that I have just mentioned, as well
as the findings of Bell quoted in the footnote, p. 40, show that children
between the ages of three and five are capable of very clear object-
choice, accompanied by strong affects.—[In 1910 only, this footnote
continued as follows: 'Another addition to our knowledge of infantile
sexual life which has not yet been mentioned in the text relates to the
sexual researches of children, to the theories to which children are led
by them (cf. my paper on the subject, 1908*c*), to the important bearing
of these theories upon later neuroses, to the outcome of these infantile
researches and to their relation to the development of children's intellectual powers.']

[1] [The whole of this section on the sexual researches of children first
appeared in 1915.]

of the arrival of a new baby and the fear that he may, as a result of it, cease to be cared for and loved, make him thoughtful and clear-sighted. And this history of the instinct's origin is in line with the fact that the first problem with which it deals is not the question of the distinction between the sexes but the riddle of where babies come from.[1] (This, in a distorted form which can easily be rectified, is the same riddle that was propounded by the Theban Sphinx.) On the contrary, the existence of two sexes does not to begin with arouse any difficulties or doubts in children. It is self-evident to a male child that a genital like his own is to be attributed to everyone he knows, and he cannot make its absence tally with his picture of these other people.

CASTRATION COMPLEX AND PENIS ENVY   This conviction is energetically maintained by boys, is obstinately defended against the contradictions which soon result from observation, and is only abandoned after severe internal struggles (the castration complex). The substitutes for this penis which they feel is missing in women play a great part in determining the form taken by many perversions.[2]

The assumption that all human beings have the same (male) form of genital is the first of the many remarkable and momentous sexual theories of children. It is of little use to a child that the science of biology justifies his prejudice and has been obliged to recognize the female clitoris as a true substitute for the penis.

Little girls do not resort to denial of this kind when they see that boys' genitals are formed differently from their own. They are ready to recognize them immediately and are overcome by envy for the penis—an envy culminating in the wish, which is so important in its consequences, to be boys themselves.

[1] [In a later work, Freud (1925j) corrected this statement, saying that it is not true of girls, and not always true of boys.]

[2] [Footnote added 1920:] We are justified in speaking of a castration complex in women as well. Both male and female children form a theory that women no less than men originally had a penis, but that they have lost it by castration. The conviction which is finally reached by males that women have no penis often leads them to an enduringly low opinion of the other sex.

THEORIES   Many people can remember clearly what an
OF BIRTH   intense interest they took during the prepubertal
           period in the question of where babies come from.
The anatomical answers to the question were at the time very
various: babies come out of the breast, or are cut out of the
body, or the navel opens to let them through.[1] Outside analysis,
there are very seldom memories of any similar researches having
been carried out in the *early* years of childhood. These earlier
researches fell a victim to repression long since, but all their
findings were of a uniform nature: people get babies by eating
some particular thing (as they do in fairy tales) and babies are
born through the bowel like a discharge of faeces. These infantile
theories remind us of conditions that exist in the animal king-
dom—and especially of the cloaca in types of animals lower
than mammals.

SADISTIC VIEW   If children at this early age witness sexual
OF SEXUAL   intercourse between adults—for which an op-
INTERCOURSE   portunity is provided by the conviction of
                grown-up people that small children cannot
understand anything sexual—they inevitably regard the sexual
act as a sort of ill-treatment or act of subjugation: they view
it, that is, in a sadistic sense. Psycho-analysis also shows us that
an impression of this kind in early childhood contributes a great
deal towards a predisposition to a subsequent sadistic displacement of the sexual aim. Furthermore, children are much concerned with the problem of what sexual intercourse—or, as
they put it, being married—consists in: and they usually seek
a solution of the mystery in some common activity concerned
with the function of micturition or defaecation.

TYPICAL FAILURE   We can say in general of the sexual
OF INFANTILE   theories of children that they are reflec-
SEXUAL RESEARCHES tions of their own sexual constitution,
                   and that in spite of their grotesque errors
the theories show more understanding of sexual processes than
one would have given their creators credit for. Children also

_____

[1] [*Footnote added* 1924:] In these later years of childhood there is a
great wealth of sexual theories, of which only a few examples are given
in the text.

perceive the alterations that take place in their mother owing
to pregnancy and are able to interpret them correctly. The
fable of the stork is often told to an audience that receives
it with deep, though mostly silent, mistrust. There are, however, two elements that remain undiscovered by the sexual
researches of children: the fertilizing role of semen and the existence of the female sexual orifice—the same elements, incidentally, in which the infantile organization is itself undeveloped.
It therefore follows that the efforts of the childish investigator
are habitually fruitless, and end in a renunciation which not
infrequently leaves behind it a permanent injury to the instinct
for knowledge. The sexual researches of these early years of
childhood are always carried out in solitude. They constitute a
first step towards taking an independent attitude in the world,
and imply a high degree of alienation of the child from the
people in his environment who formerly enjoyed his complete
confidence.

[6] THE PHASES OF DEVELOPMENT OF THE SEXUAL ORGANIZATION [1]

The characteristics of infantile sexual life which we have
hitherto emphasized are the facts that it is essentially auto-
erotic (i.e. that it finds its object in the infant's own body) and
that its individual component instincts are upon the whole dis-
connected and independent of one another in their search for
pleasure. The final outcome of sexual development lies in what
is known as the normal sexual life of the adult, in which the
pursuit of pleasure comes under the sway of the reproductive
function and in which the component instincts, under the
primacy of a single erotogenic zone, form a firm organization
directed towards a sexual aim attached to some extraneous
sexual object.

PREGENITAL   The study, with the help of psycho-analysis,
ORGANIZATIONS   of the inhibitions and disturbances of this pro-
                 cess of development enables us to recognize
abortive beginnings and preliminary stages of a firm organization of the component instincts such as this—preliminary stages

[1] [The whole of this section, too, first appeared in 1915. The concept
of a 'pregenital organization' of sexual life seems to have been first

which themselves constitute a sexual régime of a sort. These phases of sexual organization are normally passed through smoothly, without giving more than a hint of their existence. It is only in pathological cases that they become active and recognizable to superficial observation.

We shall give the name of 'pregenital' to organizations of sexual life in which the genital zones have not yet taken over their predominant part. We have hitherto identified two such organizations, which almost seem as though they were harking back to early animal forms of life.

The first of these is the oral or, as it might be called, cannibalistic pregenital sexual organization. Here sexual activity has not yet been separated from the ingestion of food; nor are opposite currents within the activity differentiated. The *object* of both activities is the same; the sexual *aim* consists in the incorporation of the object—the prototype of a process which, in the form of identification, is later to play such an important psychological part. A relic of this constructed phase of organization, which is forced upon our notice by pathology, may be seen in thumb-sucking, in which the sexual activity, detached from the nutritive activity, has substituted for the extraneous object one situated in the subject's own body.[1]

A second pregenital phase is that of the sadistic-anal organization. Here the opposition between two currents, which runs through all sexual life, is already developed: they cannot yet, however, be described as 'masculine' and 'feminine', but only as 'active' and 'passive'. The *activity* is put into operation by the instinct for mastery through the agency of the somatic musculature; the organ which, more than any other, represents the *passive* sexual aim is the erotogenic mucous membrane of the anus. Both of these currents have objects, which, however, are not identical. Alongside these, other component instincts operate in an auto-erotic manner. In this phase, therefore, sexual

introduced by Freud in his paper on 'The Predisposition to Obsessional Neurosis' (1913*i*), which, however, deals only with the sadistic-anal organization. The oral organization was apparently recognized as such for the first time in the present passage.]

[1] [*Footnote added* 1920:] For remnants of this phase in adult neurotics, cf. Abraham (1916). [*Added* 1924:] In another, later work (1924) the same writer has divided both this oral phase, and also the later sadistic-anal one, into two sub-divisions, which are characterized by differing attitudes towards the object.

polarity and an extraneous object are already observable. But organization and subordination to the reproductive function are still absent.[1]

AMBIVALENCE This form of sexual organization can persist throughout life and can permanently attract a large portion of sexual activity to itself. The predominance in it of sadism and the cloacal part played by the anal zone give it a quite peculiarly archaic colouring. It is further characterized by the fact that in it the opposing pairs of instincts are developed to an approximately equal extent, a state of affairs described by Bleuler's happily chosen term 'ambivalence'.

The assumption of the existence of pregenital organizations of sexual life is based on the analysis of the neuroses, and without a knowledge of them can scarcely be appreciated. Further analytic investigation may be expected to provide us with far more information on the structure and development of the normal sexual function.

In order to complete our picture of infantile sexual life, we must also suppose that the choice of an object, such as we have shown to be characteristic of the pubertal phase of development, has already frequently or habitually been effected during the years of childhood: that is to say, the whole of the sexual currents have become directed towards a single person in relation to whom they seek to achieve their aims. This then is the closest approximation possible in childhood to the final form taken by sexual life after puberty. The only difference lies in the fact that in childhood the combination of the component instincts and their subordination under the primacy of the genitals have been effected only very incompletely or not at all. Thus the establishment of that primacy in the service of reproduction is the last phase through which the organization of sexuality passes.[2]

[1] [*Footnote added* 1924:] Abraham, in the paper last quoted (1924), points out that the anus is developed from the embryonic blastopore—a fact which seems like a biological prototype of psychosexual development.

[2] [*Footnote added* 1924:] At a later date (1923), I myself modified this account by inserting a third phase in the development of childhood, subsequent to the two pregenital organizations. This phase, which already deserves to be described as genital, presents a sexual object and some degree of convergence of the sexual impulses upon that object; but it

DIPHASIC CHOICE   It may be regarded as typical of the choice
OF OBJECT   of an object that the process is diphasic, that
          is, that it occurs in two waves. The first of
these begins between the ages of two [1] and five, and is brought to
a halt or to a retreat by the latency period; it is characterized
by the infantile nature of the sexual aims. The second wave sets
in with puberty and determines the final outcome of sexual life.

Although the diphasic nature of object-choice comes down in
essentials to no more than the operation of the latency period,
it is of the highest importance in regard to disturbances of that
final outcome. The resultants of infantile object-choice are
carried over into the later period. They either persist as such
or are revived at the actual time of puberty. But as a consequence of the repression which has developed between the
two phases they prove unutilizable. Their sexual aims have become mitigated and they now represent what may be described
as the 'affectionate current' of sexual life. Only psycho-analytic
investigation can show that behind this affection, admiration
and respect there lie concealed the old sexual longings of the
infantile component instincts which have now become unser-
viceable. The object-choice of the pubertal period is obliged
to dispense with the objects of childhood and to start afresh as a
'sensual current'. Should these two currents fail to converge,
the result is often that one of the ideals of sexual life, the focusing
of all desires upon a single object, will be unattainable. [2]

[7] THE SOURCES OF INFANTILE SEXUALITY

Our efforts to trace the origins of the sexual instinct have
shown us so far that sexual excitation arises (a) as a reproduction
of a satisfaction experienced in connection with other organic
processes, (b) through appropriate peripheral stimulation of
erotogenic zones and (c) as an expression of certain 'instincts'

is differentiated from the final organization of sexual maturity in one
essential respect. For it knows only one kind of genital: the male one.
For that reason I have named it the 'phallic' stage of organization. (Freud,
1923e.) According to Abraham [1924], it has a biological prototype in
the embryo's undifferentiated genital disposition, which is the same for
both sexes.

  [1] [In 1915 this figure was 'three'; it was altered to 'two' in 1920. Cf.
also the end of the footnote on p. 88.]   [2] [See Addenda, p. 112.]

(such as the scopophilic instinct and the instinct of cruelty) of which the origin is not yet completely intelligible. Psychoanalytic investigation, reaching back into childhood from a later time, and contemporary observation of children combine to indicate to us still other regularly active sources of sexual excitation. The direct observation of children has the disadvantage of working upon data which are easily misunderstandable; psycho-analysis is made difficult by the fact that it can only reach its data, as well as its conclusions, after long détours. But by co-operation the two methods can attain a satisfactory degree of certainty in their findings.

We have already discovered in examining the erotogenic zones that these regions of the skin merely show a special intensification of a kind of susceptibility to stimulus which is possessed in a certain degree by the whole cutaneous surface. We shall therefore not be surprised to find that very definite erotogenic effects are to be ascribed to certain kinds of general stimulation of the skin. Among these we may especially mention thermal stimuli, whose importance may help us to understand the therapeutic effects of warm baths.

MECHANICAL EXCITATIONS   At this point we must also mention the production of sexual excitation by rhythmic mechanical agitation of the body. Stimuli of this kind operate in three different ways: on the sensory apparatus of the vestibular nerves, on the skin, and on the deeper parts (e.g. the muscles and articular structures). The existence of these pleasurable sensations—and it is worth emphasizing the fact that in this connection the concepts of 'sexual excitation' and 'satisfaction' can to a great extent be used without distinction, a circumstance which we must later endeavour to explain [p. 78] —the existence, then, of these pleasurable sensations, caused by forms of mechanical agitation of the body, is confirmed by the fact that children are so fond of games of passive movement, such as swinging and being thrown up into the air, and insist on such games being incessantly repeated.[1] It is well known

[1] Some people can remember that in swinging they felt the impact of moving air upon their genitals as an immediate sexual pleasure. [A specific instance of this is quoted in a footnote to a passage in *The Interpretation of Dreams* (1900a, near the end of Chapter V) in which this whole topic is discussed (Standard Ed., **4**, 272).]

that rocking is habitually used to induce sleep in restless children. The shaking produced by driving in carriages and later by railway-travel exercises such a fascinating effect upon older children that every boy, at any rate, has at one time or other in his life wanted to be an engine driver or a coachman. It is a puzzling fact that boys take such an extraordinarily intense interest in things connected with railways, and, at the age at which the production of phantasies is most active (shortly before puberty), use those things as the nucleus of a symbolism that is peculiarly sexual. A compulsive link of this kind between railway-travel and sexuality is clearly derived from the pleasurable character of the sensations of movement. In the event of repression, which turns so many childish preferences into their opposite, these same individuals, when they are adolescents or adults, will react to rocking or swinging with a feeling of nausea, will be terribly exhausted by a railway journey, or will be subject to attacks of anxiety on the journey and will protect themselves against a repetition of the painful experience by a dread of railway-travel.

Here again we must mention the fact, which is not yet understood, that the combination of fright and mechanical agitation produces the severe, hysteriform, traumatic neurosis. It may at least be assumed that these influences, which, when they are of small intensity, become sources of sexual excitation, lead to a profound disorder in the sexual mechanism or chemistry[1] if they operate with exaggerated force.

MUSCULAR   We are all familiar with the fact that children
ACTIVITY   feel a need for a large amount of active muscular
              exercise and derive extraordinary pleasure from
satisfying it. Whether this pleasure has any connection with sexuality, whether it itself comprises sexual satisfaction or whether it can become the occasion of sexual excitation—all of this is open to critical questioning, which may indeed also be directed against the view maintained in the previous paragraphs that the pleasure derived from sensations of *passive* movement is of a sexual nature or may produce sexual excitation. It is, however, a fact that a number of people report that they experienced the first signs of excitement in their genitals while they were romping or wrestling with playmates—a situation in

[1] [The last two words were added in 1924.]

which, apart from general muscular exertion, there is a large amount of contact with the skin of the opponent. An inclination to physical struggles with some one particular person, just as in later years an inclination to *verbal* disputes,[1] is a convincing sign that object-choice has fallen on him. One of the roots of the sadistic instinct would seem to lie in the encouragement of sexual excitation by muscular activity. In many people the infantile connection between romping and sexual excitation is among the determinants of the direction subsequently taken by their sexual instinct.[2]

AFFECTIVE   The further sources of sexual excitation in chil-
PROCESSES   dren are open to less doubt. It is easy to establish,
                   whether by contemporary observation or by sub-
sequent research, that all comparatively intense affective processes, including even terrifying ones, trench upon sexuality—
a fact which may incidentally help to explain the pathogenic
effect of emotions of that kind. In schoolchildren dread of going
in for an examination or tension over a difficult piece of work
can be important not only in affecting the child's relations at
school but also in bringing about an irruption of sexual manifestations. For quite often in such circumstances a stimulus may
be felt which urges the child to touch his genitals, or something
may take place akin to a nocturnal emission with all its bewildering consequences. The behaviour of children at school,
which confronts a teacher with plenty of puzzles, deserves in
general to be brought into relation with their budding sexuality.
The sexually exciting effect of many emotions which are in
themselves unpleasurable, such as feelings of apprehension,
fright or horror, persists in a great number of people throughout
their adult life. There is no doubt that this is the explanation
of why so many people seek opportunities for sensations of this
kind, subject to the proviso that the seriousness of the unpleasurable feeling is damped down by certain qualifying facts, such

[1] 'Was sich liebt, das neckt sich.' [Lovers' quarrels are proverbial.]
[2] [*Footnote added* 1910:] The analysis of cases of neurotic abasia and agoraphobia removes all doubt as to the sexual nature of pleasure in movement. Modern education, as we know, makes great use of games in order to divert young people from sexual activity. It would be more correct to say that in these young people it replaces sexual enjoyment by pleasure in movement—and forces sexual activity back to one of its auto-erotic components.

as its occurring in an imaginary world, in a book or in a play.

If we assume that a similar erotogenic effect attaches even to intensely painful feelings, especially when the pain is toned down or kept at a distance by some accompanying condition, we should here have one of the main roots of the masochistic-sadistic instinct, into whose numerous complexities we are very gradually gaining some insight.[1]

INTELLECTUAL WORK
Finally, it is an unmistakable fact that concentration of the attention upon an intellectual task and intellectual strain in general produce a concomitant sexual excitation in many young people as well as adults. This is no doubt the only justifiable basis for what is in other respects the questionable practice of ascribing nervous disorders to intellectual 'overwork'.[2]

If we now cast our eyes over the tentative suggestions which I have made as to the sources of infantile sexual excitation, though I have not described them completely nor enumerated them fully, the following conclusions emerge with more or less certainty. It seems that the fullest provisions are made for setting in motion the process of sexual excitation—a process the nature of which has, it must be confessed, become highly obscure to us. The setting in motion of this process is first and foremost provided for in a more or less direct fashion by the excitations of the sensory surfaces—the skin and the sense organs—and, most directly of all, by the operation of stimuli on certain areas known as erotogenic zones. The decisive element in these sources of sexual excitation is no doubt the *quality* of the stimuli, though the factor of intensity, in the case of pain, is not a matter of complete indifference. But apart from these sources there are present in the organism contrivances which bring it about that in the case of a great number of internal processes sexual excitation arises as a concomitant effect, as soon as the intensity

---

[1] [*Footnote added* 1924:] I am here referring to what is known as 'erotogenic' masochism. [See footnote 2, p. 24.]

[2] [Some earlier remarks by Freud on this subject will be found in the middle of his first paper on 'Sexuality in the Aetiology of the Neuroses' (1898a), and some later ones in a footnote to Section III of 'Analysis Terminable and Interminable' (1937c).]

of those processes passes beyond certain quantitative limits. What we have called the component instincts of sexuality are either derived directly from these internal sources or are composed of elements both from those sources and from the erotogenic zones. It may well be that nothing of considerable importance can occur in the organism without contributing some component to the excitation of the sexual instinct.[1]

It does not seem to me possible at present to state these general conclusions with any greater clarity or certainty. For this I think two factors are responsible: first, the novelty of the whole method of approach to the subject, and secondly, the fact that the whole nature of sexual excitation is completely unknown to us. Nevertheless I am tempted to make two observations which promise to open out wide future prospects:

VARIETIES OF SEXUAL CONSTITUTION (a) Just as we saw previously [p. 37] that it was possible to derive a multiplicity of innate sexual constitutions from variety in the development of the erotogenic zones, so we can now make a similar attempt by including the *indirect* sources of sexual excitation. It may be assumed that, although contributions are made from these sources in the case of everyone, they are not in all cases of equal strength, and that further help towards the differentiation of sexual constitutions may be found in the varying development of the individual sources of sexual excitation.[2]

PATHWAYS OF MUTUAL INFLUENCE (b) If we now drop the figurative expression that we have so long adopted in speaking of the 'sources' of sexual excitation, we are led to the suspicion that all the connecting pathways that lead from other functions to sexuality must also be traversable in the reverse direction. If, for instance, the common possession

---

[1] [Freud quoted this passage in his paper on 'The Economic Problem of Masochism' (1924c), *Standard Ed.*, **19**, 163.]

[2] [*Footnote added* 1920:] An inevitable consequence of these considerations is that we must regard each individual as possessing an oral erotism, an anal erotism, a urethral erotism, etc., and that the existence of mental complexes corresponding to these implies no judgement of abnormality or neurosis. The differences separating the normal from the abnormal can lie only in the relative strength of the individual components of the sexual instinct and in the use to which they are put in the course of development.

of the labial zone by the two functions is the reason why sexual satisfaction arises during the taking of nourishment, then the same factor also enables us to understand why there should be disorders of nutrition if the erotogenic functions of the common zone are disturbed. Or again, if we know that concentration of attention may give rise to sexual excitation, it seems plausible to assume that by making use of the same path, but in a contrary direction, the condition of sexual excitation may influence the possibility of directing the attention. A good portion of the symptomatology of the neuroses, which I have traced to disturbances of the sexual processes, is expressed in disturbances of other, non-sexual, somatic functions; and this circumstance, which has hitherto been unintelligible, becomes less puzzling if it is only the counterpart of the influences which bring about the production of sexual excitation.[1]

The same pathways, however, along which sexual disturbances trench upon the other somatic functions must also perform another important function in normal health. They must serve as paths for the attraction of sexual instinctual forces to aims that are other than sexual, that is to say, for the sublimation of sexuality. But we must end with a confession that very little is as yet known with certainty of these pathways, though they certainly exist and can probably be traversed in both directions.

[1] [Freud took up this point, with special reference to disorders of vision, in his paper on 'The Psycho-Analytic View of Psychogenic Disturbance of Vision' (1910i), *Standard Ed.*, **11**, 215-17.]

III

THE TRANSFORMATIONS OF PUBERTY

WITH the arrival of puberty, changes set in which are destined to give infantile sexual life its final, normal shape. The sexual instinct has hitherto been predominantly auto-erotic; it now finds a sexual object. Its activity has hitherto been derived from a number of separate instincts and erotogenic zones, which, independently of one another, have pursued a certain sort of pleasure as their sole sexual aim. Now, however, a new sexual aim appears, and all the component instincts combine to attain it, while the erotogenic zones become subordinated to the primacy of the genital zone.[1] Since the new sexual aim assigns very different functions to the two sexes, their sexual development now diverges greatly. That of males is the more straightforward and the more understandable, while that of females actually enters upon a kind of involution. A normal sexual life is only assured by an exact convergence of the two currents directed towards the sexual object and the sexual aim, the affectionate current and the sensual one.[2] (The former, the affectionate current, comprises what remains of the infantile efflorescence of sexuality.)[3] It is like the completion of a tunnel which has been driven through a hill from both directions.

The new sexual aim in men consists in the discharge of the sexual products. The earlier one, the attainment of pleasure, is by no means alien to it; on the contrary, the highest degree of pleasure is attached to this final act of the sexual process. The sexual instinct is now subordinated to the reproductive function; it becomes, so to say, altruistic. If this transformation is to succeed, the original dispositions and all the other characteristics of the instincts must be taken into account in the process. Just as on any other occasion on which the organism should by

---

[1] [*Footnote added* 1915:] The schematic picture which I have given in the text aims at emphasizing differences. I have already shown on p. 65 the extent to which infantile sexuality approximates to the final sexual organization, owing to its choice of object [*added* 1924:] and to the development of the phallic phase.

[2] [Cf. Addenda, p. 112.]   [3] [This sentence as added in 1920.]

rights make new combinations and adjustments leading to complicated mechanisms, here too there are possibilities of pathological disorders if these new arrangements are not carried out. Every pathological disorder of sexual life is rightly to be regarded as an inhibition in development.

[1] THE PRIMACY OF THE GENITAL ZONES AND FORE-PLEASURE

The starting-point and the final aim of the process which I have described are clearly visible. The intermediate steps are still in many ways obscure to us. We shall have to leave more than one of them as an unsolved riddle.

The most striking of the processes at puberty has been picked upon as constituting its essence: the manifest growth of the external genitalia. (The latency period of childhood is, on the other hand, characterized by a relative cessation of their growth.) In the meantime the development of the internal genitalia has advanced far enough for them to be able to discharge the sexual products or, as the case may be, to bring about the formation of a new living organism. Thus a highly complicated apparatus has been made ready and awaits the moment of being put into operation.

This apparatus is to be set in motion by stimuli, and observation shows us that stimuli can impinge on it from three directions: from the external world by means of the excitation of the erotogenic zones with which we are already familiar, from the organic interior by ways which we have still to explore, and from mental life, which is itself a storehouse for external impressions and a receiving-post for internal excitations. All three kinds of stimuli produce the same effect, namely a condition described as 'sexual excitement', which shows itself by two sorts of indication, mental and somatic. The mental indications consist in a peculiar feeling of tension of an extremely compelling character; and among the numerous somatic ones are first and foremost a number of changes in the genitals, which have the obvious sense of being preparations for the sexual act— the erection of the male organ and the lubrication of the vagina.

SEXUAL   The fact that sexual excitement possesses the char-
TENSION   acter of tension raises a problem the solution of which
                 is no less difficult than it would be important in help-
ing us to understand the sexual processes. In spite of all the
differences of opinion that reign on the subject among psycho-
logists, I must insist that a feeling of tension necessarily involves
unpleasure. What seems to me decisive is the fact that a feeling
of this kind is accompanied by an impulsion to make a change
in the psychological situation, that it operates in an urgent way
which is wholly alien to the nature of the feeling of pleasure. If,
however, the tension of sexual excitement is counted as an unpleasurable feeling, we are at once brought up against the fact
that it is also undoubtedly felt as pleasurable. In every case in
which tension is produced by sexual processes it is accompanied
by pleasure; even in the preparatory changes in the genitals a
feeling of satisfaction of some kind is plainly to be observed.
How, then, are this unpleasurable tension and this feeling of
pleasure to be reconciled?

Everything relating to the problem of pleasure and unpleasure touches upon one of the sorest spots of present-day
psychology. It will be my aim to learn as much as possible from
the circumstances of the instance with which we are at present
dealing, but I shall avoid any approach to the problem as a
whole.[1]

Let us begin by casting a glance at the way in which the
erotogenic zones fit themselves into the new arrangement. They
have to play an important part in introducing sexual excitation.
The eye is perhaps the zone most remote from the sexual object,
but it is the one which, in the situation of wooing an object, is
liable to be the most frequently stimulated by the particular
quality of excitation whose cause, when it occurs in a sexual
object, we describe as beauty. (For the same reason the merits
of a sexual object are described as 'attractions'.)[2] This stimulation is on the one hand already accompanied by pleasure, while
on the other hand it leads to an increase of sexual excitement
or produces it if it is not yet present. If the excitation now
spreads to another erotogenic zone—to the hand, for instance,

---

[1] [*Footnote added* 1924:] I have made an attempt at solving this problem
in the first part of my paper on 'The Economic Problem of Masochism'
(1924c).

[2] [See footnote 2, p. 22.]

through tactile sensations—the effect is the same: a feeling of pleasure on the one side, which is quickly intensified by pleasure arising from the preparatory changes [in the genitals], and on the other side an increase of sexual tension, which soon passes over into the most obvious unpleasure if it cannot be met by a further accession of pleasure. Another instance will perhaps make this even clearer. If an erotogenic zone in a person who is not sexually excited (e.g. the skin of a woman's breast) is stimulated by touch, the contact produces a pleasurable feeling; but it is at the same time better calculated than anything to arouse a sexual excitation that demands an increase of pleasure. The problem is how it can come about that an experience of pleasure can give rise to a need for greater pleasure.

THE MECHANISM OF   The part played in this by the eroto-
FORE-PLEASURE   genic zones, however, is clear. What is
                       true of one of them is true of all. They
are all used to provide a certain amount of pleasure by being stimulated in the way appropriate to them. This pleasure then leads to an increase in tension which in its turn is responsible for producing the necessary motor energy for the conclusion of the sexual act. The penultimate stage of that act is once again the appropriate stimulation of an erotogenic zone (the genital zone itself, in the glans penis) by the appropriate object (the mucous membrane of the vagina); and from the pleasure yielded by this excitation the motor energy is obtained, this time by a reflex path, which brings about the discharge of the sexual substances. This last pleasure is the highest in intensity, and its mechanism differs from that of the earlier pleasure. It is brought about entirely by discharge: it is wholly a pleasure of satisfaction and with it the tension of the libido is for the time being extinguished.

This distinction between the one kind of pleasure due to the excitation of erotogenic zones and the other kind due to the discharge of the sexual substances deserves, I think, to be made more concrete by a difference in nomenclature. The former may be suitably described as 'fore-pleasure' in contrast to the 'end-pleasure' or pleasure of satisfaction derived from the sexual act. Fore-pleasure is thus the same pleasure that has already been produced, although on a smaller scale, by the infantile sexual instinct; end-pleasure is something new and is thus probably conditioned by circumstances that do not arise till puberty. The formula for the new function of the erotogenic zones runs therefore: they are used to make possible, through the medium of the fore-pleasure which can be derived from them (as it was during infantile life), the production of the greater pleasure of satisfaction.

I was able recently to throw light upon another instance, in a quite different department of mental life, of a slight feeling of pleasure similarly making possible the attainment of a greater resultant pleasure, and thus operating as an 'incentive bonus'. In the same connection I was also able to go more deeply into the nature of pleasure.[1]

DANGERS OF FORE-PLEASURE   The connection between fore-pleasure and infantile sexual life is, however, made clearer by the pathogenic part which it can come to play. The attainment of the normal sexual aim can clearly be endangered by the mechanism in which fore-pleasure is involved. This danger arises if at any point in the preparatory sexual processes the fore-pleasure turns out to be too great and the element of tension too small. The motive for proceeding further with the sexual process then disappears, the whole path is cut short, and the preparatory act in question takes the place of the normal sexual aim. Experience has shown that the precondition for this damaging event is that the erotogenic zone concerned or the corresponding component instinct shall already during childhood have contributed an unusual amount of pleasure. If further factors then come into play, tending to bring about a fixation, a compulsion may easily arise in later life which resists the incorporation of this particular fore-pleasure into a new context. Such is in fact the mechanism of many perversions, which consist in a lingering over the preparatory acts of the sexual process.

This failure of the function of the sexual mechanism owing to fore-pleasure is best avoided if the primacy of the genitals too

---

[1] See my volume on *Jokes and their Relation to the Unconscious* which appeared in 1905 [near the end of Chapter IV]. The 'fore-pleasure' attained by the technique of joking is used in order to liberate a greater pleasure derived from the removal of internal inhibitions. [In a later paper, on creative writing (1908e), Freud attributed a similar mechanism to aesthetic pleasure.]

is adumbrated in childhood; and indeed things seem actually arranged to bring this about in the second half of childhood (from the age of eight to puberty). During these years the genital zones already behave in much the same way as in maturity; they become the seat of sensations of excitation and of preparatory changes whenever any pleasure is felt from the satisfaction of other erotogenic zones, though this result is still without a purpose—that is to say, contributes nothing to a continuation of the sexual process. Already in childhood, therefore, alongside of the pleasure of satisfaction there is a certain amount of sexual tension, although it is less constant and less in quantity. We can now understand why, in discussing the sources of sexuality, we were equally justified in saying of a given process that it was sexually satisfying or sexually exciting. [See p. 67.] It will be noticed that in the course of our enquiry we began by exaggerating the distinction between infantile and mature sexual life, and that we are now setting this right. Not only the deviations from normal sexual life but its normal form as well are determined by the infantile manifestations of sexuality.

[2] THE PROBLEM OF SEXUAL EXCITATION

We remain in complete ignorance both of the origin and of the nature of the sexual tension which arises simultaneously with the pleasure when erotogenic zones are satisfied.[1] The most obvious explanation, that this tension arises in some way out of the pleasure itself, is not only extremely improbable in itself but becomes untenable when we consider that in connection with the greatest pleasure of all, that which accompanies the discharge of the sexual products, no tension is produced, but on the contrary all tension is removed. Thus pleasure and sexual tension can only be connected in an indirect manner.

---

[1] It is a highly instructive fact that the German language in its use of the word '*Lust*' takes into account the part played by the preparatory sexual excitations which, as has been explained above, simultaneously produce an element of satisfaction and a contribution to sexual tension. '*Lust*' has two meanings, and is used to describe the sensation of sexual tension ('*Ich habe Lust*' = 'I should like to', 'I feel an impulse to') as well as the feeling of satisfaction. [Cf. footnote 2, p. 1.]

PART PLAYED   Apart from the fact that normally it is only
BY THE SEXUAL the discharge of the sexual substances that
SUBSTANCES   brings sexual excitation to an end, there are
               other points of contact between sexual ten-
sion and the sexual products. In the case of a man living a
continent life, the sexual apparatus, at varying intervals, which,
however, are not ungoverned by rules, discharges the sexual
substances during the night, to the accompaniment of a pleasurable feeling and in the course of a dream which hallucinates
a sexual act. And in regard to this process (nocturnal emission)
it is difficult to avoid the conclusion that the sexual tension,
which succeeds in making use of the short cut of hallucination as
a substitute for the act itself, is a function of the accumulation
of semen in the vesicles containing the sexual products. Our
experience in connection with the exhaustibility of the sexual
mechanism argues in the same sense. If the store of semen is
exhausted, not only is it impossible to carry out the sexual act,
but the susceptibility of the erotogenic zones to stimulus ceases,
and their appropriate excitation no longer gives rise to any
pleasure. We thus learn incidentally that a certain degree
of sexual tension is required even for the excitability of the
erotogenic zones.

This would seem to lead to what is, if I am not mistaken, the
fairly wide-spread hypothesis that the accumulation of the
sexual substances creates and maintains sexual tension; the
pressure of these products upon the walls of the vesicles containing them might be supposed to act as a stimulus upon a
spinal centre, the condition of which would be perceived by
higher centres and would then give rise in consciousness to the
familiar sensation of tension. If the excitation of the erotogenic
zones increases sexual tension, this could only come about on
the supposition that the zones in question are in an anatomical
connection that has already been laid down with these centres,
that they increase the tonus of the excitation in them, and, if
the sexual tension is sufficient, set the sexual act in motion or,
if it is insufficient, stimulate the production of the sexual substances.[1]

The weakness of this theory, which we find accepted, for
instance, in Krafft-Ebing's account of the sexual processes, lies

[1] [This hypothesis had been discussed by Freud earlier: in Section
III of his first paper on anxiety neurosis (1895*b*).]

in the fact that, having been designed to account for the sexual activity of adult males, it takes too little account of three sets of conditions which it should also be able to explain. These are the conditions in children, in females and in castrated males. In none of these three cases can there be any question of an accumulation of sexual products in the same sense as in males, and this makes a smooth application of the theory difficult. Nevertheless it may at once be admitted that it is possible to find means by which the theory may be made to cover these cases as well. In any case we are warned not to lay more weight on the factor of the accumulation of the sexual products than it is able to bear.

IMPORTANCE OF THE INTERNAL SEXUAL ORGANS　　Observations on castrated males seem to show that sexual excitation can occur to a considerable degree independently of the production of the sexual substances. The operation of castration occasionally fails to bring about a limitation of libido, although such limitation, which provides the motive for the operation, is the usual outcome. Moreover, it has long been known that diseases which abolish the production of the masculine sex-cells leave the patient, though he is now sterile, with his libido and potency undamaged.[1] It is therefore by no means as astonishing as Rieger [1900] represents it to be that the loss of the masculine sex-glands in an adult may have no further effect upon his mental behaviour.[2] It is true that if castration is performed at a tender age, before puberty, it approximates in its effect to the aim of obliterating the sexual characters; but here too it is possible that what is in question is, besides the actual loss of the sex-glands, an inhibition (connected with that loss) in the development of other factors.

----

[1] [This sentence was added in 1920.]

[2] [The following sentence occurs at this point in editions before 1920, when it was omitted: 'For the sex-glands do not constitute sexuality, and the observations on castrated males merely confirm what had been shown long before by removal of the ovaries—namely that it is impossible to obliterate the sexual characters by removing the sex-glands.' Before 1920, too, the second half of the next sentence began: 'but it seems that what is in question here is not the actual loss of the sex-glands but an inhibition . . .']

CHEMICAL   Experiments in the removal of the sex-glands
THEORY   (testes and ovaries) of animals, and in the grafting
                into vertebrates of sex-glands from other individuals
of the opposite sex,[1] have at last thrown a partial light on the
origin of sexual excitation, and have at the same time still
further reduced the significance of a possible accumulation of
cellular sexual products. It has become experimentally possible
(E. Steinach) to transform a male into a female, and conversely
a female into a male. In this process the psychosexual behaviour
of the animal alters in accordance with the somatic sexual
characters and simultaneously with them. It seems, however,
that this sex-determining influence is not an attribute of that
part of the sex-glands which gives rise to the specific sex-cells
(spermatozoa and ovum) but of their interstitial tissue, upon
which special emphasis is laid by being described in the literature as the 'puberty-gland'. It is quite possible that further
investigation will show that this puberty-gland has normally a
hermaphrodite disposition. If this were so, the theory of the
bisexuality of the higher animals would be given anatomical
foundation. It is already probable that the puberty-gland is not
the only organ concerned with the production of sexual excitation and sexual characters. In any case, what we already know
of the part played by the thyroid gland in sexuality fits in with
this new biological discovery. It seems probable, then, that
special chemical substances are produced in the interstitial portion of the sex-glands; these are then taken up in the blood
stream and cause particular parts of the central nervous
system to be charged with sexual tension. (We are already
familiar with the fact that other toxic substances, introduced
into the body from outside, can bring about a similar transformation of a toxic condition into a stimulus acting on a
particular organ.) The question of how sexual excitation arises
from the stimulation of erotogenic zones, when the central apparatus has been previously charged, and the question of what
interplay arises in the course of these sexual processes between
the effects of purely toxic stimuli and of physiological ones—
none of this can be treated, even hypothetically, in the present
state of our knowledge. It must suffice us to hold firmly to what
is essential in this view of the sexual processes: the assumption

[1] Cf. Lipschütz's work (1919), quoted on p. 43 n.

that substances of a peculiar kind arise from the sexual meta-
bolism.[1] For this apparently arbitrary supposition is supported
by a fact which has received little attention but deserves the
closest consideration. The neuroses, which can be derived only
from disturbances of sexual life, show the greatest clinical simi-
larity to the phenomena of intoxication and abstinence that
arise from the habitual use of toxic, pleasure-producing substances (alkaloids).

[1] [The whole of this paragraph as far as this point dates in its present
form from 1920. In the first edition (1905) and the two subsequent ones
the following passage appears in its place: 'The truth is that we can
give no information on the nature of sexual excitation, especially since
(having found that the importance of the sex-glands in this respect has
been over-estimated) we are in the dark as to the organ or organs to
which sexuality is attached. After the surprising discoveries of the important part played by the thyroid gland in sexuality, it is reasonable
to suspect that we are still ignorant of the essential factors of sexuality.
Anyone who feels the need of a provisional hypothesis to fill this wide
gap in our knowledge may well take as his starting-point the powerful
substances which have been found to be present in the thyroid gland and
may proceed along some such lines as the following. It may be supposed
that, as a result of an appropriate stimulation of erotogenic zones, or in
other circumstances that are accompanied by an onset of sexual excitation, some substance that is disseminated generally throughout the
organism becomes decomposed and the products of its decomposition
give rise to a specific stimulus which acts on the reproductive organs
or upon a spinal centre related to them. (We are already familiar with
the fact that other toxic substances, introduced into the body from
outside, can bring about a similar transformation of a toxic condition
into a stimulus acting on a particular organ.) The question of what
interplay arises in the course of the sexual processes between the effects
of purely toxic stimuli and of physiological ones cannot be treated, even
hypothetically, in the present state of our knowledge. I may add that I
attach no importance to this particular hypothesis and should be ready
to abandon it at once in favour of another, provided that its fundamental nature remained unchanged—that is, the emphasis which it lays
upon sexual chemistry.'—It is worth remarking how small a modification was made necessary in Freud's hypothesis by the discovery of
the sex-hormones, which, indeed, he had anticipated not merely in
1905 but at least as early as in 1896, as may be seen from his two letters
to Fliess, of March 1 and April 2 of that year (Freud, 1950a, Letters 42
and 44). He further insisted upon the importance of the chemical factor
in his second paper on the part played by sexuality in the neuroses,
published at about the same time as the first edition of the *Three Essays*
(1906a, *Standard Ed.*, **7**, 279). See Addenda, p. 112.]

[3] THE LIBIDO THEORY [1]

The conceptual scaffolding which we have set up to help us in dealing with the psychical manifestations of sexual life tallies well with these hypotheses as to the chemical basis of sexual excitation. We have defined the concept of libido as a quantitatively variable force which could serve as a measure of processes and transformations occurring in the field of sexual excitation. We distinguish this libido in respect of its special origin from the energy which must be supposed to underlie mental processes in general, and we thus also attribute a *qualitative* character to it. In thus distinguishing between libidinal and other forms of psychical energy we are giving expression to the presumption that the sexual processes occurring in the organism are distinguished from the nutritive processes by a special chemistry. The analysis of the perversions and psychoneuroses has shown us that this sexual excitation is derived not from the so-called sexual parts alone, but from all the bodily organs. We thus reach the idea of a quantity of libido, to the mental representation of which we give the name of 'ego-libido', and whose production, increase or diminution, distribution and displacement should afford us possibilities for explaining the psychosexual phenomena observed.

This ego-libido is, however, only conveniently accessible to analytic study when it has been put to the use of cathecting sexual objects, that is, when it has become object-libido. We can then perceive it concentrating upon objects,[2] becoming fixed upon them or abandoning them, moving from one object to another and, from these situations, directing the subject's sexual activity, which leads to the satisfaction, that is, to the partial and temporary extinction, of the libido. The psychoanalysis of what are termed transference neuroses (hysteria and obsessional neurosis) affords us a clear insight at this point.

We can follow the object-libido through still further vicissitudes. When it is withdrawn from objects, it is held in suspense

[1] [This whole section, except for its last paragraph, dates from 1915. It is largely based on Freud's paper on narcissism (1914c).]

[2] [It is scarcely necessary to explain that here as elsewhere, in speaking of the libido concentrating on 'objects', withdrawing from 'objects', etc., Freud has in mind the mental presentations (*Vorstellungen*) of objects and not, of course, objects in the external world.]

in peculiar conditions of tension and is finally drawn back into the ego, so that it becomes ego-libido once again. In contrast to object-libido, we also describe ego-libido as 'narcissistic' libido. From the vantage-point of psycho-analysis we can look across a frontier, which we may not pass, at the activities of narcissistic libido, and may form some idea of the relation between it and object-libido.[1] Narcissistic or ego-libido seems to be the great reservoir from which the object-cathexes are sent out and into which they are withdrawn once more; the narcissistic libidinal cathexis of the ego is the original state of things, realized in earliest childhood, and is merely covered by the later extrusions of libido, but in essentials persists behind them.

It should be the task of a libido theory of neurotic and psychotic disorders to express all the observed phenomena and inferred processes in terms of the economics of the libido. It is easy to guess that the vicissitudes of the ego-libido will have the major part to play in this connection, especially when it is a question of explaining the deeper psychotic disturbances. We are then faced by the difficulty that our method of research, psycho-analysis, for the moment affords us assured information only on the transformations that take place in the object-libido,[2] but is unable to make any immediate distinction between the ego-libido and the other forms of energy operating in the ego.[3]

For the present, therefore,[4] no further development of the libido theory is possible, except upon speculative lines. It would, however, be sacrificing all that we have gained hitherto from psycho-analytic observation, if we were to follow the example of C. G. Jung and water down the meaning of the concept of libido itself by equating it with psychical instinctual force in general. The distinguishing of the sexual instinctual impulses from the rest and the consequent restriction of the concept of libido to the former receives strong support from the assumption

[1] [*Footnote added* 1924:] Since neuroses other than the transference neuroses have become to a greater extent accessible to psycho-analysis, this limitation has lost its earlier validity.

[2] [*Footnote added* 1924:] See the previous footnote.

[3] [*Footnote added* 1915:] Cf. my paper on narcissism (1914c). [*Added* 1920:] The term 'narcissism' was not introduced, as I erroneously stated in that paper, by Näcke, but by Havelock Ellis. [Ellis himself subsequently (1928) discussed this point in detail and considered that the honours should be divided.]

[4] [This paragraph was added in 1920.]

which I have already discussed that there is a special chemistry of the sexual function.

[4] THE DIFFERENTIATION BETWEEN MEN AND WOMEN

As we all know, it is not until puberty that the sharp distinction is established between the masculine and feminine characters. From that time on, this contrast has a more decisive influence than any other upon the shaping of human life. It is true that the masculine and feminine dispositions are already easily recognizable in childhood. The development of the inhibitions of sexuality (shame, disgust, pity, etc.) takes place in little girls earlier and in the face of less resistance than in boys; the tendency to sexual repression seems in general to be greater; and, where the component instincts of sexuality appear, they prefer the passive form. The auto-erotic activity of the erotogenic zones is, however, the same in both sexes, and owing to this uniformity there is no possibility of a distinction between the two sexes such as arises after puberty. So far as the auto-erotic and masturbatory manifestations of sexuality are concerned, we might lay it down that the sexuality of little girls is of a wholly masculine character. Indeed, if we were able to give a more definite connotation to the concepts of 'masculine' and 'feminine', it would even be possible to maintain that libido is invariably and necessarily of a masculine nature, whether it occurs in men or in women and irrespectively of whether its object is a man or a woman.[1]

[1] [Before 1924 the words from 'libido' to the end of the sentence were printed in spaced type.—*Footnote added* 1915:] It is essential to understand clearly that the concepts of 'masculine' and 'feminine', whose meaning seems so unambiguous to ordinary people, are among the most confused that occur in science. It is possible to distinguish at least three uses. 'Masculine' and 'feminine' are used sometimes in the sense of activity and passivity, sometimes in a biological, and sometimes, again, in a sociological sense. The first of these three meanings is the essential one and the most serviceable in psycho-analysis. When, for instance, libido was described in the text above as being 'masculine', the word was being used in this sense, for an instinct is always active even when it has a passive aim in view. The second, or biological, meaning of 'masculine' and 'feminine' is the one whose applicability can be determined most easily. Here 'masculine' and 'feminine' are characterized by the presence of spermatozoa or ova respectively and by the

Since I have become acquainted [1] with the notion of bisexuality I have regarded it as the decisive factor, and without taking bisexuality into account I think it would scarcely be possible to arrive at an understanding of the sexual manifestations that are actually to be observed in men and women.

LEADING ZONES IN MEN AND WOMEN   Apart from this I have only the following to add. The leading erotogenic zone in female children is located at the clitoris, and is thus homologous to the masculine genital zone of the glans penis. All my experience concerning masturbation in little girls has related to the clitoris and not to the regions of the external genitalia that are important in later sexual functioning. I am even doubtful whether a female child can be led by the influence of seduction to anything other than clitoridal masturbation. If such a thing occurs, it is quite exceptional. The spontaneous discharges of sexual excitement which occur so often precisely in little girls are expressed in spasms of the clitoris. Frequent erections of that organ make it possible for girls to form a correct judgement, even without any instruction, of the sexual manifestations of the other sex: they merely transfer on to boys the sensations derived from their own sexual processes.

If we are to understand how a little girl turns into a woman, we must follow the further vicissitudes of this excitability of the clitoris. Puberty, which brings about so great an accession of libido in boys, is marked in girls by a fresh wave of *repression*, in which it is precisely clitoridal sexuality that is affected. What is

functions proceeding from them. Activity and its concomitant phenomena (more powerful muscular development, aggressiveness, greater intensity of libido) are as a rule linked with biological masculinity; but they are not necessarily so, for there are animal species in which these qualities are on the contrary assigned to the female. The third, or sociological, meaning receives its connotation frcm the observation of actually existing masculine and feminine individuals. Such observation shows that in human beings pure masculinity or femininity is not to be found either in a psychological or a biological sense. Every individual on the contrary displays a mixture of the character-traits belonging to his own and to the opposite sex; and he shows a combination of activity and passivity whether or not these last character-traits tally with his biological ones. [A later discussion of this point will be found in a footnote at the end of Chapter IV of *Civilization and its Discontents* (1930a).]

[1] [In 1905 only: 'through Wilhelm Fliess'. Cf. end of footnote, p. 9.]

thus overtaken by repression is a piece of masculine sexuality. The intensification of the brake upon sexuality brought about by pubertal repression in women serves as a stimulus to the libido in men and causes an increase of its activity. Along with this heightening of libido there is also an increase of sexual over-valuation which only emerges in full force in relation to a woman who holds herself back and who denies her sexuality. When at last the sexual act is permitted and the clitoris itself becomes excited, it still retains a function: the task, namely, of transmitting the excitation to the adjacent female sexual parts, just as—to use a simile—pine shavings can be kindled in order to set a log of harder wood on fire. Before this transference can be effected, a certain interval of time must often elapse, during which the young woman is anaesthetic. This anaesthesia may become permanent if the clitoridal zone refuses to abandon its excitability, an event for which the way is prepared precisely by an extensive activity of that zone in childhood. Anaesthesia in women, as is well known, is often only apparent and local. They are anaesthetic at the vaginal orifice but are by no means incapable of excitement originating in the clitoris or even in other zones. Alongside these erotogenic determinants of anaes-thesia must also be set the psychical determinants, which equally arise from repression.

When erotogenic susceptibility to stimulation has been suc-cessfully transferred by a woman from the clitoris to the vaginal orifice, it implies that she has adopted a new leading zone for the purposes of her later sexual activity. A man, on the other hand, retains his leading zone unchanged from childhood. The fact that women change their leading erotogenic zone in this way, together with the wave of repression at puberty, which, as it were, puts aside their childish masculinity, are the chief determinants of the greater proneness of women to neurosis and especially to hysteria. These determinants, therefore, are intim-ately related to the essence of femininity.[1]

------

[1] [The course of development of sexuality in women was further examined by Freud more particularly on four later occasions: in his case history of a homosexual woman (1920a), in his discussion of the conse-quences of the anatomical distinction between the sexes (1925j), in his paper on female sexuality (1931b), and in Lecture XXXIII of his *New Introductory Lectures* (1933a).—See also Addenda, p. 112, below.]

[5] THE FINDING OF AN OBJECT

The processes at puberty thus establish the primacy of the genital zones; and, in a man, the penis, which has now become capable of erection, presses forward insistently towards the new sexual aim—penetration into a cavity in the body which excites his genital zone. Simultaneously on the psychical side the process of finding an object, for which preparations have been made from earliest childhood, is completed. At a time at which the first beginnings of sexual satisfaction are still linked with the taking of nourishment, the sexual instinct has a sexual object outside the infant's own body in the shape of his mother's breast. It is only later that the instinct loses that object, just at the time, perhaps, when the child is able to form a total idea of the person to whom the organ that is giving him satisfaction belongs. As a rule the sexual instinct then becomes auto-erotic, and not until the period of latency has been passed through is the original relation restored. There are thus good reasons why a child sucking at his mother's breast has become the prototype of every relation of love. The finding of an object is in fact a refinding of it.[1]

THE SEXUAL OBJECT DURING EARLY INFANCY   But even after sexual activity has become detached from the taking of nourishment, an important part of this first and most significant of all sexual relations is left over, which helps to prepare for the choice of an object and thus to restore the happiness that has been lost. All through the period of latency children learn to feel for other people who help them in their helplessness and satisfy their needs a love which is on the model of, and a continuation of, their relation as sucklings

---

[1] [*Footnote added* 1915:] Psycho-analysis informs us that there are two methods of finding an object. The first, described in the text, is the 'anaclitic' or 'attachment' one, based on attachment to early infantile prototypes. The second is the narcissistic one, which seeks for the subject's own ego and finds it again in other people. This latter method is of particularly great importance in cases where the outcome is a pathological one, but it is not relevant to the present context. [The point is elaborated in the later part of Section II of Freud's paper on narcissism (1914*c*).—The paragraph in the text above, written in 1905, does not appear to harmonize with the remarks on the subject on pp. 66 and 100, written in 1915 and 1920 respectively.]

to their nursing mother. There may perhaps be an inclination to dispute the possibility of identifying a child's affection and esteem for those who look after him with sexual love. I think, however, that a closer psychological examination may make it possible to establish this identity beyond any doubt. A child's intercourse with anyone responsible for his care affords him an unending source of sexual excitation and satisfaction from his erotogenic zones. This is especially so since the person in charge of him, who, after all, is as a rule his mother, herself regards him with feelings that are derived from her own sexual life: she strokes him, kisses him, rocks him and quite clearly treats him as a substitute for a complete sexual object.[1] A mother would probably be horrified if she were made aware that all her marks of affection were rousing her child's sexual instinct and preparing for its later intensity. She regards what she does as asexual, 'pure' love, since, after all, she carefully avoids applying more excitations to the child's genitals than are unavoidable in nursery care. As we know, however, the sexual instinct is not aroused only by direct excitation of the genital zone. What we call affection will unfailingly show its effects one day on the genital zones as well. Moreover, if the mother understood more of the high importance of the part played by instincts in mental life as a whole—in all its ethical and psychical achievements—she would spare herself any self-reproaches even after her enlightenment. She is only fulfilling her task in teaching the child to love. After all, he is meant to grow up into a strong and capable person with vigorous sexual needs and to accomplish during his life all the things that human beings are urged to do by their instincts. It is true that an excess of parental affection does harm by causing precocious sexual maturity and also because, by spoiling the child, it makes him incapable in later life of temporarily doing without love or of being content with a smaller amount of it. One of the clearest indications that a child will later become neurotic is to be seen in an insatiable demand for his parents' affection. And on the other hand neuropathic parents, who are inclined as a rule to display excessive affection, are precisely those who are most likely by their caresses to arouse the child's disposition to neurotic illness.

[1] Anyone who considers this 'sacrilegious' may be recommended to read Havelock Ellis's views [1913, 18] on the relation between mother and child, which agree almost completely with mine.

Incidentally, this example shows that there are ways more direct than inheritance by which neurotic parents can hand their disorder on to their children.

INFANTILE   Children themselves behave from an early age
ANXIETY   as though their dependence on the people looking
after them were in the nature of sexual love. Anxiety in children is originally nothing other than an expression of the fact that they are feeling the loss of the person they love. It is for this reason that they are frightened of every stranger. They are afraid in the dark because in the dark they cannot see the person they love; and their fear is soothed if they can take hold of that person's hand in the dark. To attribute to bogeys and blood-curdling stories told by nurses the responsibility for making children timid is to over-estimate their efficacy. The truth is merely that children who are inclined to be timid are affected by stories which would make no impression whatever upon others, and it is only children with a sexual instinct that is excessive or has developed prematurely or has become vociferous owing to too much petting who are inclined to be timid. In this respect a child, by turning his libido into anxiety when he cannot satisfy it, behaves like an adult. On the other hand an adult who has become neurotic owing to his libido being unsatisfied behaves in his anxiety like a child: he begins to be frightened when he is alone, that is to say when he is away from someone of whose love he had felt secure, and he seeks to assuage this fear by the most childish measures.[1]

[1] For this explanation of the origin of infantile anxiety I have to thank a three-year-old boy whom I once heard calling out of a dark room: 'Auntie, speak to me! I'm frightened because it's so dark.' His aunt answered him: 'What good would that do? You can't see me.' 'That doesn't matter,' replied the child, 'if anyone speaks, it gets light.' Thus what he was afraid of was not the dark, but the absence of someone he loved; and he could feel sure of being soothed as soon as he had evidence of that person's presence. [*Added* 1920:] One of the most important results of psycho-analytic research is this discovery that neurotic anxiety arises out of libido, that it is the product of a transformation of it, and that it is thus related to it in the same kind of way as vinegar is to wine. A further discussion of this problem will be found in my *Introductory Lectures on Psycho-Analysis* (1916–17), Lecture XXV, though even there, it must be confessed, the question is not finally cleared up. [For Freud's latest views on the subject of anxiety see his *Inhibitions, Symptoms and Anxiety* (1926d) and his *New Introductory Lectures* (1933a), Chapter XXXII.]

THE BARRIER   We see, therefore, that the parents' affec-
AGAINST INCEST [1] tion for their child may awaken his sexual
instinct prematurely (i.e. before the somatic
conditions of puberty are present) to such a degree that the
mental excitation breaks through in an unmistakable fashion to
the genital system. If, on the other hand, they are fortunate
enough to avoid this, then their affection can perform its task
of directing the child in his choice of a sexual object when he
reaches maturity. No doubt the simplest course for the child
would be to choose as his sexual objects the same persons
whom, since his childhood, he has loved with what may be
described as damped-down libido.[2] But, by the postponing of
sexual maturation, time has been gained in which the child can
erect, among other restraints on sexuality, the barrier against
incest, and can thus take up into himself the moral precepts
which expressly exclude from his object-choice, as being blood-
relations, the persons whom he has loved in his childhood.
Respect for this barrier is essentially a cultural demand made
by society. Society must defend itself against the danger that
the interests which it needs for the establishment of higher
social units may be swallowed up by the family; and for this
reason, in the case of every individual, but in particular of
adolescent boys, it seeks by all possible means to loosen their
connection with their family—a connection which, in their
childhood, is the only important one.[3]

It is in the world of ideas, however, that the choice of an
object is accomplished at first; and the sexual life of maturing

[1] [This side-heading was omitted, probably by an oversight, from
1924 onwards.]

[2] [*Footnote added* 1915:] Cf. what has been said on p. 66 about
children's object-choice and the 'affectionate current'.

[3] [*Footnote added* 1915:] The barrier against incest is probably among
the historical acquisitions of mankind, and, like other moral taboos, has
no doubt already become established in many persons by organic inheritance. (Cf. my *Totem and Taboo*, 1912–13.) Psycho-analytic investigation shows, however, how intensely the individual struggles with the
temptation to incest during his period of growth and how frequently the
barrier is transgressed in phantasies and even in reality.—[Though this
is its first published appearance, the 'horror of incest' had been discussed by Freud on May 31, 1897 (Draft N in Freud, 1950a)—some
months, that is, before his first revelation of the Oedipus complex.
In that draft too he accounts for it on the ground that incest is
'antisocial'.]

youth is almost entirely restricted to indulging in phantasies, that is, in ideas that are not destined to be carried into effect.[1] In these phantasies the infantile tendencies invariably emerge

[1] [*Footnote added* 1920:] The phantasies of the pubertal period have as their starting-point the infantile sexual researches that were abandoned in childhood. No doubt, too, they are also present before the end of the latency period. They may persist wholly, or to a great extent, unconsciously and for that reason it is often impossible to date them accurately. They are of great importance in the origin of many symptoms, since they precisely constitute preliminary stages of these symptoms and thus lay down the forms in which the repressed libidinal components find satisfaction. In the same way, they are the prototypes of the nocturnal phantasies which become conscious as dreams. Dreams are often nothing more than revivals of pubertal phantasies of this kind under the influence of, and in relation to, some stimulus left over from the waking life of the previous day (the 'day's residues'). [See Chapter VII, Section I, of *The Interpretation of Dreams* (1900*a*); Standard Ed., **5**, 492 f.] Some among the sexual phantasies of the pubertal period are especially prominent, and are distinguished by their very general occurrence and by being to a great extent independent of individual experience. Such are the adolescent's phantasies of overhearing his parents in sexual intercourse, of having been seduced at an early age by someone he loves and of having been threatened with castration [cf. the discussion of 'primal phantasies' in Lecture XXIII of Freud's *Introductory Lectures* (1916–17)]; such, too, are his phantasies of being in the womb, and even of experiences there, and the so-called 'Family Romance', in which he reacts to the difference between his attitude towards his parents now and in his childhood. The close relations existing between these phantasies and myths has been demonstrated in the case of the last instance by Otto Rank (1909). [Cf. also Freud's own paper on 'Family Romances' (1909*c*) and his long footnote to Section G of Part I of his case history of the 'Rat Man' (1909*d*).]

It has justly been said that the Oedipus complex is the nuclear complex of the neuroses, and constitutes the essential part of their content. It represents the peak of infantile sexuality, which, through its after-effects, exercises a decisive influence on the sexuality of adults. Every new arrival on this planet is faced by the task of mastering the Oedipus complex; anyone who fails to do so falls a victim to neurosis. With the progress of psycho-analytic studies the importance of the Oedipus complex has became more and more clearly evident; its recognition has become the shibboleth that distinguishes the adherents of psycho-analysis from its opponents.

[*Added* 1924:] In another work (1924), Rank has traced attachment to the mother back to the prehistoric intra-uterine period and has thus indicated the biological foundation of the Oedipus complex. He differs from what has been said above, by deriving the barrier against incest from the traumatic effect of anxiety at birth. [See Chapter X of *Inhibitions, Symptoms and Anxiety* (1926*d*).]

once more, but this time with intensified pressure from somatic sources. Among these tendencies the first place is taken with uniform frequency by the child's sexual impulses towards his parents, which are as a rule already differentiated owing to the attraction of the opposite sex—the son being drawn towards his mother and the daughter towards her father.[1] At the same time as these plainly incestuous phantasies are overcome and repudiated, one of the most significant, but also one of the most painful, psychical achievements of the pubertal period is completed: detachment from parental authority, a process that alone makes possible the opposition, which is so important for the progress of civilization, between the new generation and the old. At every stage in the course of development through which all human beings ought by rights to pass, a certain number are held back; so there are some who have never got over their parents' authority and have withdrawn their affection from them either very incompletely or not at all. They are mostly girls, who, to the delight of their parents, have persisted in all their childish love far beyond puberty. It is most instructive to find that it is precisely these girls who in their later marriage lack the capacity to give their husbands what is due to them; they make cold wives and remain sexually anaesthetic. We learn from this that sexual love and what appears to be non-sexual love for parents are fed from the same sources; the latter, that is to say, merely corresponds to an infantile fixation of the libido.

The closer one comes to the deeper disturbances of psychosexual development, the more unmistakably the importance of incestuous object-choice emerges. In psychoneurotics a large portion or the whole of their psychosexual activity in finding an object remains in the unconscious as a result of their repudiation of sexuality. Girls with an exaggerated need for affection and an equally exaggerated horror of the real demands made by sexual life have an irresistible temptation on the one hand to realize the ideal of asexual love in their lives and on the other hand to conceal their libido behind an affection which they can express without self-reproaches, by holding fast throughout their lives to their infantile fondness, revived at

[1] Cf. my remarks in *The Interpretation of Dreams* (1900a), on the inevitability of Fate in the fable of Oedipus [Chapter V, Section D (β); Standard Ed., **4**, 260 ff.].

puberty, for their parents or brothers and sisters. Psycho-analysis has no difficulty in showing persons of this kind that they are *in love*, in the everyday sense of the word, with these blood-relations of theirs; for, with the help of their symptoms and other manifestations of their illness, it traces their unconscious thoughts and translates them into conscious ones. In cases in which someone who has previously been healthy falls ill after an unhappy experience in love it is also possible to show with certainty that the mechanism of his illness consists in a turning-back of his libido on to those whom he preferred in his infancy.

AFTER-EFFECTS   Even a person who has been fortunate
OF INFANTILE   enough to avoid an incestuous fixation of his
OBJECT-CHOICE   libido does not entirely escape its influence. It
often happens that a young man falls in love seriously for the first time with a mature woman, or a girl with an elderly man in a position of authority; this is clearly an echo of the phase of development that we have been discussing, since these figures are able to re-animate pictures of their mother or father.[1] There can be no doubt that every object-choice whatever is based, though less closely, on these prototypes. A man, especially, looks for someone who can represent his picture of his mother, as it has dominated his mind from his earliest childhood; and accordingly, if his mother is still alive, she may well resent this new version of herself and meet her with hostility. In view of the importance of a child's relations to his parents in determining his later choice of a sexual object, it can easily be understood that any disturbance of those relations will produce the gravest effects upon his adult sexual life. Jealousy in a lover is never without an infantile root or at least an infantile reinforcement. If there are quarrels between the parents or if their marriage is unhappy, the ground will be prepared in their children for the severest predisposition to a disturbance of sexual development or to a neurotic illness.

A child's affection for his parents is no doubt the most important infantile trace which, after being revived at puberty, points the way to his choice of an object; but it is not the only one. Other starting-points with the same early origin enable a

[1] [*Footnote added* 1920:] Cf. my paper 'A Special Type of Choice of Object made by Men' (1910*h*).

man to develop more than one sexual line, based no less upon his childhood, and to lay down very various conditions for his object-choice.[1]

PREVENTION OF   One of the tasks implicit in object-choice is
INVERSION   that it should find its way to the opposite sex.
This, as we know, is not accomplished without a certain amount of fumbling. Often enough the first impulses after puberty go astray, though without any permanent harm resulting. Dessoir [1894] has justly remarked upon the regularity with which adolescent boys and girls form sentimental friendships with others of their own sex. No doubt the strongest force working against a permanent inversion of the sexual object is the attraction which the opposing sexual characters exercise upon one another. Nothing can be said within the framework of the present discussion to throw light upon it.[2] This factor is not in itself, however, sufficient to exclude inversion; there are no doubt a variety of other contributory factors. Chief among these is its authoritative prohibition by society. Where inversion is not regarded as a crime it will be found that it answers fully to the sexual inclinations of no small number of people. It may be presumed, in the next place, that in the case of men a childhood recollection of the affection shown them by their mother and others of the female sex who looked after them when they were children contributes powerfully to directing their choice towards women;[3] on the other hand their early experience of being deterred by their father from sexual activity and their competitive relation with him deflect them from their own sex. Both of these two factors apply equally to girls, whose sexual

[1] [*Footnote added* 1915:] The innumerable peculiarities of the erotic life of human beings as well as the compulsive character of the process of falling in love itself are quite unintelligible except by reference back to childhood and as being residual effects of childhood.

[2] [*Footnote added* 1924:] This is the place at which to draw attention to Ferenczi's *Versuch einer Genitaltheorie* (1924), a work which, though somewhat fanciful, is nevertheless of the greatest interest, and in which the sexual life of the higher animals is traced back to their biological evolution.

[3] [The rest of this sentence and the two following ones date from 1915. In the editions of 1905 and 1910 the following passage takes their place: 'while in the case of girls, who in any case enter a period of repression at puberty, impulses of rivalry play a part in discouraging them from loving members of their own sex.']

activity is particularly subject to the watchful guardianship of their mother. They thus acquire a hostile relation to their own sex which influences their object-choice decisively in what is regarded as the normal direction. The education of boys by male persons (by slaves, in antiquity) seems to encourage homosexuality. The frequency of inversion among the present-day aristocracy is made somewhat more intelligible by their employment of menservants, as well as by the fact that their mothers give less personal care to their children. In the case of some hysterics it is found that the early loss of one of their parents, whether by death, divorce or separation, with the result that the remaining parent absorbs the whole of the child's love, determines the sex of the person who is later to be chosen as a sexual object, and may thus open the way to permanent inversion.

SUMMARY

THE time has arrived for me to attempt to summarize what I have said. We started out from the aberrations of the sexual instinct in respect of its object and of its aim and we were faced by the question of whether these arise from an innate disposition or are acquired as a result of experiences in life. We arrived at an answer to this question from an understanding, derived from psycho-analytic investigation, of the workings of the sexual instinct in psychoneurotics, a numerous class of people and one not far removed from the healthy. We found that in them tendencies to every kind of perversion can be shown to exist as unconscious forces and betray their presence as factors leading to the formation of symptoms. It was thus possible to say that neurosis is, as it were, the negative of perversion. In view of what was now seen to be the wide dissemination of tendencies to perversion we were driven to the conclusion that a disposition to perversions is an original and universal disposition of the human sexual instinct and that normal sexual behaviour is developed out of it as a result of organic changes and psychical inhibitions occurring in the course of maturation; we hoped to be able to show the presence of this original disposition in childhood. Among the forces restricting the direction taken by the sexual instinct we laid emphasis upon shame, disgust, pity and the structures of morality and authority erected by society. We were thus led to regard any established aberration from normal sexuality as an instance of developmental inhibition and infantilism. Though it was necessary to place in the foreground the importance of the variations in the original disposition, a co-operative and not an opposing relation was to be assumed as existing between them and the influences of actual life. It appeared, on the other hand, that since the original disposition is necessarily a complex one, the sexual instinct itself must be something put together from various factors, and that in the perversions it falls apart, as it were, into its components. The perversions were thus seen to be on the one hand inhibitions, and on the other hand dissociations, of normal development. Both these aspects were brought together in the supposition that the sexual instinct of adults arises from a combination of a number of impulses of childhood into a unity, an impulsion with a single aim.

After having explained the preponderance of perverse tendencies in psychoneurotics by recognizing it as a collateral filling of subsidiary channels when the main current of the instinctual stream has been blocked by 'repression',[1] we proceeded to a consideration of sexual life in childhood. We found it a regrettable thing that the existence of the sexual instinct in childhood has been denied and that the sexual manifestations not infrequently to be observed in children have been described as irregularities. It seemed to us on the contrary that children bring germs of sexual activity with them into the world, that they already enjoy sexual satisfaction when they begin to take nourishment and that they persistently seek to repeat the experience in the familiar activity of 'thumb-sucking'. The sexual activity of children, however, does not, it appeared, develop *pari passu* with their other functions, but, after a short period of efflorescence from the ages of two to five,[2] enters upon the so-called period of latency. During that period the production of sexual excitation is not by any means stopped but continues and produces a store of energy which is employed to a great extent for purposes other than sexual—namely, on the one hand in contributing the sexual components to social feelings and on the other hand (through repression and reaction-forming) in building up the subsequently developed barriers against sexuality. On this view, the forces destined to retain the sexual instinct upon certain lines are built up in childhood chiefly at the cost of perverse sexual impulses and with the assistance of education. A certain portion of the infantile sexual impulses would seem to evade these uses and succeed in expressing itself as sexual activity. We next found that sexual excitation in children springs from a multiplicity of forces. Satis-

---

[1] [*Footnote added* 1915:] This does not apply only to the 'negative' tendencies to perversion which appear in neuroses but equally to the 'positive', properly so-called, perversions. Thus these latter are to be derived not merely from a fixation of infantile tendencies but also from a regression to those tendencies as a result of other channels of the sexual current being blocked. It is for this reason that the positive perversions also are accessible to psycho-analytic therapy.

[2] [The last seven words were first inserted in 1915. In the edition of that year, however, the ages given were 'three to five'. The 'two' was substituted in 1920.]

faction arises first and foremost from the appropriate sensory excitation of what we have described as erotogenic zones. It seems probable that any part of the skin and any sense-organ —probably, indeed, *any* organ[1]—can function as an erotogenic zone, though there are some particularly marked erotogenic zones whose excitation would seem to be secured from the very first by certain organic contrivances. It further appears that sexual excitation arises as a by-product, as it were, of a large number of processes that occur in the organism, as soon as they reach a certain degree of intensity, and most especially of any relatively powerful emotion, even though it is of a distressing nature. The excitations from all these sources are not yet combined; but each follows its own separate aim, which is merely the attainment of a certain sort of pleasure. In childhood, therefore, the sexual instinct is not unified and is at first[2] without an object, that is, auto-erotic.

The erotogenic zone of the genitals begins to make itself noticeable, it seems, even during the years of childhood. This may happen in two ways. Either, like any other erotogenic zone, it yields satisfaction in response to appropriate sensory stimulation; or, in a manner which is not quite understandable, when satisfaction is derived from other sources, a sexual excitation is simultaneously produced which has a special relation to the genital zone. We were reluctantly obliged to admit that we could not satisfactorily explain the relation between sexual satisfaction and sexual excitation, or that between the activity of the genital zone and the activity of the other sources of sexuality.

We found from the study of neurotic disorders[3] that beginnings of an organization of the sexual instinctual components can be detected in the sexual life of children from its very beginning. During a first, very early phase, oral erotism occupies most of the picture. A second of these pregenital organizations is characterized by the predominance of sadism and anal erotism. It is not until a third phase has been reached that the genital zones proper contribute their share in determining sexual life, and in children this last phase is developed only so far as to a primacy of the phallus.[4]

[1] [This parenthesis was added in 1915.]
[2] [The words 'not unified and is at first' were added in 1920.]
[3] [This and the next two paragraphs were added in 1920.]
[4] [The last clause was added in 1924.]

We were then obliged to recognize, as one of our most surprising findings, that this early efflorescence of infantile sexual life (between the ages of two and five) already gives rise to the choice of an object, with all the wealth of mental activities which such a process involves.[1] Thus, in spite of the lack of synthesis between the different instinctual components and the uncertainty of the sexual aim, the phase of development corresponding to that period must be regarded as an important precursor of the subsequent final sexual organization.

The fact that the onset of sexual development in human beings occurs in two phases, i.e. that the development is interrupted by the period of latency, seemed to call for particular notice. This appears to be one of the necessary conditions of the aptitude of men for developing a higher civilization, but also of their tendency to neurosis. So far as we know, nothing analogous is to be found in man's animal relatives. It would seem that the origin of this peculiarity of man must be looked for in the prehistory of the human species.

It was not possible to say what amount of sexual activity can occur in childhood without being described as abnormal or detrimental to further development. The nature of these sexual manifestations was found to be predominantly masturbatory. Experience further showed that the external influences of seduction are capable of provoking interruptions of the latency period or even its cessation, and that in this connection the sexual instinct of children proves in fact to be polymorphously perverse; it seems, moreover, that any such premature sexual activity diminishes a child's educability.

In spite of the gaps in our knowledge of infantile sexual life, we had to proceed to an attempt at examining the alterations brought about in it by the arrival of puberty. We selected two of these as being the decisive ones: the subordination of all the other sources of sexual excitation under the primacy of the genital zones and the process of finding an object. Both of these are already adumbrated in childhood. The first is accomplished by the mechanism of exploiting fore-pleasure: what were formerly self-contained sexual acts, attended by pleasure and excitation, become acts preparatory to the new sexual aim (the discharge of the sexual products), the attainment of which enormously pleasurable, brings the sexual excitation to an end.

[1] [Cf. the end of the footnote on p. 88.]

In this connection we had to take into account the differentiation of sexuality into masculine and feminine; and we found
that in order to become a woman a further stage of repression
is necessary, which discards a portion of infantile masculinity
and prepares the woman for changing her leading genital zone.
As regards object-choice, we found that it is given its direction
by the childhood hints (revived at puberty) of the child's
sexual inclination towards his parents and others in charge of
him, but that it is diverted away from them, on to other people
who resemble them, owing to the barrier against incest which
has meanwhile been erected. Finally it must be added that
during the transition period of puberty the processes of somatic
and of psychical development continue for a time side by side
independently, until the irruption of an intense mental erotic
impulse, leading to the innervation of the genitals, brings about
the unity of the erotic function which is necessary for normality.

FACTORS   Every step on this long path of development
INTERFERING   can become a point of fixation, every juncture
WITH   in this involved combination can be an occasion
DEVELOPMENT   for a dissociation of the sexual instinct, as we
                            have already shown from numerous instances.[1]
It remains for us to enumerate the various factors, internal and
external, that interfere with development, and to indicate the
place in the mechanism on which the disturbance arising from
each of them impinges. The factors that we shall enumerate can
evidently not be of equal importance, and we must be prepared
for difficulties in assigning an appropriate value to each.

CONSTITUTION   First and foremost we must name the innate
AND HEREDITY   variety of sexual constitutions, upon which it
                            is probable that the principal weight falls, but
which can clearly only be inferred from their later manifestations and even then not always with great certainty. We picture
this variety as a preponderance of one or another of the many

---

[1] [The further problem of a possible relation between the point of
fixation and the type of neurosis developed—the problem of the 'choice
of neurosis'—is not dealt with in these essays, though it had long been
in Freud's thoughts. See, for instance, his letters to Fliess of May 30,
1896, and of December 9, 1899 (Freud, 1950a, Letters 46 and 125). The
subject was touched on in a paper almost contemporary with the

sources of sexual excitation, and it is our view that a difference in disposition of this kind is always bound to find expression in the final result, even though that result may not overstep the limits of what is normal. No doubt it is conceivable that there may also be variations in the original disposition of a kind which must necessarily, and without the concurrence of any other factors, lead to the development of an abnormal sexual life. These might be described as 'degenerative' and be regarded as an expression of inherited degeneracy. In this connection I have a remarkable fact to record. In more than half of the severe cases of hysteria, obsessional neurosis, etc., which I have treated psychotherapeutically, I have been able to prove with certainty that the patient's father suffered from syphilis before marriage, whether there was evidence of tabes or general para- lysis, or whether the anamnesis indicated in some other way the presence of syphilitic disease. I should like to make it per- fectly plain that the children who later became neurotic bore no physical signs of hereditary syphilis, so that it was their abnormal sexual constitution that was to be regarded as the last echo of their syphilitic heritage. Though I am far from wishing to assert that descent from syphilitic parents is an invariable or indispensable aetiological condition of a neuro- pathic constitution, I am nevertheless of opinion that the co- incidence which I have observed is neither accidental nor unimportant.

The hereditary conditions in the case of positive perverts are less well known, for they know how to avoid investigation. Yet there are good reasons to suppose that what is true of the neuroses applies also to the perversions. For it is no rare thing to find perversions and psychoneuroses occurring in the same family, and distributed between the two sexes in such a way that the male members of the family, or one of them, are positive perverts, while the females, true to the tendency of their sex to repression, are negative perverts, that is, hysterics.[1] This is good evidence of the essential connections which we have shown to exist between the two disorders.

present work (1906a, _Standard Ed._, **7**, 275) and discussed more fully in a later paper on 'The Predisposition to Obsessional Neurosis' (1913i).]

[1] [A detailed family tree of this kind is given in a letter to Fliess of January 11, 1897 (Freud, 1950a, Letter 55).]

FURTHER   On the other hand, it is not possible to adopt
MODIFICATION   the view that the form to be taken by sexual
                          life is unambiguously decided, once and for all,
with the inception of the different components of the sexual constitution. On the contrary, the determining process continues,
and further possibilities arise according to the vicissitudes of the
tributary streams of sexuality springing from their separate
sources. This further modification is clearly what brings the
decisive outcome, and constitutions which might be described
as the same can lead to three different final results:—

[1] If the relation between all the different dispositions—a
relation which we will assume to be abnormal—persists and
grows stronger at maturity, the result can only be a perverse
sexual life. The analysis of abnormal constitutional dispositions
of this kind has not yet been properly taken in hand. But we
already know cases which can easily be explained on such a basis
as this. Writers on the subject, for instance, have asserted [see
p. 8] that the necessary precondition of a whole number of
perverse fixations lies in an innate weakness of the sexual
instinct. In this form the view seems to me untenable. It makes
sense, however, if what is meant is a constitutional weakness of
one particular factor in the sexual instinct, namely the genital
zone—a zone which takes over the function of combining the
separate sexual activities for the purposes of reproduction. For
if the genital zone is weak, this combination, which is required
to take place at puberty, is bound to fail, and the strongest of
the other components of sexuality will continue its activity as
a perversion.[1]

REPRESSION   [2] A different result is brought about if in the
                          course of development some of the components
which are of excessive strength in the disposition are submitted
to the process of repression (which, it must be insisted, is not
equivalent to their being abolished). If this happens, the excitations concerned continue to be generated as before; but they are
prevented by psychical obstruction from attaining their aim and

---

[1] [*Footnote added* 1915:] In such circumstances one often finds that
at puberty a normal sexual current begins to operate at first, but that,
as a result of its internal weakness, it breaks down in face of the first
external obstacles and is then replaced by regression to the perverse
fixation.

are diverted into numerous other channels till they find their way to expression as symptoms. The outcome may be an approximately normal sexual life—though usually a restricted one —but there is in addition psychoneurotic illness. These particular cases have become familiar to us from the psycho-analytic investigation of neurotics. Their sexual life begins like that of perverts, and a considerable part of their childhood is occupied with perverse sexual activity which occasionally extends far into maturity. A reversal due to repression then occurs, owing to internal causes (usually before puberty, but now and then even long afterwards), and from that time onwards neurosis takes the place of perversion, without the old impulses being extinguished. We are reminded of the proverb 'Junge Hure, alte Betschwester',[1] only that here youth has lasted all too short a time. The fact that perversion can be replaced by neurosis in the life of the same person, like the fact which we have already mentioned that perversion and neurosis can be distributed among different members of the same family, tallies with the view that neurosis is the negative of perversion.

SUBLIMATION   [3] The third alternative result of an abnormal constitutional disposition is made possible by the process of sublimation. This enables excessively strong excitations arising from particular sources of sexuality to find an outlet and use in other fields, so that a not inconsiderable increase in psychical efficiency results from a disposition which in itself is perilous. Here we have one of the origins of artistic activity; and, according to the completeness or incompleteness of the sublimation, a characterological analysis of a highly gifted individual, and in particular of one with an artistic disposition, may reveal a mixture, in every proportion, of efficiency, perversion and neurosis. A sub-species of sublimation is to be found in suppression by reaction-formation, which, as we have seen, begins during a child's period of latency and continues in favourable cases throughout his whole life. What we describe as a person's 'character' is built up to a considerable extent from the material of sexual excitations and is composed of instincts that have been fixed since childhood, of constructions achieved by means of sublimation, and of other constructions, employed for

---

[1] ['A young whore makes an old nun.']

effectively holding in check perverse impulses which have been recognized as being unutilizable.[1] The multifariously perverse sexual disposition of childhood can accordingly be regarded as the source of a number of our virtues, in so far as through reaction-formation it stimulates their development.[2]

ACCIDENTAL   No other influences on the course of sexual
EXPERIENCES   development can compare in importance with
                   releases of sexuality, waves of repression and sub-limations—the two latter being processes of which the inner causes are quite unknown to us. It might be possible to include repressions and sublimations as a part of the constitutional disposition, by regarding them as manifestations of it in life; and anyone who does so is justified in asserting that the final shape taken by sexual life is principally the outcome of the innate constitution. No one with perception will, however, dispute that an interplay of factors such as this also leaves room for the modifying effects of accidental events experienced in childhood and later. It is not easy [3] to estimate the relative efficacy of the constitutional and accidental factors. In theory one is always inclined to overestimate the former; therapeutic practice emphasizes the importance of the latter. It should, however, on no account be forgotten that the relation between the two is a co-operative and not a mutually exclusive one. The constitutional factor must await experiences before it can make itself felt; the accidental factor must have a constitutional basis in order to come into operation. To cover the majority of cases we can picture what has been described as a 'complemental

---

[1] [*Footnote added* 1920:] In the case of some character-traits it has even been possible to trace a connection with particular erotogenic components. Thus, obstinacy, thrift and orderliness arise from an exploitation of anal erotism, while ambition is determined by a strong urethral-erotic disposition. [See Freud, 1908*b* (last paragraph).]

[2] Emile Zola, a keen observer of human nature, describes in *La joie de vivre* how a girl, cheerfully and selflessly and without thought of reward, sacrificed to those she loved everything that she possessed or could lay claim to—her money and her hopes. This girl's childhood was dominated by an insatiable thirst for affection, which was transformed into cruelty on an occasion when she found herself slighted in favour of another girl.

[3] [The remainder of this paragraph and the whole of the next one were added in 1915.]

series',[1] in which the diminishing intensity of one factor is balanced by the increasing intensity of the other; there is, however, no reason to deny the existence of extreme cases at the two ends of the series.

We shall be in even closer harmony with psycho-analytic research if we give a place of preference among the accidental factors to the experiences of early childhood. The single aetiological series then falls into two, which may be called the dispositional and the definitive. In the first the constitution and the accidental experiences of childhood interact in the same manner as do the disposition and later traumatic experiences in the second. All the factors that impair sexual development show their effects by bringing about a regression, a return to an earlier phase of development.

Let us now resume our task of enumerating the factors which we have found to exercise an influence on sexual development, whether they are themselves operative forces or merely manifestations of such forces.

PRECOCITY   One such factor is spontaneous sexual precocity, whose presence at least can be demonstrated with certainty in the aetiology of the neuroses though, like other factors, it is not in itself a sufficient cause. It is manifested in the interruption, abbreviation or bringing to an end of the infantile period of latency; and it is a cause of disturbances by occasioning sexual manifestations which, owing on the one hand to the sexual inhibitions being incomplete and on the other hand to the genital system being undeveloped, are bound to be in the nature of perversions. These tendencies to perversion may thereafter either persist as such or, after repressions have set in, become the motive forces of neurotic symptoms. In any case sexual precocity makes more difficult the later control of the sexual instinct by the higher mental agencies which is so desirable, and it increases the impulsive quality which, quite apart from this, characterizes the psychical representations of

---

[1] [In 1915 the term used was 'aetiological series', which was altered to 'complemental series' in 1920. The latter term seems to have been first used by Freud in Lecture XXII of his *Introductory Lectures* (1916–17). The correction of the phrase was not carried out where it occurs again a few lines lower down.]

the instinct. Sexual precocity often runs parallel with premature intellectual development and, linked in this way, is to be found in the childhood history of persons of the greatest eminence and capacity; under such conditions its effects do not seem to be so pathogenic as when it appears in isolation.[1]

TEMPORAL   Other factors which, along with precocity, may
FACTORS   be classed as temporal also deserve attention. The
            order in which the various instinctual impulses come into activity seems to be phylogenetically determined; so, too, does the length of time during which they are able to manifest themselves before they succumb to the effects of some freshly emerging instinctual impulse or to some typical repression. Variations, however, seem to occur both in temporal sequence and in duration, and these variations must exercise a determining influence upon the final result. It cannot be a matter of indifference whether a given current makes its appearance earlier or later than a current flowing in the opposite direction, for the effect of a repression cannot be undone. Divergences in the temporal sequence in which the components come together invariably produce a difference in the outcome. On the other hand, instinctual impulses which emerge with special intensity often run a surprisingly short course—as, for instance, the heterosexual attachment of persons who later become manifest homosexuals. There is no justification for the fear that trends which set in with the greatest violence in childhood will permanently dominate the adult character; it is just as likely that they will disappear and make way for an opposite tendency. ('Gestrenge Herren regieren nicht lange.')[2]

We are not in a position to give so much as a hint as to the causes of these temporal disturbances of the process of development. A prospect opens before us at this point upon a whole phalanx of biological and perhaps, too, of historical problems of which we have not even come within striking distance.

---

[1] [Cf. some remarks on this point in the case history of 'Little Hans' (1909b), near the beginning of the third section of Chapter III.—The paragraph which follows was added in 1915.]

[2] ['Harsh rulers have short reigns.']

PERTINACITY   The importance of all early sexual manifesta-
OF EARLY   tions is increased by a psychical factor of un-
IMPRESSIONS   known origin, which at the moment, it must be
                admitted, can only be brought forward as a pro-
visional psychological concept. I have in mind the fact that,
in order to account for the situation, it is necessary to assume
that these early impressions of sexual life are characterized by
an increased pertinacity or susceptibility to fixation in persons
who are later to become neurotics or perverts. For the same
premature sexual manifestations, when they occur in other persons, fail to make so deep an impression; they do not tend in
a compulsive manner towards repetition nor do they lay down
the path to be taken by the sexual instinct for a whole lifetime.
Part of the explanation of this pertinacity of early impressions
may perhaps lie in another psychical factor which we must not
overlook in the causation of the neuroses, namely the preponderance attaching in mental life to memory-traces in comparison
with recent impressions. This factor is clearly dependent on
intellectual education and increases in proportion to the degree
of individual culture. The savage has been described in contrast
as 'das unglückselige Kind des Augenblickes'.[1] In consequence
of the inverse relation holding between civilization and the free
development of sexuality, of which the consequences can be
followed far into the structure of our existences, the course taken
by the sexual life of a child is just as unimportant for later life
where the cultural or social level is relatively low as it is important where that level is relatively high.

FIXATION   The ground prepared by the psychical factors
                which have just been enumerated affords a favour-
able basis for such stimulations of infantile sexuality as are
experienced accidentally. The latter (first and foremost, seduction by other children or by adults) provide the material which,
with the help of the former, can become fixated as a permanent
disorder. A good proportion of the deviations from normal
sexual life which are later observed both in neurotics and in
perverts are thus established from the very first by the impressions of childhood—a period which is regarded as being devoid

[1] ['The hapless child of the moment.'] Increase in pertinacity may
also possibly be the effect of an especially intense somatic manifestation
of sexuality in early years. [See Addenda, p. 112, below.]

of sexuality. The causation is shared between a compliant constitution, precocity, the characteristic of increased pertinacity of early impressions and the chance stimulation of the sexual instinct by extraneous influences.

The unsatisfactory conclusion, however, that emerges from these investigations of the disturbances of sexual life is that we know far too little of the biological processes constituting the essence of sexuality to be able to construct from our fragmentary information a theory adequate to the understanding alike of normal and of pathological conditions.

APPENDIX

[*References to sexuality are, of course, to be found in a large majority of Freud's writings. The following list comprises those which are more directly concerned with the subject. The date at the beginning of each entry gives the year of publication. Fuller particulars of each work will be found in the bibliography at the end of the present volume.*]

1898*a*.   'Sexuality in the Aetiology of the Neuroses.'

1905*d*.   *Three Essays on the Theory of Sexuality.*

1906*a*.   'My Views on the Part Played by Sexuality in the Aetiology of the Neuroses.'

1907*c*.   'The Sexual Enlightenment of Children.'

1908*b*.   'Character and Anal Erotism.'

1908*c*.   'On the Sexual Theories of Children.'

1908*d*.   ' "Civilized" Sexual Morality and Modern Nervous Sickness.'

1910*a*.   *Five Lectures on Psycho-Analysis*, Lecture IV.

1910*c*.   *Leonardo da Vinci*, Chapter III.

1910*h*.   'A Special Type of Choice of Object made by Men.'

1912*d*.   'On the Universal Tendency to Debasement in the Sphere of Love.'

1912*f*.   'Contributions to a Discussion on Masturbation.'

1913*i*.   'The Disposition to Obsessional Neurosis.'

1913*j*.   'The Claims of Psycho-Analysis to Scientific Interest', Part II (C).

1913*k*.   Preface to Bourke's *Scatalogic Rites of All Nations*.

1914*c*.   'On Narcissism: an Introduction.'

1916–17.   *Introductory Lectures on Psycho-Analysis*, Lectures XX, XXI, XXII and XXVI.

1917*c*.   'On the Transformation of Instincts, with Special Reference to Anal Erotism.'

1918*a*.   'The Taboo of Virginity.'

1919*e*.   ' "A Child is Being Beaten." '

1920*a*.   'The Psychogenesis of a Case of Female Homosexuality.'

1922*b*.   'Some Neurotic Mechanisms in Jealousy, Paranoia and
              Homosexuality', Section C.

1923*a*.   Two Encyclopaedia Articles: (2) 'The Libido Theory.'

1923*e*.   'The Infantile Genital Organization.'

1924*c*.   'The Economic Problem of Masochism.'

1924*d*.   'The Dissolution of the Oedipus Complex.'

1925*j*.   'Some Psychical Consequences of the Anatomical Dis-
              tinction between the Sexes.'

1927*e*.   'Fetishism.'

1931*a*.   'Libidinal Types.'

1931*b*.   'Female Sexuality.'

1933*a*.   *New Introductory Lectures on Psycho-Analysis*, Lectures
              XXXII and XXXIII.

1940*a* [1938].   *An Outline of Psycho-Analysis*, Chapters III and
                      VII.

1940*e* [1938].   'Splitting of the Ego in the Process of Defence.'

ADDENDA

Page xiii According to Ernest Jones, on Jung's suggestion.

31-2 *n*. [Freud had pointed out this coincidence in *The Psychopathology of Everyday Life* (1901*b*), *Standard Ed.*, v. 255 *n*. 2.]

42 [The connection between hysterical and infantile amnesia had been pointed out by Freud in a letter to Fliess of March 10, 1898 (Freud, 1950*a*, Letter 84).]

66 *n*. 2 [The two currents had been discussed at length in the second of Freud's 'Contributions to the Psychology of Love' (1912*d*), *Standard Ed.*, **11**, 180-7.]

73 *n*. 2 [The last seven words were added in 1915.]

82 *n*. [Cf. also some remarks at the end of Section III of the paper on 'Female Sexuality' (1931*b*), *Standard Ed.*, **21**, 240.]

87 *n*. [The importance of the clitoris in the childhood of girls is already mentioned in a letter to Fliess of November 14, 1897 (Freud, 1950*a*, Letter 75).]

108 *n*. [What Freud here describes as 'pertinacity of early impressions' and 'susceptibility to fixation' was also termed by him elsewhere 'adhesiveness of the libido'. An account of his use of these terms will be found in an Editor's footnote to 'A Case of Paranoia' (1915*f*), *Standard Ed.*, **14**, 272. A further reference should be added to Chapter V of *Civilization and its Discontents* (1930*a*), ibid., **21**, 108.]

LIST OF ABBREVIATIONS

G.S.   = Freud, *Gesammelte Schriften* (12 vols.), Vienna 1924–34
G.W.   = Freud, *Gesammelte Werke* (18 vols.), London, from 1940
C.P.   = Freud, *Collected Papers* (5 vols.), London, 1924–50
S.E.   ⎫ = Freud, *Standard Edition* (24 vols.), London, from
Standard Ed.⎬   1953
Basic Writings = Freud, *The Basic Writings of Sigmund Freud*, New York, 1938
I.P.L.   = *International Psycho-Analytical Library*, Hogarth Press and Institute of Psycho-Analysis, London, from 1921

BIBLIOGRAPHY

[Titles of books and periodicals are in italics; titles of papers are in inverted commas. Abbreviations are in accordance with the *World List of Scientific Periodicals* (Oxford, 1950). Further abbreviations used in this volume will be found in the List on page 113. Numerals in thick type refer to volumes; ordinary numerals refer to pages. The figures in round brackets at the end of each entry indicate the page or pages of this volume on which the work in question is mentioned. In the case of the Freud entries, the letters attached to the dates of publication are in accordance with the corresponding entries in the complete bibliography of Freud's writings to be included in the last volume of the *Standard Edition*.

For non-technical authors, and for technical authors where no specific work is mentioned, see the *General Index*.]

ABRAHAM, K. (1916) 'Untersuchungen über die früheste prägenitale Entwicklungsstufe der Libido', *Int. Z. Psychoanal.*, **4**, 71. (64.) [*Trans.:* 'The First Pregenital Stage of the Libido', *Selected Papers*, London, 1927, Chap. XII.]
  (1924) *Versuch einer Entwicklungsgeschichte der Libido*, Vienna. (64, 65–6)
  [Trans.: 'A Short Study of the Development of the Libido', *Selected Papers*, London, 1927, Chap. XXVI.]
ADLER, A. (1907) *Studie über Minderwertigkeit von Organen*, Vienna. (50)
ANDREAS-SALOMÉ, L. (1916) ' "Anal" und "Sexual" ', *Imago*, **4**, 249. (53)
ARDUIN (1900) 'Die Frauenfrage und die sexuellen Zwischenstufen', *Jb. sex. Zwischenst.*, **2.** (9)
BALDWIN, J. M. (1895) *Mental Development in the Child and the Race*, New York. (39–40)
BAYER, H. (1902) 'Zur Entwicklungsgeschichte der Gebärmutter', *Dtsch. Arch. klin. Med.*, **73**, 422. (43)
BELL, J. SANFORD (1902) 'A Preliminary Study of the Emotion of Love between the Sexes', *Amer. J. Psychol.*, **13**, 325. (39–40, 60)
BINET, A. (1888) *Études de psychologie expérimentale: le fétichisme dans l'amour*, Paris. (20, 37)
BLEULER, E. (1908) 'Sexuelle Abnormitäten der Kinder', *Jb. schweiz. Ges. Schulgesundh. Pfl.*, **9**, 623. (39–40)
  (1913) 'Der Sexualwiderstand', *Jb. psychoanal. psychopath. Forsch.*, **5**, 442. (55)
BLOCH, I. (1902–3) *Beiträge zur Ätiologie der Psychopathia sexualis* (2 vols.), Dresden. (5)
BREUER, J., and FREUD, S. (1893) See FREUD, S. (1893a)
  (1895) See FREUD, S. (1895d)

CHEVALIER, J. (1893) *L'inversion sexuelle*, Lyon. (7, 9)

DESSOIR, M. (1894) 'Zur Psychologie der Vita sexualis', *Allg. Z. Psychiat.*, **50**, 941. (95)

DISKUSSIONEN DER WIENER PSYCHOANALYTISCHEN VEREINIGUNG (1912) II, 'Die Onanie', Wiesbaden. (51, 54)

ELLIS, HAVELOCK (1910) *Studies in the Psychology of Sex*, Vol. I: *The Evolution of Modesty; the Phenomena of Sexual Periodicity; and Auto-erotism*, 3rd ed., Philadelphia. (1st ed., 'Leipzig' [London], 1899.) (47)

(1913) *Studies in the Psychology of Sex*, Vol. III: *Analysis of the Sexual Impulse; Love and Pain; the Sexual Impulse in Women*, 2nd ed., Philadelphia. (1st ed., Philadelphia, 1903.) (25, 39–40, 56, 89)

(1915) *Studies in the Psychology of Sex*, Vol. II: *Sexual Inversion*, 3rd ed., Philadelphia. (1st Engl. ed., London, 1897.) (6, 8)

(1928) 'The Conception of Narcissism', *Studies in the Psychology of Sex*, Vol. VII: *Eonism, etc.*, Philadelphia, Chap. VI. (84)

FERENCZI, S. (1909) 'Introjektion und Übertragung', *Jb. psychoanal. psychopath. Forsch.*, **1**, 422. (16)

[*Trans.*: 'Introjection and Transference', *First Contributions to Psycho-Analysis*, London, 1952, Chap. II.]

(1914) 'Zur Nosologie der männlichen Homosexualität (Homoërotik)', *Int. Z. Psychoanal.*, **2**, 131 (12)

[*Trans.*: 'The Nosology of Male Homosexuality (Homoerotism)', *First Contributions to Psycho-Analysis*, London, 1952, Chap. XII.]

(1920) Review of Lipschütz, *Die Pubertätsdrüse*, *Int. Z. Psychoanal.*, **6**, 84. (43)

[*Trans.*: *Int. J. Psycho-Anal.*, **2** (1921), 143.]

(1924) *Versuch einer Genitaltheorie*, Vienna. (95)

[*Trans.*: *Thalassa, a Theory of Genitality*, New York, 1938.]

FLIESS, W. (1906) *Der Ablauf des Lebens*, Vienna. (9)

FREUD, S. (1893*a*) With BREUER, J., 'Über den psychischen Mechanismus hysterischer Phänomene: Vorläufige Mitteilung', *G.S.*, **1**, 7; *G.W.*, **1**, 81. (xi)

[*Trans.*: 'On the Psychical Mechanism of Hysterical Phenomena: A Preliminary Communication', *C.P.*, **1**, 24; *Standard Ed.*, **2**, 3.]

(1895*b*) 'Über die Berechtigung, von der Neurasthenie einen bestimmten Symptomenkomplex als "Angstneurose" abzutrennen', *G.S.*, **1**, 306; *G.W.*, **1**, 313. (xi, 79)

[*Trans.*: 'On the Grounds for Detaching a Particular Syndrome from Neurasthenia under the Description "Anxiety Neurosis" ', *C.P.*, **1**, 76; *Standard Ed.*, **3**, 87.]

(1895*d*) With BREUER, J., *Studien über Hysterie*, Vienna. (*G.S.*, **1**; *G.W.*, **1**, 75. Omitting Breuer's contributions.) (30)

[*Trans.*: *Studies on Hysteria*, *Standard Ed.*, **2**; *I.P.L.*, **50.**]

(1896*b*) 'Weitere Bemerkungen über die Abwehr-Neuropsychosen' *G.S.*, **1**, 363; *G.W.*, **1**, 377. (xii)

[*Trans.*: 'Further Remarks on the Neuro-Psychoses of Defence', *C.P.*, **1**, 155; *Standard Ed.*, **3**, 159.]

(1896*c*) 'Zur Ätiologie der Hysterie', *G.S.*, **1**, 404; *G.W.*, **1**, 423. (42, 56)

FREUD, S. (*cont.*)

    [*Trans.:* 'The Aetiology of Hysteria', *C.P.*, **1**, 183; *Standard Ed.*, **3**, 189.]

(1898*a*) 'Die Sexualität in der Ätiologie der Neurosen', *G.S.*, **1**, 439; *G.W.*, **1**, 489. (xii, 70)

    [*Trans.:* 'Sexuality in the Aetiology of the Neuroses', *C.P.*, **1**, 220; *Standard Ed.*, **3**, 261.]

(1899*a*) 'Über Deckerinnerungen', *G.S.*, **1**, 465; *G.W.*, **1**, 529. (41)

    [*Trans.:* 'Screen Memories', *C.P.*, **5**, 47; *Standard Ed.*, **3**, 301.]

(1900*a*) *Die Traumdeutung*, Vienna. (*G.S.*, **2–3**; *G.W.*, **2–3**.) (x–xiii, 50–1, 58, 67, 92, 93)

    [*Trans.: The Interpretation of Dreams*, London and New York, 1955; *Standard Ed.*, **4–5**.]

(1901*a*) *Über den Traum*. Wiesbaden. (*G.S.*, **3**, 189; *G.W.*, **2–3**, 643.) (xiii)

    [*Trans.: On Dreams*, London, 1951; *Standard Ed.*, **5**, 629.]

(1901*b*) *Zur Psychopathologie des Alltagslebens*, Berlin. (*G.S.*, **4**; *G.W.*, **4**.) (xiii, 9, 41, 112)

    [*Trans.: The Psychopathology of Everyday Life*, Standard, Ed., **6**.]

(1905*b*) 'Psychische Behandlung (Seelenbehandlung)', *G.W.*, **5**, 289. (16)

    [*Trans.:* 'Psychical (or Mental) Treatment', *Standard Ed.*, **7**, 283.]

(1905*c*) *Der Witz und seine Beziehung zum Unbewussten*, Vienna. (*G.S.*, **9**, 5; *G.W.*, **6**.) (xiii, 77)

    [*Trans.: Jokes and their Relation to the Unconscious*, London, 1960; *Standard Ed.*, **8**.]

(1905*d*) *Drei Abhandlungen zur Sexualtheorie*, Vienna. (*G.S.*, **5**, 3; *G.W.*, **5**, 29.)

    [*Trans.: Three Essays on the Theory of Sexuality*, *Standard Ed.*, **7**, 125; *I.P.L.*, **57**.]

(1905*e*) 'Bruchstück einer Hysterie-Analyse', *G.S.*, **8**, 3; *G.W.*, **5**, 163. (xiii, 22, 29, 31, 33)

    [*Trans.:* 'Fragment of an Analysis of a Case of Hysteria', *C.P.*, **3**, 13; *Standard Ed.*, **7**, 3.]

(1906*a*) 'Meine Ansichten über die Rolle der Sexualität in der Ätiologie der Neurosen', *G.S.*, **5**, 123; *G.W.*, **5**, 149. (xii, 56, 82, 101–2)

    [*Trans.:* 'My Views on the Part played by Sexuality in the Aetiology of the Neuroses', *C.P.*, **1**, 272; *Standard Ed.*, **7**, 271.]

(1907*c*) 'Zur sexuellen Aufklärung der Kinder', *G.S.*, **5**, 134; *G.W.*, **7**, 19. (110)

    [*Trans.:* 'The Sexual Enlightenment of Children', *C.P.*, **2**, 36; *Standard Ed.*, **9**, 131.]

(1908*b*) 'Charakter und Analerotik', *G.S.*, **5**, 261; *G.W.*, **7**, 203. (51, 105)

    [*Trans.:* 'Character and Anal Erotism', *C.P.*, **2**, 45; *Standard Ed.*, **9**, 169.]

(1908*c*) 'Über infantile Sexualtheorien', *G.S.*, **5**, 168; *G.W.*, **7**, 171. (60)

FREUD, S. (*cont.*)
　　[*Trans.:* 'On the Sexual Theories of Children', *C.P.*, **2**, 59; *Standard Ed.*, **9**, 207.]
　(1908d) 'Die "kulturelle" Sexualmoral und die moderne Nervosität', *G.S.*, **5**, 143; *G.W.*, **7**, 143 (110)
　　[*Trans.:* ' "Civilized" Sexual Morality and Modern Nervous Illness', *C.P.*, **2**, 76; *Standard Ed.*, **9**, 179.]
　(1908e) 'Der Dichter und das Phantasieren', *G.S.*, **10**, 229; *G.W.*, **7**, 213. (77)
　　[*Trans.:* 'Creative Writers and Day-Dreaming', *C.P.*, **4**, 173; *Standard Ed.*, **9**, 143.]
　(1909b) 'Analyse der Phobie eines fünfjährigen Knaben', *G.S.*, **8**, 129; *G.W.*, **7**, 243. (60, 107)
　　[*Trans.:* 'Analysis of a Phobia in a Five-Year-Old Boy', *C.P.*, **3**, 149; *Standard Ed.*, **10**, 3.]
　(1909c) 'Der Familienroman der Neurotiker', *G.S.*, **12**, 371; *G.W.*, **7**, 227. (92)
　　[*Trans.:* 'Family Romances', *C.P.*, **5**, 74; *Standard Ed.*, **9**, 237.]
　(1909d) 'Bemerkungen über einen Fall von Zwangsneurose', *G.S.*, **8**, 269; *G.W.*, **7**, 381. (21, 92)
　　[*Trans.:* 'Notes on a Case of Obsessional Neurosis', *C.P.*, **3**, 293; *Standard Ed.*, **10**, 155.]
　(1910a) *Über Psychoanalyse*, Vienna. (*G.S.*, **4**, 349; *G.W.*, **8**, 3.) (110)
　　[*Trans.: Five Lectures on Psycho-Analysis, Standard Ed.*, **11**, 3.]
　(1910c) *Eine Kindheitserinnerung des Leonardo da Vinci*, Vienna. (*G.S.*, **9**, 371; *G.W.*, **8**, 128.) (110)
　　[*Trans.: Leonardo da Vinci and a Memory of his Childhood*, New York, 1916; *Standard Ed.*, **11**, 59.]
　(1910h) 'Über einen besonderen Typus der Objektwahl beim Manne', *G.S.*, **5**, 186; *G.W.*, **8**, 66. (94)
　　[*Trans.:* 'A Special Type of Choice of Object made by Men', *C.P.*, **4**, 192; *Standard Ed.*, **11**, 165.]
　(1912c) 'Über neurotische Erkrankungstypen', *G.S.*, **5**, 400; *G.W.*, **8**, 322. (31)
　　[*Trans.:* 'Types of Onset of Neurosis', *C.P.*, **2**, 113; *Standard Ed.*, **12**, 229.]
　(1912d) 'Über die allgemeinste Erniedrigung des Liebeslebens', *G.S.*, **5**, 198; *G.W.*, **8**, 78. (110, 112)
　　[*Trans.:* 'On the Universal Tendency to Debasement in the Sphere of Love', *C.P.*, **4**, 203; *Standard Ed.*, **11**, 179.]
　(1912f) 'Zur Onanie-Diskussion', *G.S.*, **3**, 324; *G.W.*, **8**, 332. (51, 54)
　　[*Trans.:* 'Contributions to a Discussion on Masturbation', *Standard Ed.*, **12**, 243.]
　(1912–13) *Totem und Tabu*, Vienna, 1913. (*G.S.*, **10**, 3; *G.W.*, **9**.) (91)
　　[*Trans.: Totem and Taboo*, London, 1950; *Standard Ed.*, **13**, 13.]
　(1913i) 'Die Disposition zur Zwangsneurose', *G.S.*, **5**, 277; *G.W.*, **8**, 442. (63–4, 101–2)
　　[*Trans.:* 'The Disposition to Obsessional Neurosis', *C.P.*, **2**, 122; *Standard Ed.*, **12**, 313.]

FREUD, S. (*cont.*)

(1913*j*) 'Das Interesse an der Psychoanalyse', *G.S.*, **4**, 313; *G.W.*, **8**, 390. (110)
[*Trans.*: 'The Claims of Psycho-Analysis to Scientific Interest', *Standard Ed.*, **13**, 165.]

(1913*k*) 'Geleitwort zu Bourke *Der Unrat in Sitte, Brauch, Glauben und Gewohnheitsrecht der Völker*', Leipzig. (*G.S.*, **11**, 249; *G.W.*, **10**, 453.) (110)
[*Trans.*: 'Preface to Bourke's *Scatalogic Rites of All Nations*', *C.P.*, **5**, 88; *Standard Ed.*, **12**, 335.]

(1914*c*) 'Zur Einführung des Narzissmus', *G.S.*, **6**, 155; *G.W.*, **10**, 138. (45, 48, 83, 84, 88)
[*Trans.*: 'On Narcissism: an Introduction', *C.P.*, **4**, 30; *Standard Ed.*, **14**, 69.]

(1914*d*) 'Zur Geschichte der psychoanalytischen Bewegung', *G.S.*, **4**, 411; *G.W.*, **10**, 44. (xii)
[*Trans.*: 'On the History of the Psycho-Analytic Movement', *C.P.*, **1**, 287; *Standard Ed.*, **14**, 3.]

(1915*c*) 'Triebe und Triebschicksale', *G.S.*, **5**, 443; *G.W.*, **10**, 210. (34)
[*Trans.*: 'Instincts and their Vicissitudes', *C.P.*, **4**, 60; *Standard Ed.*, **14**, 111.]

(1915*d*) 'Die Verdrängung', *G.S.*, **5**, 466; *G.W.*, **10**, 248. (42)
[*Trans.*: 'Repression', *C.P.*, **4**, 84; *Standard Ed.*, **14**, 143.]

(1915*f*) 'Mitteilung eines der psychoanalytischen Theorie widersprechenden Falles von Paranoia', *G.S.*, **5**, 288; *G.W.*, **10**, 234. (112)
[*Trans.*: 'A Case of Paranoia Running Counter to the Psycho-Analytic Theory of the Disease', *C.P.*, **2**, 150; *Standard Ed.*, **14**, 263.]

(1916–17) *Vorlesungen zur Einführung in die Psychoanalyse*, Vienna. (*G.S.*, **7**; *G.W.*, **11**.) (90, 92, 106)
[*Trans.*: *Introductory Lectures on Psycho-Analysis*, revised ed., London, 1929; *Standard Ed.*, **15–16**.]

(1917*c*) 'Über Triebumsetzungen insbesondere der Analerotik', *G.S.*, **5**, 268; *G.W.*, **10**, 402. (51, 52)
[*Trans.*: 'On the Transformation of Instincts with Special Reference to Anal Erotism', *C.P.*, **2**, 164; *Standard Ed.*, **17**, 127.]

(1918*a*) 'Das Tabu der Virginität, *G.S.*, **5**, 212; *G.W.*, **12**, 161. (110)
[*Trans.*: 'The Taboo of Virginity', *C.P.*, **4**, 217; *Standard Ed.*, **11**, 193.]

(1919*e*) ' "Ein Kind wird geschlagen" ', *G.S.*, **5**, 344; *G.W.*, **12**, 197. (9)
[*Trans.*: ' "A Child is being Beaten" ', *C.P.*, **2**, 172; *Standard Ed.*, **17**, 177.]

(1920*a*) 'Über die Psychogenese eines Falles von weiblicher Homosexualität', *G.S.*, **5**, 312; *G.W.*, **12**, 271. (87)
[*Trans.*: 'The Psychogenesis of a Case of Female Homosexuality', *C.P.*, **2**, 202; *Standard Ed.*, **18**, 147.]

FREUD, S. (*cont.*)

(1920g) *Jenseits des Lustprinzips*, Vienna. (*G.S.*, **6**, 191; *G.W.*, **13**, 3. (2, 34)
[*Trans.*: *Beyond the Pleasure Principle*, Standard Ed., **18**, 3; *I.P.L.*, **4.**]

(1921c) *Massenpsychologie und Ich-Analyse*, Vienna. (*G.S.*, **6**, 261; *G.W.*, **13**, 73.) (16)
[*Trans.*: *Group Psychology and the Analysis of the Ego, Standard Ed.*, **18**, 67; *I.P.L.*, **6.**]

(1922b) 'Über einige neurotische Mechanismen bei Eifersucht, Paranoia und Homosexualität', *G.S.*, **5**, 387; *G.W.*, **13**, 195. (112)
[*Trans.*: 'Some Neurotic Mechanisms in Jealousy, Paranoia and Homosexuality', C.P., **2**, 232; *Standard Ed.*, **18**, 223.]

(1923a [1922]) ' "Psychoanalyse" und "Libido Theorie" ', *G.S.*, **11**, 201; *G.W.*, **13**, 211. (111)
[*Trans.*: 'Two Encyclopaedia Articles', *C.P.*, **5**, 107; *Standard Ed.*, **18**, 235.]

(1923b) *Das Ich und das Es*, Vienna. (*G.S.*, **6**, 353; *G.W.*, **13**, 237.) (34, 45)
[*Trans.*: *The Ego and the Id, Standard Ed.*, **19**, 3; *I.P.L.*, **12.**]

(1923e) 'Die infantile Genitalorganization', *G.S.*, **5**, 232; *G.W.*, **13**, 293. (x, 65-6)
[*Trans.*: 'The Infantile Genital Organization', *C.P.*, **2**, 244; *Standard Ed.*, **19**, 141.]

(1924c) 'Das ökonomische Problem des Masochismus', *G.S.*, **5**, 374; *G.W.*, **13**, 371. (24, 71, 75)
[*Trans.*: 'The Economic Problem of Masochism', *C.P.*, **2**, 255; *Standard Ed.*, **19**, 157.]

(1924d) 'Der Untergang des Ödipuskomplexes', *G.S.*, **5**, 423; *G.W.*, **13**, 395. (111)
[*Trans.*: 'The Dissolution of the Oedipus Complex', *C.P.*, **2**, 269; *Standard Ed.*, **19**, 173.]

(1925d [1924]) '*Selbstdarstellung*', Vienna, 1934. (*G.S.*, **11**, 119; *G.W.*, **14**, 33.) (xii)
[*Trans.*: *An Autobiographical Study*, London and New York, 1935; *Standard Ed.*, **20**, 3.]

(1925h) 'Die Verneinung', *G.S.*, **11**, 3; *G.W.*, **14**, 11. (51)
[*Trans.*: 'Negation', *C.P.*, **5**, 181; *Standard Ed.*, **19**, 235.]

(1925j) 'Einige psychische Folgen des anatomischen Geschlechtsunterschieds', *G.S.*, **11**, 8; *G.W.*, **14**, 19. (61, 87)
[*Trans.*: 'Some Psychical Consequences of the Anatomical Distinction between the Sexes', *C.P.*, **5**, 186; *Standard Ed.*, **19**, 243.]

(1926d) *Hemmung, Symptom und Angst*, Vienna. (*G.S.*, **11**, 23; *G.W.*, **13**, 113.) (90, 92)
[*Trans.*: *Inhibitions, Symptoms and Anxiety, Standard Ed.*, **20**, 77; *I.P.L.*, **28.**]

(1927e) 'Fetischismus', *G.S.*, **11**, 395; *G.W.*, **14**, 311. (21)
[*Trans.*: 'Fetishism', *C.P.*, **5**, 198; *Standard Ed.*, **21**, 149.]

(1930a) *Das Unbehagen in der Kultur*, Vienna. (*G.S.*, **12**, 29; *G.W.*, **14**, 421.) (21, 86, 112)

I*

FREUD, S. (*cont.*)
　　[*Trans.: Civilization and its Discontents*, London, 1930; New York, 1961; *Standard Ed.*, **21**, 59.]
　(1931*a*) 'Über libidinöse Typen', *G.S.*, **12**, 115; *G.W.*, **14**, 509. (111)
　　[*Trans.:* 'Libidinal Types', *C.P.*, **5**, 247; *Standard Ed.*, **21**, 215.]
　(1931*b*) 'Über die weibliche Sexualität', G.S., **12**, 120; *G.W.*, **14**, 517. (87, 112)
　　[*Trans.:* 'Female Sexuality', *C.P.*, **5**, 252; *Standard Ed.*, **21**, 223.]
　(1933*a*) *Neue Folge der Vorlesungen zur Einführung in die Psychoanalyse*, Vienna. (*G.S.*, **12**, 151; *G.W.*, **15**.) (87, 90)
　　[*Trans.: New Introductory Lectures on Psycho-Analysis*, London and New York, 1933; *Standard Ed.*, **22**.]
　(1937*c*) 'Die endliche und die unendliche Analyse', *G.W.*, **16**, 59. (70)
　　[*Trans.:* 'Analysis Terminable and Interminable', *C.P.*, **5**, 316; *Standard Ed.*, **23**.]
　(1940*a* [1938]) *Abriss der Psychoanalyse*, *G.W.*, **17**, 67. (21)
　　[*Trans.: An Outline of Psycho-Analysis*, London and New York, 1949; *Standard Ed.*, **23**.]
　(1940*e* [1938]) 'Die Ichspaltung im Abwehrvorgang', *G.W.*, **17**, 59. (21)
　　[*Trans.:* 'Splitting of the Ego in the Process of Defence', *C.P.* **5**, 372; *Standard Ed.*, **23**.]
　(1950*a* [1887–1902]) *Aus den Anfängen der Psychoanalyse*, London. Includes 'Entwurf einer Psychologie' (1895). (x–xiii, 9, 22, 28, 31, 33, 50–1, 82, 91, 101, 102)
　　[*Trans.: The Origins of Psycho-Analysis*, London and New York, 1954. (Partly, including 'A Project for a Scientific Psychology', in *Standard Ed.*, **1.**)]
GALANT, S. (1919) 'Sexualleben im Säuglings- und Kindesalter', *Neurol. Zbl.*, **38**, 652. Reprinted, *Int. Z. Psychoanal.*, **6** (1920), 164. (47)
GLEY, E. (1884) 'Les aberrations de l'instinct sexuel', *Revue philosophique*, **17**, 66. (9)
GROOS, K. (1899) *Die Spiele der Menschen*, Jena. (39–40)
　(1904) *Das Seelenleben des Kindes*, Berlin. (39–40)
HALBAN, J. (1903) 'Die Entstehung der Geschlechtscharaktere', *Arch. Gynaek.*, **70**, 205. (8)
　(1904) 'Schwangerschaftsreaktionen der fötalen Organe und ihre puerperale Involution', *Z. Geburtsh. Gynäk.*, **53**, 191. (43)
HALL, G. STANLEY (1904) *Adolescence: its Psychology and its relations to Physiology, Anthropology, Sociology, Sex, Crime, Religion and Education*, 2 vols., New York. (39–40)
HELLER, T. (1904) *Grundriss der Heilpädagogik*, Leipzig. (39–40)
HERMAN, G. (1903) '*Genesis*', *das Gesetz der Zeugung*, Bd. 5, *Libido und Mania*, Leipzig. (9)
HIRSCHFELD, M. (1899) 'Die objecktive Diagnose der Homosexualität', *Jb. sex. Zwischenst.*, **1**, 8. (9)

HIRSCHFELD, M. (*cont.*)

(1904) 'Statistiche Untersuchungen über den Prozentsatz der Homosexuellen', *Jb. sex. Zwischenst.*, **6**. (2)

HUG-HELLMUTH, H. VON (1913) *Aus dem Seelenleben des Kindes*, Vienna. (39–40)

[*Trans.*: *A Study of the Mental Life of the Child*, New York, 1919.]

JAHRBUCH FÜR SEXUELLE ZWISCHENSTUFEN (1, 7, 9)

KIERNAN, J. G. (1888) *Med. Stand.* (Chicago), Nov. and Dec. (7)

KINDERFEHLER, DIE (39–40)

KRAFFT-EBING, R. VON (1895) 'Zur Erklärung der conträren Sexualempfindung', *Jb. Psychiat. Neurol.*, **13**, 1. (8, 9)

LINDNER, S. (1879) 'Das Saugen an den Fingern, Lippen, etc., bei den Kindern (Ludeln)', *Jb. Kinderheilk.*, N.F., **14**, 68. (45)

LIPSCHÜTZ, A. (1919) *Die Pubertätsdrüse und ihre Wirkungen*, Bern. (13, 43, 81)

LYDSTON, G. F. (1889) *Philadelphia Med. Surg. Rep.*, Sept. 7. (7)

MOEBIUS, P. J. (1900) 'Über Entartung', *Grenzfr, Nerv.-u. Seelenleb.*, **3**. (4)

MOLL, A. (1898) *Untersuchungen über die Libido sexualis*, Bd. I, Berlin. (35, 46)

(1909) *Das Sexualleben des Kindes*, Berlin. (39–40, 46)

NACHMANSOHN, M. (1915) 'Freuds Libidotheorie verglichen mit der Eroslehre Platos', *Int. Z. Psychoanal.*, **3**, 65. (xviii)

PÉREZ, B. (1886) *L'enfant de trois à sept ans*, Paris. (39–40)

PREYER, W. (1882) *Die Seele des Kindes*, Leipzig. (39–40)

RANK, O. (1909) *Der Mythus von der Geburt des Helden*, Vienna. (92)

[*Trans.*: *The Myth of the Birth of the Hero*, New York, 1914.]

(1924) *Das Trauma der Geburt*, Vienna. (92)

[*Trans.*: *The Trauma of Birth*, London, 1929.]

RIEGER, C. (1900) *Die Castration*, Jena. (80)

ROHLEDER, H. (1899) *Die Masturbation*, Berlin. (51)

SCHRENCK-NOTZING, A. VON (1899) 'Literaturzusammenstellung über die Psychologie und Psychopathologie der Vita sexualis', *Z. Hypnot.*, **9**, Heft 2, 98. (23)

STRÜMPELL, L. (1899) *Die pädagogische Pathologie*, Leipzig. (39–40)

SULLY, J. (1895) *Studies of Childhood*, London. (39–40)

TARUFFI, C. (1903) *Hermaphroditismus und Zeugungsunfähigkeit* (German trans. by R. Teuscher), Berlin. (7)

WEININGER, O. (1903) *Geschlecht und Charakter*, Vienna. (9)

[*Trans.*: *Sex and Character*, London, 1906.]

ADDENDUM

FREUD, S. (1910*i*) 'Die psychogene Sehstörung in psychoanalytischer Auffassung', *G.S.*, **5**, 310; *G.W.*, **8**, 94. (72)

[*Trans.*: 'The Psycho-Analytic View of Psychogenic Disturbance of Vision', *C.P.*, **2**, 105; *Standard Ed.*, **11**, 211.]

GENERAL INDEX

This index includes the names of non-technical authors. It also includes the names of technical authors where no reference is made in the text to particular works. For references to particular technical works, the Bibliography should be consulted.

Abasia, 69 *n.* 2

Aberrations, sexual (*see also* Inversion; Perversions), 1–38, 97, 102
  literature of, 1 *n.* 1

Activity and passivity (*see also* Masculine and feminine), xii, 24–6, 32, 64, 85 *n.*

Adult sexuality
  and infantile sexuality, 65, 73 *n.* 1, 78, 94–5, 100, 108
  and Oedipus complex, 92 *n.*
  sexual aim of, 15–16, 73, 76–7, 87–8, 100

Aesthetic pleasure (*see also* Art and sublimation), 77 *n.*

Affect and sexual excitation, 69, 99

Affection and sexuality, 66, 73, 89–90, 91 *n.* 2, 93, 112

Aggressiveness (*see also* Mastery, instinct for; Sadism), 23–6, 64, 68–9, 85–6 *n.*

Agoraphobia, 69 *n.* 2

Algolagnia, 23

Ambivalence, 26 *n.* 1, 65

Amnesia
  hysterical, 3 *n.* 2, 41–2, 112
  infantile, 3 *n.* 2, 40–2, 55, 112

Anaclitic (attachment) relation of libidinal to self-preservative instinct, 24–5, 47–8, 51, 64, 71, 88–9, 98

Anaclitic (attachment) type of object-choice, 88–9

Anaclitic object-choice, 88 *n.*

Anaesthesia, sexual, 87, 93

Anal erotism, 11, 18, 32, 35, 51–3, 64–5, 71 *n.* 2, 99, 105 *n.* 1
  and character-traits, 105 *n.* 1
  and constipation, 51–3
  and repression, 53 *n.*
  in neuroses, 32

Analogies
  Great Pyramid, 41–2 *n.*
  inter-communicating pipes, 17 *n.* 1

pine-shavings for kindling wood, 87
  Plato's myth of bisexuality, 2
  tunnel pierced from two sides, 73

Analytic (*see* Psycho-analytic)

Animals, sexuality in, 1, 43 *n.*, 64, 95 *n.* 2, 100

Antiquity
  glorification of sexual instinct in, 15 *n.*
  inversion in, 5, 10, 11 *n.*, 96

Anxiety, neurotic, x–xi, 90

Aristophanes, 2 *n.*

Art and sublimation (*see also* Aesthetic pleasure), 22–3, 104

Attachment (*see* Anaclitic)

Auto-erotism (*see also* Masturbation), 47–8, 60 *n.*, 63–4, 69 *n.* 2, 73, 85, 88, 99

Beauty and sexual attraction, 22 *n.* 2, 75

Bed-wetting (*see* Enuresis)

Bestiality, 14

Binet, A. (*see also* Bibliography), 37

Biological factors, xv, xvii, 1, 23–4, 43 *n.*, 50, 61, 65 *n.* 1, 65–6 *n.*, 81, 85 *n.*, 92 *n.*, 95 *n.* 2, 107, 109

Birth
  infantile theories of, 52, 61–3
  trauma, 92 *n.*

Bisexuality, xi, 2, 7–14, 9 *n.*, 26, 81, 86
  literature of, 9 *n.*

Bladder disturbances, 56

Bleuler, E. (*see also* Bibliography), 65

Bloch, I., 1 *n.* 1, 5, 17

Boys
  and railway interests, 68
  inversion in, 95–6
  masturbation in, 54, 85
  sexual researches of, 61

Breast, child's relation to, 47–8, 50–51 *n.*, 88

Breuer, J. (*see also* Bibliography), 29

Brill, A. A., xvi *n.*
Buttocks, 59

Cannibalism, 25, 64
Castration
  complex, 23 *n.* 2, 24, 61
  effects of, 13 *n.*, 80–1
  threat of, 19 *n.*, 21–2, 23 *n.* 2, 92 *n.*, 95
Catharsis, 29
Character, structure of, 104–5
Chemistry, sexual, x–xi, 13, 34, 68, 81–2, 84–5
Childhood
  experiences, 6, 106, 109
  impressions, pertinacity of, 108–9, 112
Children (see also Infantile; Infantile sexuality; Parents and children)
  neurotic anxiety in, 90
  psycho-analysis of, xvii–xviii
  sexual abuse of (*see also* Seduction), 14
Clitoris, 53, 61, 86–7, 112
Cloaca, 53 *n.*, 62, 65
Complemental series, 36, 97, 105–6
Component instincts
  and character, 104–5
  and erotogenic zones, 32–7, 57–9, 71, 77
  and perversions, 28, 32–3
  and sexual constitution, 37, 71 *n.* 2, 101–2
  convergence of, at puberty, 63–4, 66, 73, 98, 100, 103
  in girls, 85
  independent pursuit of pleasure by, 63, 65, 73, 99–100
  order of emergence of, 107
  repression of, and neurosis, 48, 68, 103, 104
Compulsive behaviour, 3, 55, 58, 77
Confessions of *Rousseau*, 59
Consciousness, 30–1, 41, 55, 94
Constitutional factors (*see* Heredity and experience)
Contrectation, 35 *n.* 2, 46 *n.* 2
Conversion, hysterical, 30
Coprophilia, 21 *n.* 2, 27
Corporal punishment, 59
Cruelty (*see also* Sadism), 23–6, 32–3, 35, 58–9, 66–7, 105 *n.* 2
Cultural development, 15, 43–4, 59, 91–3, 100, 108

Cunnilinctus, 17
Curiosity (*see also* Infantile sexual researches; Knowledge, instinct for; Scopophilia), 22–3, 58

Dark, children's fear of, 90
Day's residues as dream-sources, 92 *n.*
Defaecation (*see also* Faeces), 18, 23, 52–3, 58, 62
Degeneracy, 4–5, 26, 40 *n.*, 102
Delusions, 31–2 *n.*
Dementia praecox, 29
Detumescence, 35 *n.* 2, 46 *n.* 2
Diphasic choice of object, 66
Diphasic onset of sexuality, 100
Disgust
  and perversions, 17–18, 23–5, 48
  as force opposing sexual instinct, xi, 23, 25, 27–8, 30, 43–4, 57, 85, 97
Displacement, 83
  from lower to upper part of body, 49–50
'*Dora*', case of, xiii
Dream of Irma's injection, xi
Dream-instigators, day's residues as, 92 *n.*
Dreams, 79, 92 *n.*
Drinking, 48

Education, 28 *n.* 2, 43–6, 52, 59, 69 *n.* 2, 96, 98, 100, 108
Ego and libido, 29 *n.* 3, 83–4
Ellis, Havelock (*see also* Bibliography), 1 *n.* 1, 84 *n.* 3
Emissions, nocturnal, 56, 69, 79
End-pleasure, 15–16, 76–7
Enuresis, 56
Epilepsy, 56
Erection, 35
Eros, xviii
Erotogenic zones
  and component instincts, 32–7, 57–9, 71, 77
  and hysterogenic zones, 50
  and infantile sexuality, xi, 44, 47–9, 57–9, 73, 89, 98–9
  and sexual constitution, 37, 71, 101–2
  and sexual excitation, 50–4, 66–7, 70–1, 74–81, 99
  predestined, 18–19, 49–52, 99
Erotogenicity, 47–59, 70–1
Eulenburg, A., 1 *n.* 1

Examinations, 69
Exhibitionism, 23, 32–3, 35, 58
Experimental transformation of sex, 13 *n.*, 81
Eye as erotogenic zone, 35, 75

Faeces equated with gift, penis, baby, 52, 62
Family, 91–3
Father, 12 *n.*, 93–5
Faust (Goethe), 20, 28
Fellatio, 17
Féré, C. S., 25–6 *n.*
Fetishism, 19–21, 28 *n.* 3, 33 *n.* 1, 37
Fixation
  and hypnosis, 16 *n.*
  causation of, 77, 101, 108
  determinant of inversion, 6
  determinant of perversions, 15–16, 20–5, 27, 28 *n.* 3, 37, 98 *n.* 1, 108
  of incestuous object-choice, 93–4
  of preliminary sexual aim, 15–16, 21–6, 104–5
  susceptibility to, 108, 112
  to mother in homosexuals, 11 *n.*
Fliess, Wilhelm (see also Bibliography), xi, 9 *n.*, 13 *n.*, 32 *n.* 1, 44 *n.* 1, 86 *n.* 1
Foot fetishism, 19, 21
Fore-pleasure, 15–16, 21–2, 76–8, 100
Fur, 21

Generations, opposition between succeeding, 93
General paralysis of the insane, 102
Genital
  erotism, provoking factors of, 53–57, 78, 89–91, 99
  primacy, 54, 63, 65, 73–8, 88, 100
  zone, 35, 53–6, 73, 78, 86–9, 99–101, 103, 106
Genitals
  and extension of sexual aim, 16–18, 21 *n.* 2, 22–3, 32, 49–50
  symbols for, 21 *n.* 1
Girls
  inversion in, 95–6
  masturbation in, 55–6, 85–7
  relation to parents, 93–4
  repression in, 85–7, 93–4, 101
  sexual researches of, 61 *n.* 1
  sexuality of, 85–7
Giza, Great Pyramid of, 41–2 *n.*

Glands, 13 *n.*, 81, 82 *n.*
Glans penis, 53, 76, 86, 88
Globus hystericus, 48
Goethe, 19, 28
Grasping instinct, 46
Guilt, sense of, 24

Hair, 19, 21
'*Hans, Little*', case of, 59–60 *n.*
Heredity and experience as aetiological factors in
  fetishism, 19 *n.*
  forces inhibiting sexuality, 28 *n.* 2, 43–4, 91 *n.* 3
  incest barrier, 91 *n.* 3
  inversion, 4–7, 12 *n.*
  neuroses, 36–7, 56, 89–90, 102
  perversions, 102
  pubertal phantasies, 92 *n.*
  scopophilia, 58
  sexual development, xv, 20–1, 39, 97, 101–9
  symbolism, 21
Hermaphroditism, somatic (*see also* Bisexuality), 7–8
Heterosexual attraction (*see* Object-choice, heterosexual)
Hirschfeld, M. (*see also* Bibliography), 1 *n.* 1, 13 *n.*
Hoche, A., 17 *n.*
Homosexuality (*see* Inversion)
Hormones, 82 *n.*
Hunger, 1, 14, 15
Hydropathy, 67
Hypnosis
  as psychotherapy, 6
  relation to hypnotist in, 16 *n.*
Hysteria
  and inversion, 96
  and perversions, 35, 49–50
  in men, 32
  proneness of women to, 87, 102
  psycho-analytical treatment of, 29–31, 83
  sexual aetiology of, xi–xiii, 30–1
  universality of, 37
Hysterical phantasies, 31–2 *n.*
Hysterical symptoms (*see* Abasia; Amnesia, Anaesthesia; *Globus hystericus*; Vomiting)
Hysterogenic zones, 50

Identification, 64
Impotence, 2, 14, 19, 21
'Incentive bonus', pleasure as, 77

Incest, 91–4, 101
Incestuous phantasies, 91 n. 3, 92–3
Infantile sexual
  disposition, perverse, 57–8, 100, 105
  researches, 59–60 n., 60–3, 92 n.
  satisfaction, contrivances for guaranteeing, 50–4, 70–1, 89, 99
  theories, x, 21 n. 2, 52, 59–60 n., 61–3
Infantile sexuality (see also Childhood; Children), xi–xii, 39–72, 78, 89–91, 98–100, 108–9
  and object-choice, 20 n. 2, 40 n., 46–8, 57–8, 59–60 n., 64–6, 73 n. 1, 100
  and Oedipus complex, 92 n.
  auto-erotic nature of, 47–9, 59–60 n., 64, 73, 88, 99–100
  based on erotogenic zones, 47–58, 73, 99
  first efflorescence of, 42–3, 55, 60, 65, 73, 98, 100
  literature of, 39, 39 n. 2
  sexual aim of, 49–51, 73
  sources of, 66–72
Insane, sexual impulses in the (see also Psychoses), 15, 27
Insomnia, 46 n.
Instincts, theory of the, 34
Intellectual
  development and inversion, 5
  development and sexual precocity, 106–7
  work as source of sexual excitation, 70–2
Intestinal disturbances, 51–2, 54
Inversion, sexual (see also Aberrations, sexual; Perversions), 1 n. 1, 2–14, 18, 26, 32, 95–6, 107
  and bisexuality, 7–11, 13 n.
  and intellectual development, 5
  and neuroses, 31–3
  at puberty, 3
  determinants of, 3–10, 10 n., 95–6
  in antiquity, 5, 10, 11 n., 96
  in primitive races, 5, 11 n.
  in women, 8, 11–12, 87 n., 95–6
  object-choice in, 2, 10–11, 107
  prevention of, 95–6
  sexual aim in, 11–12

Jahrbuch für sexuelle Zwischenstufen, 1 n. 1, 7 n., 9 n.
Jealousy, 40, 94

Joie de vivre, la (Zola), 105 n. 2
Jokes, 77 n.
Jones, Ernest, 112
Jung, C. G., 84, 112

Kinderfehler, Die, 40 n.
Kissing, 16, 17, 47 n., 48, 89
Knowledge, instinct for, 60–3
Krafft-Ebing, R. von. (see also Bibliography), 1 n. 1, 23, 25–6 n., 79
Kris, Ernst, 9 n.

Latency period, 42–5, 56, 66, 74, 88–9, 92 n., 98, 100, 104, 106
Libido (see also Sexual excitation; Sexual instinct)
  adhesiveness of, 112
  and anxiety, 90
  and hunger, 1, 14
  collateral flow of, 17 n., 36, 59, 98
  definition of, 1, 83
  increase at puberty, 45, 87
  theory, x, 83–4
Love, 27, 32–3, 40, 88–90, 95 n. 1
Löwenfeld, L., 1 n. 1

Magnan, J., 4
Masculine and feminine (see also Activity and passivity; Men; Women), 8–11, 26, 64, 73, 85–87, 101
Masochism, 16 n., 23–6, 33, 35, 59, 70
  feminine, 24 n. 2
  moral, 24 n. 2
  primary (erotogenic), 24 n. 2
  secondary, 24 n. 2
Mastery, instinct for (see also Aggressiveness; Sadism), 25, 54, 59, 60, 64
Masturbation (see also Auto-erotism), 6, 11, 18, 39, 46, 51–6, 58, 85–7, 100
  literature of, 51 n. 1
Memory (see Amnesia)
Men, sexuality of, 73, 79–80, 85–7, 94
Micturition, 18, 23, 53, 58, 62
Moebius, P. J. (see also Bibliography) 1 n. 1, 37
Moll, A. (see also Bibliography), 1 n. 1, 35 n. 2
Morality, xi, 28 n. 2, 30, 43–4, 57, 91 n. 3, 97
Mother, 11 n., 88–9, 93–6

Mucous membrane
of anal zone, 18–19, 32, 34 *n*. 1, 35, 52, 64
of genital zone, 34 *n*. 1, 53, 76
of oral zone, 12, 16–17, 32, 34 *n*. 1, 49
Muscular movement, 64, 67–9
Myths 21, 92 *n*.

Näcke, P., 84 *n*. 3
Narcissism, 11 *n*., 50 *n*. 1, 84, 88 *n*.
Narcissistic object choice, 88 *n*.
Necrophilia, 27
Neugebauer, F. von, 7 *n*.
Neurasthenia, x–xi
Neuroses
aetiology of, 29, 36–7, 89, 101–9
and anal erotism, 52–3
and diphasic onset of sexuality, 66, 100
and femininity, 87
and infantile sexuality, x–xii, 37–8, 41–2
and masturbation, 55–6
and parents, 88–90, 93–4
psycho-analytic treatment of, 29–31, 57 *n*. 2, 59 *n*.
sexual instinct in, 29–38
and repression, xvii, 30, 36, 48, 68, 87, 93, 98, 103–7
and toxic states, 82
negative of perversions, 31, 36–8, 97, 102
Neurosis, choice of, 101 *n*.
Neurotics, perverse tendencies in, 31–3, 36, 97–8, 102–4
Night fears (*Pavor nocturnus*), 90
Normal and abnormal sexuality, no hard and fast line between, 5, 7, 9 *n*., 10, 11 *n*., 14–17, 19–24, 26–8, 37–8, 42 *n*. 2, 71 *n*.
Normal sexuality, abortive beginnings of, in perversions, 3, 11 *n*., 19–20 *n*., 28 *n*. 3
Nutritional instinct, 1, 46, 83, 88, 98
and oral erotism, 45–8, 64, 71–2, 88, 98

Object-choice (*see also* Infantile sexuality; Sexual object)
accidental determinants of, 12 *n*.
anaclitic, 88 *n*.
diphasic, 66
early beginnings of, 40 *n*., 57–8, 60 *n*., 65, 73 *n*. 1, 88, 100

heterosexual, 1, 11 *n*., 93, 94–6, 107
incestuous, 91–4, 101
narcissistic, 11 *n*., 50 *n*. 1, 84, 88 *n*.
pubertal, 63, 65–6, 87, 91–4, 100–1
Obsessional neurosis, xii, 29, 65, 83, 102
Oedipus complex, xiii, 28 *n*. 3, 92 *n*., 93 *n*.
Oral erotism, 12, 16–18, 25, 32, 35, 45–51, 64, 71 *n*. 2, 88, 98–9
Orgasm, 46
Ossipow, N., xvi
Overvaluation, sexual, 17–20, 24 *n*. 1, 87
Overwork, 70

Paedicatio, 11, 18
Pain, 23–7, 32, 35, 58–9, 70, 99
Paralysis of the insane, 102
Paranoia (*see also* Psychoses), 29, 31–2 *n*., 33, 35
Parental intercourse, 62, 92 *n*.
Parents and children, relations between, 12 *n*., 16 *n*., 62–3, 88–96, 101
Passive sexual attitude (*see* Activity and Passivity)
Pavor nocturnus, 90
Penis
absence of, in women, 21 *n*. 2, 23 *n*. 2, 61
glans, 53, 76, 86, 88
Perversions (*see also* Aberrations, sexual; Inversion)
abortive beginnings of normal sexuality in, 3, 11 *n*., 19–20 *n*., 28 *n*. 3
aetiology of, 15–16, 21–8, 36–7, 57, 61, 98, 106–9
and artistic disposition, 22–3, 104
and character, 104–9
and fore-pleasure, 15–16, 21–2, 76–8, 100
and innate sexual weakness, 6, 8, 14, 19, 21–2, 103, 106
and insanity, 27
and neuroses, 31–3, 36–8, 58, 65, 97–8, 102–4, 108–9
and normal constitution, 37–8, 57, 97
and Oedipus complex, 28 *n*. 3
and psycho-analysis, xviii

Perversions (cont.)—
  and regression, 36, 98 n. 1, 104–5
  and sublimation, 27–8, 44–5, 98,
    104–5
  criterion of, 14–15, 20, 22–3, 26–8
  general character of, 15–16, 25–6
  universal disposition to, 57, 97
Phallic sexual organization, 65–6
    n., 73 n. 1, 99
Phantasies
  hysterical, 31–2 n.
  incestuous, 91 n. 3, 92–3
  of perverts, 31–2 n.
  pubertal, 68, 91–2
  unconscious, 32
Pity, 59, 85, 97
Plato, xviii, 2 n. 1
Pleasure
  and sexual excitation, 16, 47–54,
    67–8, 73, 75–6, 89
  and satisfaction, 67–8, 73, 75–8,
    98–9
  independent pursuit of, by com-
    ponent instincts, 63, 65, 73,
    99–100
Polymorphously perverse disposi-
    tion, 57, 97, 100, 105
Precocity, sexual, 39, 45–7, 51–2,
    59, 90–1, 100, 106–9
Pregenital sexuality, x, 25 n. 2, 58–9,
    63–6
Pregnancy (see also Birth), children's
    observation of, 63
Primal scene (see Parental inter-
    course)
Primitive man, 5, 11 n., 17
Prostitutes, male, 10
Psycho-analytic treatment, xvii, 3
    nn. 1 and 2, 29–31, 55, 59 n.
    2, 67, 83–4, 94, 98 n. 1, 105
Psychoses, 14–15, 27, 84
Puberty (see also Adult sexuality;
    Phantasies, pubertal)
  and genital primacy, 63, 73, 88,
    100–1
  and masturbation, 55
  and object-choice, 63, 65–6,
    87, 91–4, 100–1
  and onset of neuroses, 36
  convergence of affectionate and
    sensual currents at, 66, 73, 98,
    100, 103
  convergence of sexual aim and
    object at, 63, 65–6, 73, 101
  detachment from parents at, 91–4

  divergence of male and female
    development at, 73, 85, 100
  effect of, in boys, 68, 86
  effect of, in girls, 86–7, 101
  sexual changes at, xii, 39, 43 n.,
    73–8, 85–7, 91–6, 100–1
Puberty gland, 13 n., 43 n., 81

Quantitative factors, 12 n., 71

Railway anxiety, 68
'Rat Man', case of, 21 n. 2
Reaction-formations, 44, 98, 104–5
Reality-testing, 50–1 n.
Regression, 36, 94, 98 n. 1, 103 n.,
    106
Repression
  and amnesia, 41
  and neuroses, xvii, 30, 36, 48, 68,
    87, 93, 98, 103–7
  and Oedipus complex, 28–9 n.
  in girls, 85–7, 93–4, 101
  mechanism of, 41–2
  of component instincts, 48, 68,
    103, 104
  of infantile sexuality, 48, 53 n., 58,
    62, 66, 98
Reproductive function, 1, 15, 44,
    63–5, 73–4, 103
Rhythm, 45–7, 49, 67
Rocking, 67–8, 89
Rousseau, J. J., 59

Sadger, I., 1 n. 1
Sadism, 23–6, 32–5, 58–9, 62, 64–7,
    69–70, 99
Sadistic-anal organization, 64, 99
Scatological interest, 23, 52–3, 58,
    62
School-life, 69
Schopenhauer, A., xviii
Schrenck-Notzing, A. von (see also
    Bibliography), 1 n. 1, 23
Scott, C., 25–6 n.
Screen memories, 20 n. 2, 41 n. 1
Seduction, xi–xii, 6, 56–8, 86, 92 n.,
    100
Self-preservative instinct, 25, 48, 63
Semen, 63, 79
Sex, experimental transformation of,
    13 n., 81
Sex-distinction, infantile views on,
    61
Sexual aim
  adult, 15–16, 73, 76–7, 87–8, 100

Sexual aim (*cont.*)—
and pleasure, 49, 73, 99–100
and object, convergence of, 63–6, 73, 101
definition of, 2, 50
extension of, 15–21, 26–7, 32, 35
fixation of preliminary, 15–16, 21–6, 104–5
in inversion, 11–12
infantile, 49–50, 73
Sexual characters, secondary, 8, 10, 13 *n.*, 80–1
Sexual constitution, multiplicity of, 12 *n.*, 37, 71, 101–5
Sexual currents, affectionate and sensual, 66, 73, 98, 100, 103, 112
Sexual development (*see also* Heredity and experience), 42–3, 63–6, 73, 94, 101–9
diphasic onset of, 66
disturbances of, 63–6
in animals, 1, 43 *n.*, 64, 95 *n.* 2, 100
Sexual discharge, 56, 73, 76, 78–9, 86, 100–1
Sexual excitation (*see also* Libido)
and beauty, 22 *n.* 2
and pleasure, 16, 47–54, 67–8, 73, 75–6, 89
and satisfaction, 67–8, 73, 75–8, 98–9
and toxic substances, 81–2
and unpleasure, 75–6
chemical basis of (*see* Chemistry, sexual)
contrivances for producing, 49–54, 70–1, 89, 99
effects of, 71–2
extinguished after satisfaction, 15, 76, 78–9, 83, 101
mechanism of, 50
obscure nature of, 70–1
sources of, 50–6, 59, 66–72, 74–76, 79–82, 89–99
Sexual impressions, early, pertinacity of, 6, 106, 108–9, 112
Sexual instinct (see also Aberrations, sexual; Inversion; Libido; Perversions)
composite nature of, 28, 39, 97
forces opposing, 18, 23–5, 27–8, 30, 43–4, 57–8, 85, 91, 97–8, 106
in neuroses, 29–38
nature of, 1
popular views of, 1–2, 15–16, 39
unruly character of, 15, 27, 106

Sexual instincts, pairs of opposites, 23–6, 31–3, 64–5
Sexual object (*see also* Objectchoice)
and aim, convergence of, 63–6, 73, 101
and infantile sexuality, 20 *n.* 2, 40 *n.*, 46–8, 57–8, 59–60 *n.*, 64–6, 73 *n.* 1, 100
definition of, 1–2
infantile, not retained after maturity, 66, 91–2, 101
overvaluation of, 17–20, 24 *n.* 1, 87
relation to sexual instinct, looseness of, 7, 14
varieties of, 2–15, 19–21
whole person as, 22, 88
Sexual researches of children, 60–3, 92 *n.*
Sexual satisfaction
and pleasure, 67–8, 73, 75–8, 98–9
and perversions, 15
as soporific, 46 *n.* 1
Sexual substances, 73, 76, 78–80, 100
Sexual symbolism, 21, 59–60 *n.*, 67–8
Sexual tension, 15, 50, 74–81, 83–4, 101
Sexuality (*see also* Adult sexuality; Infantile sexuality; Normal sexuality; Puberty)
extension of concept in psychoanalysis, xviii, 47
importance for whole mental life, xvii–xviii, 89
pregenital, x, 25 *n.* 2, 58–9, 63–6
the weak spot in human development, 15
Shame, xi, 27–8, 30, 43–4, 57–8, 85, 97
Shoe as fetish, 21 *nn.* 1 and 2
Skin, 15–16, 22, 34 *n.* 1, 35, 46–9, 67–70, 76, 99
Sleep, 46 *n.* 1, 48, 68
Smell, pleasure in, 21 *n.* 2
Smoking, 48
Sphinx, riddle of the, 61
Sport, 69 *n.* 2
Steinach, E., 13 *n.*, 81
Stimuli, sensory, 34, 67–8
Strohmayer, 35 *n.* 2
Struwwelpeter, 45 *n.*
Sublimation, 22, 27, 44–5, 60, 72, 98, 104–5

Sucking (*see* Thumb-sucking)
Suggestion, 3 *n.* 1, 6, 16 *n.*
Swinging, 67–8
Symbolism, sexual, 21, 59–60 *n.*, 67–8
Symposium, Plato's, 2 *n.* 1
Symptoms (*see also* Hysterical symptoms)
   and perversion, 31–3, 35, 37, 58, 97
   as expression of repressed wish, 29–31, 38, 72, 104
   mechanism of formation of, xvii
   pubertal phantasies and 92 *n.*
Syphilis (*see* Venereal disease)

Tabes, 102
Teeth, 48
Teleological thinking, 22, 50 *n.* 2. 54 *n.* 1
Thumb-sucking, 45–51, 64, 98
Tickling, 49–50, 56
Touching (*see* Mucous membrane; Skin)
Toxic states, 81–2
Transference neuroses, 83
Traumatic experiences, 68, 106

Unconscious mental processes
   and perversions, 11 *n.*, 32–3, 97
   as origin of neurotic symptoms, 30
   made conscious in psycho-analytical treatment, 55, 94
Unconscious phantasies, 32
Unpleasure, 44, 49–50, 75–6
   sexual excitation and, 75–6
Urethral erotism, 71 *n.* 2, 105 *n.*

Vagina, 63, 76, 87
Venereal disease, 102
Virtues, basis of, 105
Vomiting, hysterical, 48

Womb, pubertal phantasies of, 92 *n.*
Women
   absence of penis in, 21 *n.* 2, 23 *n.* 2, 61
   anaesthesia in, 87, 93
   disgust in, 18
   inversion in, 8, 11–12, 87 *n.*, 95–6
   neuroses in, 87
   obscurity of sexual life of, 17, 73
   penis-envy in, 61
   sexuality of, 57, 73, 80, 85–7, 101

Zola, Emile, 105 *n.* 2